PIERCING THE FOG OF
WAR

PIERCING
THE FOG OF
WAR

Recognizing Change on the Battlefield

Lessons from Military History,
216 BC through Today

Brian L. Steed

ZENITH PRESS

First published in 2009 by Zenith Press, an imprint of MBI Publishing Company, 400 1st Avenue North, Suite 300, Minneapolis, MN 55401 USA.

Zenith Press titles are also available at discounts in bulk quantity for industrial or sales-promotional use. For details write to Special Sales Manager at MBI Publishing Company, 400 1st Avenue North, Suite 300, Minneapolis, MN 55401 USA. To find out more about our books, join us online at www.zenithpress.com.

Designer: Lindsay Haas
Jacket Designer: Simon Larkin
Maps: Courtesy Phil Schwartzberg, Meridian Mapping

Library of Congress Cataloging-in-Publication Data

Steed, Brian.
  Piercing the fog of war : recognizing change on the battlefield : lessons from military history, 216 BC through today / Brian L. Steed.
      p. cm.
  Includes bibliographical references and index.
  ISBN 978-0-7603-3523-9 (hb w/ jkt)
  1. Command of troops—Psychological aspects. 2. Command of troops—Case studies. 3. Combat—Psychological aspects. 4. Combat—Case studies. 5. Situational awareness. 6. Psychology, Military. 7. Conflict (Psychology) 8. Tactics—Case studies. 9. Decision making—Case studies. 10. Military history—Case studies. I. Title.
  UB210.S697 2009
  355.4'7—dc22
                                                              2008044744

417 3809

Front and back cover: *(main)* Marines from Company F along with engineers patrol through the thick fog in the early morning of Nov. 18 during Operation TRIFECTA. *Headquarters, U.S. Marine Corps*; *(background)* Foggy day. *iStockphoto*

Printed in the United States of America

For Jessica, Katelyn, Hunter, and B.J.
They make life worth living, and by their enthusiasm
inspire me to strive and achieve.

The great uncertainty of all data in war is a peculiar difficulty, because all action must, to a certain extent, be planned in a mere twilight, which in addition not infrequently—like the effect of a fog or moonshine—gives to things exaggerated dimensions and unnatural appearance.

—Carl von Clausewitz

For we know in part, and we prophesy in part. But when that which is perfect is come, then that which is in part shall be done away. When I was a child, I spake as a child, I understood as a child, I thought as a child: but when I became a man, I put away childish things. For now we see through a glass, darkly; but then face to face: now I know in part; but then shall I know even as also I am known.

—Paul, the Christian apostle, 1 Corinthians 13:9–12

Contents

Figures and Maps

Acknowledgments

No work of any value is a result of a single person's efforts. This is especially true in the case of this book. I began this journey with the help and indulgence of three supportive commanders—E. Scott Glasscock, J. K. Chesney, and Bryan Denny. Without their assistance in developing ideas into training and application, the foundation of this book would never have been laid. These were the men who supported this effort in the days, weeks, and months after 11 September 2001.

I need to express tremendous gratitude for all those who have assisted in this process by reading, commenting on ideas, and offering their thoughts; in so doing they have helped take the sometimes rambling path I was on and straighten it into a coherent and connected journey. As always, my wife, Sheri Steed, ranks highest in this regard. Elaine Bond dedicated numerous hours in conversation and painstaking corrections. I also thank my other friends and associates who have listened, read, and forwarded the manuscript to others. Without their help, many great ideas would not have been incorporated.

I extend a special gratitude to my Jordanian and other Arab associates, fellow officers, and friends who have taught me what it means to have a deep, ancient, and rich culture. Their examples of tolerance, patience, and thirst for explaining an often misunderstood culture have been intellectually thrilling and personally satisfying. I am honored to consider myself a soldier in the Arab Army and in the United States Army and enjoy the close associations that exist in great military organizations.

Finally, I extend my gratitude to E. J. McCarthy, who accepted this project and made it possible to bring it to light. This is the second book we have worked on together, and I am grateful for his professionalism and support.

Preface

I was serving as an instructor at a United States Army school when airplanes crashed into the World Trade Center buildings, the Pentagon, and a field in Pennsylvania. My student-officers and I spent a week in support of the military post where we were stationed. I returned to my international students, while my American students continued to assist in the establishment of a working emergency operations center. During the three weeks without my U.S. Army students, I spent a lot of time trying to determine the most important things they needed to learn. I based my thinking on what had happened and on the already circulating talk on the news channels as to what the U.S. response might be. I was responsible for teaching these officers to plan, prepare, and conduct combat operations for military units that ranged in size from sixty people to more than five thousand.

A few weeks prior to these events, I told this same group of student-officers that they would not fight another war like World War II or even Operation Desert Storm. What they heard was, "You will not fight another war." It was a running joke in our group about my supposed false prediction. I knew what I meant by my original prediction and still felt it to be true—whatever was coming would be different from the historical American military experience.

My prediction and my thoughts began to coalesce around a historical battle, the Battle of Little Bighorn. I served in the 7th United States Cavalry as a junior officer and developed not just an affection for that unit's history, but a drive to understand the actions of its most famous, and in contemporary times, infamous, commander—George Armstrong Custer. The details of this battle appear later in this book, but what is important here is my understanding of a competent battlefield commander who made a series of seemingly unexplainable decisions that led to disaster. I had read a great historical fiction on the battle in addition to numerous more scholarly selections. The historical fiction, titled *The Road We Do Not Know*, supported many of my thoughts on why Custer made certain decisions and provided a reasonable explanation to what, on the surface, were unreasonable decisions. This was not a normal battle in the historical model but what I term an *aberrational* event. Custer made mistakes, but he did so in an environment far outside his experience, and this led to his catastrophic failure.

Much of my thinking on this event was pieced together before 11 September 2001, but the application of these thoughts took place shortly thereafter. I presented a plan of training that left the norm at the school and was able to teach officers based almost entirely on experiential learning using the Battle of Little Bighorn as a starting point. The intent was to place the officers in a series of situations that presented unexpected events and to develop a method for overcoming these challenges. I cannot say how successful this effort was, since we never moved beyond test and experimentation. At that time I did not possess sufficient knowledge of the many other battles used as examples in this book. As the immediate crisis evolved into a routine, the course needed to return to its normal structure. My emphasis on teaching aberration and helping others to recognize the symptoms of an aberrational event changed to a focus on the conduct of battle analysis.

I further developed this line of thinking as I changed positions to train more junior officers who were preparing to lead at the initial level of between sixteen and fifty soldiers. I continued to use the battle analysis as a training method and tried to emphasize the importance of recognizing the aberrational cues, clues, symptoms, and indicators. The successes of these efforts are for others to determine. At the time I was greatly frustrated with my seeming inability to communicate the importance of this concept.

In this environment of teaching aberrations, I was able to participate in a forum discussing the future of conflict and received a presentation about *Creation and Destruction*, based on the thoughts and ideas of John Boyd. This introduced a variety of important methods to the line of thinking that follows in the succeeding pages of this book. Boyd's concept of "thinking outside the box" became one of the foundational principles in support of my own developing ideas. In his mind, to truly think outside the box, a person must first destroy that very box. His thinking is revolutionary and best understood through his own words, but what I learned from studying his ideas was that most of us will never be able to completely destroy our conceptual boxes. At the very best, we can only expand them to include different ideas and ways of thinking.

As I left the instructor role I became a student of the Arabic language and began an immersion in Arabic culture that has continued to the present. I have spent all of my adult life and much of my adolescence studying the history of the Middle East; in recent years that history has become reality to me. These experiences have helped me to understand the challenges I had as an instructor trying to teach students about understanding aberration. Though I tried to emphasize the personal and the importance of individual personality, I did not spend enough time on *culture* and the all-important word *empathy*. Without empathy, there can be no understanding of the opponent, and without understanding the opponent, catastrophic defeat looms large on the horizon. The importance of this word and its central role in creating the opportunity for success is discussed later, but it was my understanding of it that gave me the impetus to write this book.

I have worked in Arab culture for several years with an ever-growing understanding of how different cultures can create a different view of the same events. While serving in this environment, I have watched the debate about U.S. relations in the Middle East and the reactions to events currently transpiring. I recall hearing one of the many military experts, a retired U.S. Army general officer, say in reference to the insurgency in Iraq, "We never expected this." Though he may not have said those exact words, this is what I heard, and I thought back to Custer and his soldiers and heard the echoes from the past.

In reading the hundreds of battle analyses I have graded, I recall one of the most common lessons learned by the student authors was to expect the unexpected. This ironic and nearly impossible task is such a common mantra within U.S. society that as I heard the apparent admission of failure to achieve this coming from a retired senior officer, I was both refreshed by the honesty and recommitted to communicate my thoughts on the matter.

Introduction

ABOUT MID-MORNING on 14 November 1965, helicopters carried soldiers of the 1st Battalion, 7th United States Cavalry into a football-field-sized clearing in the Ia Drang Valley of Vietnam. The battalion commander stepped off the helicopter in a landing zone given the code name X-Ray and immediately began to order his slightly more than 150 soldiers to execute his plan. Within a matter of minutes, North Vietnamese (NVA) soldiers had been seen, tackled, and interrogated. These soldiers provided simple yet critical information about the sizable enemy force that was close and ready to fight.[1]

The battle began as U.S. squads, platoons, and companies probed forward intending to meet the enemy as far forward as possible. NVA soldiers coming down from their mountainside positions came into direct contact with the expanding U.S. forces. Helicopters lifted load after load of U.S. soldiers into the landing zone as the battle increased, and the commander expanded, reinforced, and adjusted his perimeter to accommodate the changing events created as the contest of wills between him and his opponent continued. Over three days the battle raged, and the 1st Battalion, 7th U.S. Cavalry was reinforced with more infantry, artillery fire, and air-delivered munitions. The fighting was intense, and U.S. casualties were high—the highest yet seen in the Vietnam War. By the end of the fight, two other U.S. battalions had come in to support. And the North Vietnamese had been defeated.

As the battalions left X-Ray, some soldiers were airlifted directly from the battlefield, and others were ordered to walk to other clearings where helicopters would transport them back to their respective bases. The 2nd Battalion, 7th U.S. Cavalry was one of the battalions directed to walk out. They were to go to a clearing code named Albany to be extracted. Unlike the planning and movement to X-Ray, this time there was confusion. The battalion commander did not think he was still in a high-threat environment—this was simply a movement to an extraction point. The North Vietnamese, however, were still fighting, and their forces were moving. One of the North Vietnamese regimental commanders watched the U.S. infantry battalions move from X-Ray, and he gave instructions about how to close with the Americans—to grab them by the belt and hold on in an attempt to defeat their firepower advantage.

The battle waged in and around the clearing called Albany was much different than the previous battle that had ended less than twelve hours earlier. It was a close and chaotic struggle where commanders at the battalion or company level had little opportunity to control the fight, and individual soldiers and small groups struggled to fight an enemy that they had difficulty seeing. The events of the battle around Albany are difficult to piece together, since the nature of the fight was based on the experiences of each individual.

Within hours of the battle's conclusion, the U.S. military leadership was touting the events in the Ia Drang as a tremendous victory because the U.S. forces inflicted hundreds of casualties on the enemy. At the same time, the North Vietnamese commanders had already experienced combat, faced defeat, and readjusted tactics. They were now reacting to the aberrational experience of a relatively large-scale battle against the U.S. airmobile infantry. They had been shocked and had lost, but they immediately expanded their experiential box, changed tactics, and reengaged with a new plan and so were able to inflict shock on the U.S. soldiers and commanders.

The battles at Landing Zones X-Ray and Albany demonstrate the ability of leaders to face and react successfully to aberration while in the midst of conflict. The success of the U.S. commander at X-Ray can be attributed to his grasp of and ability to demonstrate the strategies discussed in the following pages, just as the failure of the commander at Albany can be equally attributed to a failure to apply these same strategies.

CONFLICT HAS CHANGED IN THE PAST, but present and future change is happening and will continue to happen in an accelerated manner. This book focuses on how to perceive change and recognize extreme events of change immediately preceding a conflict or while in the conflict itself. Though the examples and the experiences given in this book are from armed conflict, there is significant benefit in this work for those involved in armed conflict, the business community, or anyone who faces a thinking opponent who seeks to win.

This work presents a unique historic view of the shifting nature of conflict, gives answers as to why the changes observed in conflict today are moving faster than in previous periods in human history, and explains what this means in terms of the necessity of understanding this current environment. The book also presents a new technique for observing and understanding conflict that has nearly universal application. One area of particular importance in contemporary conflict is developing empathy for the opponent.

The emphasis on truly understanding the opponent as the key for success in conflict is unique in the discussion swirling around the current military conflicts raging around the world. Much is made of history and adhering to agreements and commitments, but little is said of the importance of seeing the world from the perspective of the opponent. The simplistic dismissal of actions and behaviors outside of accepted or understood cultural norms does not help those participating in or those observing the conflicts come closer to achieving success in the conflict.

Seeing the world from a single perspective and making assessments from that perspective have resulted in failure after failure in the U.S. experience. This is especially true when the conflict occurs with an opponent from a culture significantly different from U.S. or European cultures. Korea, Vietnam, Somalia, Afghanistan, and Iraq are all examples of areas that have presented and are presenting difficulties.

The following chapters present historic examples of conflicts that involve aberrational events—events completely outside the experience of one of the opponents—to discuss the reasons behind aberrations and how to prepare to meet them. Examples come from a variety of time periods and include cross-cultural battles and battles within cultures to demonstrate the spectrum over which aberrations have occurred.

It is important to state at the very beginning what this book purports to be and what it does not. First, what it is not. Though this book involves military history and discussions of tactics and levels of strategy, it is not a history of the military, though I hope military historians can benefit from reading it. This book applies to all aspects of interpersonal relations and has direct implications for those who work in business, diplomacy, politics, and conflict resolution. The use of battle analysis provides some detailed observations and lessons about the world of conflict surrounding us. In some ways, the battles are metaphors for understanding the future, much more than specific events we can project forward.

The ideas and concepts presented here provide a different way to look at and analyze the variety of challenges facing us as individuals, businesses, cultures, and countries. Throughout the following pages there are consistent references to "the box." This is done to draw the reader to the "think outside the box" line that is so common in contemporary culture. There is much that could be said on "the box" and how we truly get outside it. In the conceptual framework used here, the notion of truly getting outside of our individual boxes is not possible for many or even the vast majority of us. Therefore the ideas presented here are designed to demonstrate some ways to expand the conceptual box and therefore operate within a larger environment of understanding. It is for this reason that the epigraph quotes Paul, the Christian apostle, who spoke using a Greek philosophical construct common in his day to express his different thoughts on religion and the nature of deity. Paul had expanded his box through the same ideas presented here, and because of this he was more effective in presenting his message to people of varying cultures and backgrounds. He specifically referred to the greater clarity and understanding that people will enjoy as they receive the greater insight that comes at the end of the road of belief that he espoused.

The insight offered through this book is a method for recognizing, understanding, and successfully competing in an aberrational enviro-nment. It would be useful to begin this discussion with a quick discussion on how the word *aberration* is and will be used throughout this book. An aberration is an event or datum that does not fit within the prescribed norm for a given problem or experiment. It is something different, unexpected, or unusual. It is a point that does not plot along a line with the other points but rather is out by itself, being a unique result. Aberrations can be successful and beneficial occurrences or detrimental and negative ones.

An aberration may sound like a surprise, since most, if not all, aberrational events do surprise those experiencing them. It is a surprise, but more than that as well. A surprise can be simple and very normal. A father jumping out from behind a door in a house can surprise his children, but there is nothing uncommon about a father being in his house. Though the event was surprising, everything else was normal. The same is true of many battles in history where surprise was achieved. Bernard Law Montgomery surprised Irwin Rommel at the Second Battle of El Alamein by changing the order of tanks and infantry in the attack. Though initial surprise was achieved, the victory by the British Army was not achieved through this surprise, but by the enormous stockpiles of men and equipment prepared beforehand. Other military examples come from the Arab army of World War I and their attacks on the cities of Aqaba and Damascus. In both cases the Arab forces used surprise through rapid movements and attacks from unexpected directions. The fact that Arab tribes conducted attacks on the edges of the deserts of Syria and Arabia was neither new nor unique. This was surprise, not aberration. In the market, one company may surprise another by a change in release date of a new product or a shift in marketing focus, but this is not outside the realm of normal practice. Aberrations are events that are not typical or predictable, and therefore reaction to them requires more than simply overcoming the surprise and then reestablishing the common defensive or offensive patterns.

It is also important to identify up front that aberrations are a matter of perspective. This is especially true in military operations, where the enactors of an aberration know what they are doing and that it is something different. Since a graph was used to help define aberration, an aberration may be defined as a plot outside the normal line of other events, but how far outside a point has to be to be considered an aberration is open for debate. Suffice it to say that there are events that are more clearly aberrations than others.

Why are there aberrations? In the natural world aberrations can come from natural mutations or from the fact that few things in nature are strictly linear or planar, and, therefore, we find the occasional five-leaf clover.

In human interaction, and in the case studies or battle analyses presented here, there are several reasons for aberrations, four of which are emphasized in this book: *means, understanding, leader,* and *target.* A progression in the presentation of these examples will be followed that is not necessarily linear through history, but flows instead from the most simple to the most radical reasons.

Means

It is easiest to imagine the impact on the marketplace or the battlefield of an opponent arriving with more resources than previously imagined. The market or the field is completely flooded with the opponent or his products, and the sudden appearance of so many things achieves a level of surprise in an order of magnitude greater than typical. Weather and natural phenomenon typically function within this area of aberration. Hurricane Katrina, which moved through the Gulf Coast of the United States in late summer 2005, can be considered an aberration. Its size and power were previously beyond contemporary precedent and clearly outside the experiential box of those struggling to manage the crisis. But the fact that a hurricane was in the Gulf of Mexico and moving toward the Gulf Coast was not unusual; what made it an aberration was the magnitude of storm resources it brought to the coast.

Resources involve material items in type or quantity. Something is brought to the event that is different and physically changes how the contest is conducted. This could be a new weapon, vastly different numbers, or new skills beyond those seen previously. This can also apply to a tactical difference in that new or old systems are employed in a significantly different manner. We see this clearly at the Battle of Little Bighorn, where an experienced commander followed his own standardized procedures despite receiving evidence that his opponent was vastly different than any he had faced previously.

There are two military events that do not appear in this book that have direct correlation to the resource aberration.[2] The Chinese offensive on the Korean Peninsula in November 1950 was one such event. This serves as a great example to elucidate the previous discussion on how an aberration may not be an aberration to one of the sides of the conflict. The Chinese planned their attack, built up a significant numerical advantage, and presented tactics different from those employed by the North Koreans against the United Nations forces. The UN, and specifically the U.S. Army, did not consider facing an opponent with tens of thousands of lightly equipped infantry moving in and among allied units to surround, separate, and destroy units in separate detail. The U.S. military was also blind, by choice, to the movement of such a force into the theater. Some analysts and commanders refused to recognize the evidence of Chinese intervention for the magnitude it represented. This could be diagnosed as a self-inflicted aberration.

Another example is the Battle of Landing Zone X-Ray in the Ia Drang Valley of Vietnam in November 1965. This battle was one of two referenced at the beginning of this chapter. The battle between the North Vietnamese Army (NVA) and the U.S. Army featured several innovations of technology, leadership, and simple surprise to create an aberrational battle. U.S. Army intelligence reports identified NVA units operating in the valley and other units were withdrawing from a siege of a U.S. Special Forces fire base. The U.S. unit used helicopters to move quickly to the area and aggressive movement once on the ground to secure a significant defensible area. Both sides were ignorant of the size and capabilities of the other. There were many more NVA units in the immediate vicinity than predicted, and the U.S. forces moved far faster than the NVA expected. The battle that was fought between the two forces created a unique environment where U.S. technology in the form of air forces provided close air support, and ground-based artillery were able to inflict maximum damage on a massed opponent of significant size. The speed of movement and aggressive actions by a commander allowed for a capable defense against which a larger

NVA force threw itself time and again. Neither side expected a battle of this magnitude, and when all was over, the lessons learned were radically different, since the NVA learned not to get into another battle like this, while the U.S. sought in vain for another similar engagement.

Understanding

Knowledge about an opponent provides the next reason for aberration. This deals with not just physical understanding and information, but something deeper and more challenging. It can also be a significantly different knowledge or understanding of the opposing individual, group, company, or enemy. This is sometimes referred to in military circles as achieving *information dominance*—when one side can gain more information about the other and, at the same time, deny information about themselves. But this is about more than information, as will be elaborated in the case studies. The Battle of Cannae is one of the great episodes in all history that can be used to illustrate this, and it will be discussed in greater detail later. At Cannae, both sides could see the opposing numbers, the initial positioning of forces, and the opening moves with complete clarity. There was no information dominance, but still one side understood the other much better, and this understanding resulted in a great victory. The second example, also receiving greater detailed discussion in a later chapter, is the Battle of Yarmouk, where information was not as clear, but understanding was even murkier, and an opponent was vastly underestimated. This touches on a variety of levels of understanding as explained in chapter 2 in the *principles of conflict* under the principle of *identification*. To truly understand involves a critical skill—empathy. This is not an establishment of moral equivalence, but a fundamental ability to understand the opponent by getting inside them and walking around in their skin, so to speak. Without this ability, real understanding is not possible. Aberrations based on an understanding of the opponent tend to happen more often when the opponents are from different cultures and have a different way of viewing victory or risk. What one side may deem to be impossible or unacceptably risky may be viewed in the opposite by people from another culture or by better-trained opponents.

Leader

The dynamic of leadership by its very nature can be aberrational. One only has to think of the likes of Alexander the Great, Galileo, Madonna, Lance Armstrong, or Bill Gates to see how a single person's vision of his or her particular area of expertise fundamentally changed the field of play in ways that contemporary observers would not have predicted. In order to understand why decisions are made, one must understand the importance of decision making on the battlefield and in the marketplace and the personalities of those making the decisions. It is not an issue of experience alone, though personal history combined with the added dimension of culture can result in a leader doing something outside the common practice for good or ill. All of the battle analyses in this book feature this aspect, but in the Battle of the Horns of Hattin it was very pronounced—here the personalities of the leaders resulted in completely unexpected outcomes. A similar situation occurred at the Battle of Trenton, where one commander through his conceptualization of second- and third-order effects was willing to risk much more than anyone expected.

Though the battles and campaigns of Alexander the Great are not included here, they overshadow almost all discussion on leaders and their ability to create aberrations through dynamic vision, personal will, and inspiration of others to execute the seemingly impossible. The fact that Alexander was able to destroy the Persian Empire—which was vastly larger in resources and geography, and deeper in culture, experience, and achievement—was a result of an aberrational person. Alexander took control of his small kingdom and within eighteen months was fighting a battle for the conquest of the known world. He marched his soldiers thousands of miles; captured impregnable cities through enormous work, willpower, and determination; and destroyed the greatest empire to that point in human history. He was living proof that one remarkable person can change the world. Almost none of us is an Alexander.

Therefore, we are not using him as an example, but instead this work includes people with simpler visions of their assignments and more attainable accomplishments.

Target
The final reason for an aberration discussed in this book is the most difficult. It might be best described as those who throw out the rules of the game but do not tell anyone about it. It is a change of target, which is most easily explained through the example of chess. If while playing chess one opponent suddenly defeats the king's knight, stands up, declares victory, and walks away, the other opponent would be completely confused at the change of target. He was protecting his king, and though he was not seeking the loss of his knight, he was willing to sacrifice it to protect what he thought were his more important pieces—king, queen, rook. In this case the king was not the object to the opponent, and a quick victory outside the rules of chess is an aberration. The idea of what is important, what needs protection, what needs emphasis, is all thrown on its head by this change. This is evidenced in the more recent Battle of Grozny, where the transition to urban terrain, use of digital/modern media, exploitation of civilians, and all the complexities associated with these changes impacted the battle in completely unexpected ways. This is most clearly demonstrated in the rapid transmogrification of warfare from a nearly complete state-versus-state affair to the current situation of non-state organizations, groups, militias, and angry individuals versus each other and state police and militaries. The board and the associated pieces are changing. Not all of these changes discussed along with the recent events are aberrations, but they set the stage for a much greater propensity for aberration as the rules continue to change and adjust to an apparently non-existent game board and unidentifiable pieces.

THIS IS CERTAINLY NOT A COMPREHENSIVE LIST, but it seeks to capture the fundamental reasons why an aberrational event can and does occur. None of the battle analyses can point exclusively to one of these reasons for success or failure; all of the battles must ascribe their outcomes to some portion of several of the elements, and many contain all four. This is true of any method for understanding why something is different. The historical battles used as the accompanying case studies are designed to assist in clarifying these elements through example.

Now that the idea of aberration in conflict has been introduced, along with the framework for how to understand some of these changes, it is time to address some of the most important questions: Why is this important? Why should anyone care about an event being an aberration? If these events are outside the norm, isn't it better just to accept them as the irregularities they are and focus on the regular and predictable events that can be more easily dealt with? These questions need to be answered through an understanding of the world in transition in which we currently live. The argument will be made that at present we live in a time where access to information is much easier than ever before. But this alone does not lead to radical changes. There is also a greater access to information transmission. The ability to disseminate information makes the present unlike any time in the history of mankind. Minutes, hours, and days are the common time frame references in conflicts and change, not the weeks, seasons, and years of previous eras.

Also, not all aberrations are human led or human contrived, though the case studies all involve human-centered events. Nature also provides aberrations, and it is important to keep this in mind.

So we live in a time of increasing potential for aberrations. So what? For anyone intent on winning on the battlefield, succeeding in the market, or even surviving the next aberrational weather phenomenon, the idea of expanding our personal boxes becomes essential to the preparation that will allow the greatest chance for overcoming whatever bizarre and unusual situation in which we find ourselves.

How does an individual, a person in business, or a leader make the necessary adjustments to function in this ever-increasing world of aberrations? This book includes strategies to achieve victory in a world of uncertainty and change. Each of these nine strategies is introduced here and will be discussed in the accompanying case studies as applicable. They are also summarized in the final chapter.

The nine strategies are as follows, with the chapters identified wherein they are featured:

1. **Introspection** (4, 5, 6, 7, 8, 9, 10, 11): This is a strategy of self-reflection. The ability to see oneself and one's abilities, skills, resources, and attributes in an honest and full manner.

2. **Empathetic Appreciation** (4, 5, 6, 7, 8, 9, 10, 11): This strategy addresses the important aspect of having empathy for the opponent. To see the opponent as he or she sees himself or herself.

3. **Empathetic Expectation** (4, 5, 6, 7, 8, 9, 10, 11): The difference from the preceding strategy lies in the ability to recognize the possibilities imagined by the opponent. What does the opponent expect? Subsequently, how will the opponent react to the actions that one plans to conduct?

4. **Study of Language** (4, 8, 10, 11): So many issues, problems, and conflicts have begun and continue because of the confusion of language. Language is how humans translate thoughts into communicable directions and intent. Language needs to be understood as the opponent understands it.

5. **Study of History** (4, 5, 8, 9, 10, 11): This is a principle of precedent. What are the precedents in this region, on this subject, in this field? How did these precedents develop in the past? The Spanish-American philosopher and poet George Santayana's great statement about those not understanding history—"Those who do not remember the past are condemned to repeat it" (*The Life of Reason, Volume 1*, 1905)—is at the heart of this strategy.

6. **Study of Culture** (4, 5, 6, 7, 8, 9, 10, 11): Language and culture are two pillars of achieving the empathy needed above. Whereas empathetic appreciation and expectation are specific to an opponent, culture deals more broadly with the society from which that opponent comes.

7. **Multiple Reserves** (5, 6, 7, 8, 10, 11): Mid- and high-level leaders can only influence events in the heat of conflict by the allocation of resources; therefore, it is critical in times of potential aberration that leaders avoid limiting themselves to a single reserve that can only be committed at a single moment.

8. **Initiative** (5, 6, 7, 8, 9, 10, 11): The participant who has the initiative and who directs the events can often determine who suffers from an aberration. The intent of this strategy is to get ahead of the decision cycle of the opponent and make him or her react to one's own decisions and actions rather than the alternative. It can also be described with the use of the word "preemption," which is the displacement of the opponent in time or space. This strategy removes the opponent from a position of advantage before he or she acts.

9. **Think Science Fiction** (10, 11): As strategy of creativity, this requires a mind open to possibilities that may, on the surface, appear to be completely unconnected with the events at hand. This is the ability to reach out and draw from a variety of sources. This includes the use of creative minds that have considered the future and proposed seemingly fanciful or far-fetched solutions or realities.

NOW THAT I HAVE EXPLAINED the purpose for developing increased insight to see more clearly and have identified the proposed strategies for succeeding in this environment, the journey begins. The following chapters expand on the concepts addressed here. Initially the work will construct a foundation on an understanding of the dynamics of change that can make these events more common, then it will establish a common framework for discussing the case studies. The framework is based on some simple principles of conflict—identify, isolate, suppress, maneuver, destroy—which have application to a wide audience. These principles help us to prepare for success and then to evaluate the case studies and see where the fundamental failures or successes occurred. The most critical principle for understanding aberration is identification. This principle is featured in a case study that seeks to demonstrate the importance of empathy in understanding the various sub-elements of identification in critical and typically misunderstood events—those involving suicide bombers.

Case studies support each of the reasons for aberration, with the last also being discussed through contemporary events dealing with the elevation of non-state actors to the world scene and their use of terror to achieve their goals. The case studies are from the battles of Little Bighorn (1876), Cannae (216 BC), Yarmouk (636), Horns of Hattin (1187), Trenton (1776), and Grozny (1994). Little Bighorn and the Horns of Hattin receive greater prominence and detail here because they provide some of the greatest insights into those points emphasized throughout the book.

The case studies are presented from a typically Western or U.S. perspective. This is done consciously for several reasons. First, it is the natural perspective of the author and makes it easier for intellectual accuracy. Second, a single perspective was chosen because aberration is a perception-based phenomenon. One experiences an aberrational event because one has a conceptual box too small to include the event. Therefore, the perspective is essential to the aberration. Third, I emphasize the importance of identifying the opponent by including their cultural perspective.

Assignment of perspective does not mean that there is a constant loser or winner in the perspective of choice. Hannibal created the aberration and also understood that he might be able to do so at the same time. Khalid bin Waleed, the one exception to the Western perspective, created an aberration but did not recognize it as such because he attributed success to divine assistance rather than clever action or opponent misunderstanding. King Guy of Jerusalem made decisions guided by an attempt to create a positive aberration, though he would have said his purpose was simply to be different; he, instead, suffered the negative effects of his self-inflicted aberration. George Washington, much like Hannibal, knew what he was seeking to accomplish and that an aberration might occur. Custer failed to recognize or accept what was happening and became a victim to aberration. The Russian army expected an action similar to an occupation and did not recognize that something had changed.

This perspective choice was not made to assign good guys and bad guys, but to establish a single perspective for each case study from which a reader can survey the events and then ask the probing personal questions on understanding, vision, and empathy that should be elicited. How would I do it differently? How could I have seen this coming? How does my box need to grow so that this does not happen to me? Or, a better question might be, how does my box need to grow so that I can create such an environment of success for me?

It was previously stated that responses and reactions to aberrations cannot rely on the same patterns. Though that may be true, it does not mean that reaction to an aberration must require the creation of a personal aberration in thinking. That would require immediate, predictable, and controllable genius. If a reader has that ability, then this book cannot provide any additional insight. Response to aberration can be through regular behaviors or actions creatively applied. Responses and ideas about preparation are part of the answers offered to the numerous questions raised here.

The path ends with conclusions drawn from the case studies and from the topic as a whole. This book is not a manual for aberration management, but rather it seeks to be a tool in a liberal arts education—to open the mind to accept new ideas and see things in a different way. The struggle to expand one's conceptual box is difficult and requires tremendous focus and effort. It may be impossible to expand that box in the heat of crisis or conflict. Leaders who could make such an adjustment are truly rare in history. Some who have successfully weathered aberrations have done so without an understanding of what they were experiencing as the events transpired, but through providence or luck, they succeeded in surviving their experiences. This is especially true in aberrational natural events. News broadcasts typically discuss those who stuck out the hurricane and survived while behaving in a normal way despite numerous others who perished. It is sometimes possible to perform in such a manner and live through the event, but the goal here is first to establish a pattern of personal conceptual box expansion before and outside of aberrational events. As noted previously, an aberrational event is mostly a matter of perception. If this first technique is applied, then aberrations will be rare in the extreme. Second, it is to create the ability not simply to survive, but to see the changes in events as they begin and as they transpire and therefore to react appropriately.

Chapter 1

The Nature of Change and
The Wizard of Oz

Understanding an aberration means being able to understand the nature of change—the regular progression of events, developments, expansion and contraction, and application of all the changes. This is regular and somewhat predictable. Then there are the events that are irregular and unpredictable—the trip to Oz as described by L. Frank Baum in his remarkable book *The Wonderful Wizard of Oz* and further elaborated in the Metro-Goldwyn-Mayer film entitled *The Wizard of Oz*. Dorothy was caught in a tornado in Kansas. This was not unpredictable or abnormal. That her house landed in a world of Technicolor and on top of a witch—that was an aberration. Here the importance lies in being able to recognize trends and where they may logically lead.

Why do we need to be able to see these things? This question is linked to the concept of shock. Shock in a medical sense causes a lack of body function through the shunting of blood from key areas, primarily the head, and can eventually lead to death if severe and left untreated. The cessation of body fluid movement is deadly.

This has, at times, led to the death of people with relatively minor injuries. It is always something of a mystery how something that has little relation to the seriousness of the injury can end a human life. Shock at the larger societal level has much the same effect on the larger body of the community. One of the primary ways to treat shock is to keep the injured person calm, which is facilitated if the person assisting is experienced with serious injuries and can act as a calming agent. At the end of this chapter is a section linking this brief discussion of first aid with the broader issue of aberration.

Military Change as Seen through the Eyes of an Ancient Time Traveler

Since the case studies contained herein come from a variety of time periods, it may be useful to reflect on the changes throughout this entire span of time. The battles are not presented chronologically, but in this chapter, the discussion follows a linear approach to understand the transitions between the various eras. All of the battles featured different technology and capability, yet that was only significant in three of the cases, including the modern example. The significance of the technology or material items was not always a benefit to the expected side; in fact, the opposite happens to be the case. All of the battles but one occurred in an open field engagement, as opposed to a siege or a fortified defense. This presents an intriguing question: In military aberration, does open-field maneuver offer more chance for freedom of thought and deployment, therefore resulting in a wider variety of scenarios? The discussion here will not encompass the answer to this important question because currently not enough data exists to form a definitive conclusion; however, it is useful to think about this possibility and its potential applications to other endeavors. Within the analogy of fortification, it is clear that being caged and static tends to force people toward consistent and regular modes of thinking. It requires an extraordinary mind to expand a conceptual box at all and one even more creative to do so in a fixed position with all of the attendant challenges of a siege. This is not to imply that creativity is nonexistent in such a case. That is not true; history is replete with examples of defenders who did so with creativity and innovation. As this chapter proceeds, the differences between innovation and aberration will hopefully become clearer. Innovation and creativity can be predicted, or at least expected, whereas an aberration cannot.

The battles begin in the middle of the Roman Republican period and the Second Punic War in the year 216 BC. The next battle occurs nearly 850 years in the future with the geographical decline of the East Roman or Byzantine Empire in 636 AD. The next time jump is only 551 years to the crusader states of *Outré Mare* (across the sea) and the Muslim response under the Ayyubids in 1187 AD. Another period of 589 years leads to the American Revolution and 1776. The next change in period is only 100 years to the post U.S. Civil War period of westward expansion in North America and the Sioux Campaign of 1876. The final battle is 118 years further along at the fracturing of the former Soviet Union and the challenges of reestablishing control by the Russian army. The last case study deals with a period from 1967 to the present with a focus on the Levant[1] and the transition from state versus state engagement to the increasing role of non-state actors. When reflecting on the various technologies visible in each of the battles, it is interesting to note that a chapter that covers a period of 40 years reflects more significant change in technology than any of the succeeding changes between battles.

When reviewing the equipment used by Hannibal Barca as he marched on the Roman legions at Cannae and the weapons used by Khalid bin Waleed in Yarmouk, there are virtually no changes. The same is true as the next leap is made, to King Guy of Jerusalem as he marched against Saladin at the Horns of Hattin; there is little difference in kind. There are differences in style and technique, but a Roman soldier transported nearly 1,400 years into the future would recognize the weapons and their attendant and appropriate uses. He would know that the swords used by the mounted knights were used for slashing opponents, that lances were for stabbing, and that crossbows were used for projecting missiles toward an opponent. He may briefly be surprised by the appearance of a crossbow or by the use of stirrups, but they would not cause an intense amount of consternation. An experienced soldier would rapidly adapt to the environment. Hannibal, for example, would easily be able to transition with only a short period of observation into the new capabilities. Each of these changes—stirrups, crossbows, lances, saddles, and personal armor, as well as other less apparent, though important, differences—represents logical and consistent change over time to adjust to transformations in culture and technology. The manner and style of leadership were also much the same. Leaders led from conspicuous places to inspire and encourage their men. Commands were given verbally or through sound as aided by instruments (drums, bugles, etc.), visually, or through messenger.

The leap forward from Hattin to Trenton would cause a greater deal of pause and observation. There was a revolutionary change in this period—the military application of gunpowder changed the primary weapon from slashing or stabbing to a projectile weapon. Projectile weapons were previously known and used from earliest antiquity, but the use of a propellant charge to provide the power was new. The crossbow mentioned in the previous paragraph presented a revolutionary change as well in projectile weapons. The power for projection no longer came from purely human-muscle power but from a combination of this and mechanical assistance with storage of that power for release at a controlled and directed time. The period between Hattin and Trenton witnessed the change from mechanical to chemical. There is human effort in loading and preparing the weapon, not unlike the effort required to crank a heavy crossbow, but now the skill set requires more training in steps because the complexity of the task has increased. Even with this revolutionary change, it is probable that a skilled soldier or commander brought forward from the ancient period would still see officers holding swords, soldiers carrying guns with bayonets on the front and at close quarters, charging forward much as infantry had done for centuries before. The sound and effect of gunpowder weapons would be surprising, but those who withstood hails of Parthian and Turkish arrows would recognize the concept and be able to adapt. George Washington commanded and directed his men before and during the battle, as did Hannibal. The one significant change was that he used time as a criterion for certain actions, and the advent and use of small, relatively precise timekeeping instruments added to his ability to control the battlefield, but in the heat of the action, the techniques were unchanged from antiquity.

From Trenton to Little Bighorn is the shortest period between cases, and the differences in technology are the smallest. Much as at Trenton, the Battle of Little Bighorn shares numerous similarities with the ancient past. There are also some differences that mark this period from the others. The soldiers riding with George Custer were not equipped with bayonets for their rifles, nor did they have their sabers with them. This was an organization that lived through the use of gunpowder. There was not, nor could there have been, a bayonet-spear charge. The Native American warriors presented a more eclectic and historically diverse set of weapons—spears, bows and arrows, and modern repeating rifles. Our ancient observer would be rather perplexed, I believe, by the transition and by the disparity of weapons, though with the benefit of traveling through the Trenton period he would recognize each of the transitions as logical and linear. If Custer had brought the Gatling guns, these would again cause a small stir, but the idea of using a repeating gunpowder weapon is not much different than the novelty crossbows that had more than one bow per stock to allow for rapid firing. Custer struggled with command and control throughout this battle as will be later discussed, but he sought command and control much as his ancient counterparts had. Because of the dispersed nature of his battle, he used messengers more than any of the other commanders, but his methods were similar to those of all his previous counterparts.

Our ancient traveler has progressed through two millennia of military development, change, and innovation. As he leaps forward to Grozny in 1996, he will now be faced with the greatest changes of his time traveling. Weapons, though larger, louder, and more powerful, will not bewilder our now experienced ancient visitor. He has already adjusted to the concept of gunpowder weapons. The appearance of armored, self-propelled chariots called tanks and armored personnel carriers would seem a logical transition as he grasps the internal combustion engine. Use of snipers, deception, ambushes, and all forms of intrigue would not be new to him because they are truly ancient in origin. The most significant and surprising change here is the advent of radio technology for communication and control. Commanders no longer see most of their soldiers in combat. They sit in relative safety while they speak into a handset and look at a map. This revolutionary change in command and control may be too much for our ancient visitor, who may not be able to accept the radical transformation. He may no longer consider it to be combat as he knows it. This may not even be considered honorable as he struggles with the idea of an enemy that is not seen but can be killed by a command through a box that can call for ammunition to be delivered from the air or miles away through long-range artillery. The evolutionary and revolutionary changes have now reached a point where conflict may no longer be recognizable or acceptable to our visitor. This is when he has stepped out of the house and into Munchkin Land. It is possible that he would look around as did Dorothy and wonder where he was. In defense of our ancient soldier, we skipped visits to World War I and World War II battlefields where he would see the introduction and use of much of this equipment. On the whole, though, the nature of warfare in Grozny presents something like a siege in ancient times. In fact it does become one. Our visitor will recognize this and understand the attitude and tactics of the besieging party, but he may be very confused by the actions of the defenders.

The defenders in Grozny no longer seek simply to defeat the enemy they see and face in their battle. Instead their efforts are designed to send messages both to the soldiers they are fighting and to people thousands of miles away through their actions. This, like the radio used by the leaders, will present a possibly insurmountable obstacle to the ancient traveler. He may make the link that it is not unlike the Roman campaign of Flavius against Hannibal, which sought to delay and slowly cause the attrition of the Carthaginian force and to send signals back to Carthage that they should withdraw Hannibal and his army. The difference is that the images of suffering are transmitted nearly simultaneous with the occurrences. The sterility of commanders' reports and the delay of weeks of cross-country and seaborne travel do not become factors. People in their homes are watching people being killed and buildings being destroyed within hours, if not in real time.

If all of this does not completely overwhelm our visitor, then multiple visits over a forty-year period of time from 1967 to 2008 most probably will. He will see the change from radio communication to the use of screens and typed messages transmitted nearly instantly. There will be the kidnappings that are common in ancient times, but also hijackings with primarily political purposes rather than for plunder. He will see the use of large remote explosives seeking destruction for the impact not on the soldiers present but entirely on a community of national-level leaders and populations far removed from the battlefield. War has truly changed in this environment. The use of non-state actors and resistance organizations was not unknown in ancient times, but the role and control of the state was also less defined, so our visitor may miss the significance of this change. He might be surprised by the fact that many state militaries seem to be less powerful and competent than the non-state organizations, yet the two organizations coexist. He is certain to shake his head at weak organizations that continue to appear to rule while strong organizations take a reduced and secondary rule. This would run contrary to his entire grasp of geopolitics.

Now, thoroughly perplexed, our traveler may be wishing for his own pair of ruby slippers so that he may return to his predictable and understandable world of Kansas-Cannae. We say goodbye to our guest and now need to discuss why the changes in forty years are more radical than the previous leaps of more than two thousand years.

Evolutionary versus Revolutionary Change and Dorothy's Problem

Both the words *evolutionary* and *revolutionary* have been used to describe changes as if they neatly fit into categories. Change is also a phenomenon based on perception and personal position, therefore it defies neat categorization. Despite its defiance, change will be placed in the two types mentioned for sake of order.

Evolutionary change is the logical next step based on use, technological advancement, or necessity. Our time-traveling guest would not be surprised by this type of change. He may not see the need based on his experience, but the change would be within the realm of understanding and acceptance. So long as he witnesses each succeeding step, there is no similar series of changes that would be shocking. The progression from spear to pike to lance to bayonet is one example.

Revolutionary change is the type that skips steps or that takes a substance, material, or technology from another field of endeavor and applies it to the field under observation. The use of gunpowder as a chemical propellant is an example where technology was brought from Chinese entertainment to military application. The use of the radio from civilian to military application is another.

Gunpowder represents a great transition where a revolutionary change then combined with evolutionary change to go from bell-shaped cannons to more sophisticated and longer barrels to lighter-weight handheld designs, etc. Once the revolutionary step was taken, then the more common evolutionary process took over to ensure the most effective use for the time.

It is interesting to note how many revolutionary military changes occurred in the twentieth century as a result of the development of civilian economies and how many revolutionary civilian changes came as a result of military research and development. The two World Wars provided impetus for change and innovation unseen in human history up to that time. The way people lived in 1910, though different in the larger cities, was greatly unchanged for the vast majority of humanity from life of centuries earlier. Life in the 1950s, however, for the majority of nations, reflected a significant leap forward in standard and style of living.

What was Dorothy's problem? She arrived in a few moments in a place entirely foreign to her knowledge and experienced aberrational change unpredicted and seemingly impossible. Can this happen in reality?

Moore's Law and the Impact on Change

In 1965 Gordon Moore, who would go on to be a cofounder of the Intel Corporation, proposed a theory in an article in *Electronics* magazine. The title of the article was "Cramming more components onto integrated circuits." The article itself is somewhat confusing for a nonelectronics person, since he stated the following:

> The complexity for minimum component costs has increased at a rate of roughly a factor of two per year. Certainly over the short term this rate can be expected to continue, if not to increase. Over the longer term, the rate of increase is a bit more uncertain, although there is no reason to believe it will not remain nearly constant for at least 10 years. That means by 1975, the number of components per integrated circuit for minimum cost will be 65,000.[2]

The gist is that every year the amount of computing components in a given space of a silicon chip would double. In 1975, Mr. Moore revised this to doubling every two years.[3] His prediction that this would remain nearly constant for ten years, with modification, has remained constant for more than forty years, and many in the industry predict that it will remain constant for the foreseeable future.

Why do we care about the technological musings of an expert on integrated circuits and silicon? This prediction, which has come to be known as Moore's Law, and the attendant reality demonstrated by the fulfillment of the prediction have fundamentally changed the world in which we live.

> If steel was the raw material for the 20th century, silicon is for the 21st century. And the silicon semiconductor industry— led in large part by Intel's technology advances—has delivered a dramatic spiral of rapid cost reduction and exponential value creation that is unequalled in history. Because of the cumulative impact of these spiraling increases in capability, silicon—the raw material of the microprocessor—powers today's economy and the Internet, running everything from digital phones and PCs to stock markets and spacecraft—and enables today's information-rich, converged, digital world.[4]

25

If change is driven by technological innovation and development, then the entry into the age of the silicon chip and the progress associated with Moore's Law mean that change is a greater part of the contemporary and future world than at any time in history. It takes only a cursory glance around society to see the radical changes brought on by this technology. The ubiquitous mobile phone has become for many in the developing world a surrogate personal computer, since they can perform ever more functions. Bedouins in the remote deserts of Jordan and Saudi Arabia have these devices, which when Gordon Moore first made his prediction were only exhibited in science fiction and fantasy. The communicator of the original *Star Trek* series pales in comparison to what a current mobile phone can do. *Star Trek* was supposed to be several centuries in the future, and within a lifetime the imagined technology has been surpassed. This represents a staggering leap forward in the speed of change.

Associated with this physical prediction was a cost prediction:

> Moore's prediction, now popularly known as Moore's Law, had some startling implications, predicting that computing technology would increase in value at the same time it would actually decrease in cost. This was an unusual idea at the time since, in a typical industry, building a faster, better widget with twice the functionality also usually means doubling the widget's cost. However, in the case of solid-state electronics, the opposite is true: Each time transistor size shrinks, integrated circuits (ICs) become cheaper and perform better.

In 1965, a single transistor cost more than a dollar. By 1975, the cost of a transistor had dropped to less than a penny, while transistor size allowed for almost 100,000 transistors on a single die. From 1979 to 1989, to 1999, processor performance went from about 1.5 million instructions per second (MIPS), to almost 50 MIPS on the i486, to over 1,000 MIPS on the Intel Pentium III. Today's Intel processors, some topping out at well above 1 billion transistors, run at 3.2 GHz and higher, deliver over 10,000 MIPS, and can be manufactured in high volumes with transistors that cost less than 1/10,000th of a cent.[5]

We all are witnesses that as computers have become faster they have also become less expensive. Computers today are many times more powerful than computers of fifteen years ago for the same or a lower price. This is true of all of the modern electronics devices— DVD players, personal music devices, wristwatches, digital cameras, and communications. The changes of the current period and the near future will continue to accelerate, place more capabilities in more people's hands, and give more power and freedom of action. This presents ever greater and greater chances for revolutionary change and creates the possibility for aberrational change for some societies.

Shock

It is only fair to answer now the question left hanging about Dorothy. Remember, Dorothy's problem was that she arrived in a few moments in a place entirely foreign to her knowledge and experienced aberrational change—unpredicted and seemingly impossible. Can this happen in reality?

It is, in fact, possible and has happened. Reflecting on Western and European history, there was a long gap between the first use of moveable type and freedom of the press as an explicit right granted to all citizens. This time can be measured in centuries, depending on the country under review. Imagine one of the millions of people who received the typeset word only forty or fifty years ago, and already they are being inundated with text messaging and digital devices. They may have adapted, but they are not unlike Dorothy walking down the Yellow Brick Road, still trying to understand if she is really in Oz.

Dorothy's experience is one of shock. Just as the medical condition causes problems in a flow of blood to nourish mind and body, social shock has a similar impact on the ability to develop cognitive thought and especially to think creatively. In the military arena, most of the situations where one army flees a battlefield are the result of shock.

This shock can happen suddenly, or it can happen gradually. Henry V achieved shock on multiple levels and at different times during the Battle of Agincourt in 1415. The battle took place in a narrow valley with woods on either side and the funnel-shaped open area narrowing as it approached Henry's position. The French forces were arrayed on the wider end but did not seek battle. Henry moved his archers forward, and they attacked the French knights and soldiers while they were unprepared for an assault. The shock of this first attack led the French to launch an attack immediately against Henry's lines. The muddy field slowed the French down, and they suffered enormous casualties as they were confined into an ever narrower space. The terrain, missile attacks, and the confined space combined with the separation of French command among several leading nobles led to a collective sense of shock among the leading forces and caused a large group to surrender. A failed second major attack led to a collective shock causing the French forces to surrender en masse.

At the Battle of Cunaxa (401 BC), Cyrus, the Persian usurping governor, attacked his brother, Artaxerxes, the Great King of Persia. Cyrus employed a mercenary Greek Phalanx in his army. Though Cyrus was killed that day, the Greek Phalanx was tremendously successful as they swept all opponents from before them through the disciplined charge of the pike-wielding and armored soldiers. In each attack the Persian forces opposite them fled before full contact was made. This was immediate shock in the ideal. The Persian soldiers had never faced Greek soldiers so arrayed and singing their war song. They were frightened and overwhelmed.

World War II demonstrated societal shock on a massive scale with the use of nuclear weapons on Japan. The casualties were certainly horrendous, but they were not an order of magnitude greater than those already suffered in the firebombing of Tokyo. The difference was the issue of experience. The Japanese had experienced bombs before. They had also experienced fire. Though this was significantly worse than regular fires in the city, it was still within the realm of comprehension. The idea of one bomb destroying an entire city, however, was outside the comprehension of the people and the government, and this led to the paralyzing shock that could only see a single option—surrender.

It is the presentation of an experience so outside a collective conceptual box that leads to shock. The opponent is overwhelmed by the experience and cannot think creatively, and therefore is forced into the fight or flight mode of thinking, which in combat usually leads to flight.

The Origin of the Box

In the world of tribal-based conflict the box is shaped through individual and mutual experience. It is safe to assume that the origin of tactics and strategy for organized violence between humans was derived from the joint hunting experience. Experience in conflict then added to each person's menu of possibilities while approaching and engaging with the opponent. Since battles tended to be rare, and writing among such cultures was limited or nonexistent, the level of complexity in group actions did not develop in sophistication. This is still true when observing current tribal-based organizations. Many of the modern nonstate organizations currently in opposition of U.S. interests follow the tribal pattern. They are loosely linked to any written and hardened doctrinal philosophy and more based on trial and error and a conglomeration of personal and collective experience. The conceptual box did not gain a rigid structure as a result of the personal experience-based model, but neither did it become a large box because each leader could at best only draw upon his experiences and the stories told of previous leaders before him.

For a state-based military, the conceptual box began in a similar fashion, since all conflict started with the same origins, but as the state coalesced into a city-based civilization with written records the manner of conflict began to be recorded as well. The civilization formed a doctrine—a written record—for how to fight. This doctrine was to become based on a variety of shifting principles of war and other platitudes on proper actions and counteractions for a given situation. The use of written books for strategy and tactics made the box more rigid in construct. The benefit of this written doctrine was that it could encompass lessons and experiences from a long period of time far in excess of what a single leader could see and do. The problem is that it placed the leader in an ever-more-rigid box.

The box's size and rigidity has direct correlation to the volume of experience used to shape it. It would seem that a state-based leader would have the benefit of his civilization's box because it encapsulates long periods of time and recorded experience. This is true in part. However, the experiences added to the recorded history are selective, and the items removed because of perceived irrelevance over time are also selective. The idea is that what is added or taken away from the collective strategic consciousness is selective and therefore not comprehensive. It funnels a leader down a specified and accepted path rather than allowing that same leader to select from a vast smorgasbord of experiential options. Therefore, the box is not free to be shaped by a sum total of experience but rather through selected experiences, which more often than not reinforce the existing box structure than challenge or expand it.

CHANGE IS A PART OF LIFE, and all people understand and accept this. Changes tend to be evolutionary, and people, though they may be impressed and amazed by the change, can conceptually grasp the next step. Sometimes revolutionary change leaps over steps to present something unique in a given environment. These changes require greater conceptualization to accept and grasp. Occasionally these changes can be presented in such a way as to be entirely outside the experience or predicted possibilities of the observer. In this case there is aberrational change. With any of these forms of change it is possible to generate shock in an opponent. There is the attrition of will that can be termed *evolutionary shock*, and there is the presentation of the unexpected that can present immediate and *revolutionary shock*. There is also the shock generated by the completely unpredicted that can create total decision-making paralysis and capitulation. This is when Dorothy accepts the munchkins and follows their advice, despite the fact she would never have done that under ordinary circumstances.

The rapid acceleration of technological developments and advancements makes it a greater likelihood that these more revolutionary and aberrational changes will become more common as time progresses. The creativity that the new access to information allows is certain to produce some very unique events.

Chapter 2

Building the Schoolhouse: Principles of Conflict

The goal in this chapter is to build a framework around which the rest of the discussion can progress. This is not to go into a military discourse on how to wage successful battle with artillery or helicopters but to establish a series of principles that apply to all forms of conflict throughout the ages. The list proposed here is designed to replace in primacy current lists of principles or fundamentals. By necessity, such a list needs to be broad and general. By design, the list is short to avoid the redundancies and contradictions that seem to exist in other similar lists.

These principles seek universal application. As a principle, it means that it is a *must do* and not just a nice idea. As a result of many years of teaching existing lists of principles and fundamentals, I have discovered that numerous items on current lists are dangerous because they tend to be confusing and, therefore, are of little benefit. It is acknowledged, for example, that many great commanders of the past have violated existing principles in favor of other principles and have been successful in battle. The argument here is that if it is a principle it should be inviolate.

The principles of conflict need to be timeless and as solid as possible. They need to be a framework upon which a variety of houses or structures can be built. This is in opposition to the current structure that requires explanatory remodeling to justify one principle over another in cases of audacity and innovation. The principles of conflict need to answer a variety of requirements, including providing current leaders and decision makers with a tool to assist in conflict preparation, understanding and evaluating previous or historical conflicts, and the comparing and contrasting of conflicts. For all of these different uses, the principles must be able to be applied across the entire spectrum of conflict.

This is a tall order and one not to be taken lightly. The new principles of conflict proposed here are focused on the crux of conflict—defeating the enemy. The list is simple. Enriching the core principles are subcomponents that support the base structure. In this current era, we need the ability to draw parallels from the past to the present and then project the lessons into the future. The focus presented by this list is crucial.

THE BASICS OF MILITARY SUCCESS are encapsulated in five elements: Identification, Isolation, Suppression, Maneuver, and Destruction. A brief definition of each element follows:

- **Identification** is the ability to define and locate the opponent.
- **Isolation** occurs when the opponent is denied the ability to gain outside resources and assistance.
- **Suppression** is the process of denying the opponent the freedom of movement and, ultimately, the ability to maneuver.
- **Maneuver** is a combination of movement and fire power— either in a physical sense, a perceived sense, or in cyberspace— to achieve a position of advantage. Advantage means the placing of strength against an opponent's weakness. Once again, this may be in reality or in the opponents' perceptions.
- **Destruction** is the end of the opponent's resistance through either physical destruction of resources or the destruction of the opponent's will. The key to this list is that

the primary components each have subordinate components that make them function and that are absolutely critical to the overall success of these principles. Each element will be further defined and subordinate components provided for each principle.

Identification

In many instances throughout this book, the word "understanding" is used. Understanding is not a replacement for identification. Identification is a principle that must be accomplished; understanding is a concept that is sought. Through understanding the opponent it is then possible to identify him. Without understanding, there can be no identification. The elements followed in the process of identification seek to provide the basis for this understanding.

The principle of identification consists of five supporting components: physical, conceptual, doctrinal, cultural, and empathy. This principle is first, since it is the foundation upon which all success is built. In fact, the greatest successes and defeats in military history have been as a result of mastery of this principle. Hannibal's victory at Cannae was a direct result of his identification of his Roman counterpart in all five elements. He knew where his opponent was; what their forces were; how he wanted to fight; what he expected to see; what his motivations, strengths, and weaknesses were; and to what tactics he would revert in times of great battlefield stress. In an equal and opposite manner, George Custer did not understand where his opponents were; what their forces were; what their intent was in terms of engagement versus retreat; or what the driving motivation was for them at this time in the larger campaign. One commander's mastery of this principle in all its aspects resulted in one of the greatest historical victories of all time, and the other, in one of the most publicized defeats in American history.

Physical

I want to explain each of the subcomponents, beginning with the most common and ending with the most challenging. The first is physical identification. This is the one with which we are most familiar. It is the physical identification of personnel; equipment; units; what their organization is; how they are positioned; their number, training, ability, and motivation; and where they are. These are the components that all intelligence officers and reconnaissance personnel have been trained on for centuries.

Physical identification has proved easiest when the opponent was a conventional force based on a similar conceptual, doctrinal, and cultural model. Operation Desert Storm (February 1991) demonstrated the capability of high technology against an opponent fighting in this typically modern, conventional manner. However, this proved extremely challenging and unsuccessful in Korea (November 1950) because the American military intelligence and national intelligence professionals could not understand the conceptual, doctrinal, or cultural model being utilized by the Chinese Communist Force moving into the peninsula to reinforce their North Korean allies. This resulted in failure to achieve physical identification because the professionals did not understand where, when, or how to find the opposing forces, or even if they would be there at all. This challenge in Korea was against a conventional opponent. The current challenges in Afghanistan and Iraq are complicated by the fact that the opponent is unconventional. When an opponent seeks unconventional tactics as a way to negate technological advantage, then the other subcomponents of identification become even more important.

Conceptual

The next subcomponent is conceptual identification. It is important to understand that the conceptual model an opponent uses often varies depending on the strategic level where the model is being applied. A simple way to look at this is to examine the division of means of engagement between conventional and unconventional (see figure 2.1). Within a conventional engagement, an opponent can seek to engage with symmetric or asymmetric methods. In a general sense, symmetric means applying strength against strength, and asymmetric is placing strength against weakness. In both the symmetric and asymmetric methods the primary target is the military or the larger opponent (logistics, support facilities, national infrastructure, etc.). Under the unconventional means of engagement, the methods expand. The targets may be military, the larger opponent, the media, or a broader audience.

In the case of the last two targets, I do not mean to imply that an opponent is engaging the media with bullets or bombs, but rather that the focus of his efforts is on influencing the media correspondents and the media outlets. The focus of each attack is to generate media coverage that is unfavorable for the opponent. The audience may be a larger international body, an ethnic group of people, or a religious affiliation. In this case the media becomes the means by which the message is transmitted, but there is a specific audience beyond the media themselves.

Desert Storm (1991) and the Falkland Islands War (1982) are examples of the symmetrical military engagement because they both featured conventional militaries fighting each other much as was done on the battlefields of Europe during World War II.

The intervention of the Chinese Communist Force (1950) in the Korean War is an example of a conventional asymmetrical engagement. In this case both sides of the conflict were standard conventional militaries, yet the Chinese Communist Force did not seek to engage the front of the U.S.-led UN forces but to rather flow around them and attack the supply lines and close the roads that would be used for withdrawal.

Means of Engagement	Conventional: *Symmetrical*	*Asymetrical*	Unconventional: *Asymetrical*
Target/ Focus of Engagement	• Military	• Military • Opponent	• Military • Opponent • Media • Audience

Fig. 2.1 Fundamentals: Identification-Conceptual

The North Vietnamese and Viet Cong attacks during the Tet Offensive (1968) would be a good example of the unconventional asymmetrical military opponent. The objective of the Tet Offensive was to gain ground through both conventional and unconventional attacks. The preparation for the North Vietnamese and Viet Cong actions focused on the unconventional. The battle itself was fighting force against force, but instead key positions were seized and command centers targeted. The major success of this entire operation was the view on the televisions in the United States. that U.S. forces were confused and overwhelmed, even though they were winning.

The Second Palestinian Intifadah and Chechnya are both excellent examples of unconventional asymmetric warfare with a media audience. Both of these engagements are described in greater detail in chapters 10 and 9 respectively, but the important detail here is that the focus of armed conflict was to influence larger audiences through the media rather than to defeat soldiers or military units on the battlefield.

None of these are clear cut, nor is this division supposed to be a clean solution for pigeonholing opponents, but rather it should provide a means to achieve a better understanding of the conceptual model or models an opponent is seeking to use so that we can better deny him success.

Doctrinal

The doctrinal element of identification is similar to the establishment of a template of behavior. The goal is to identify the opponent based on previous actions or common modes of operation. To achieve this, there needs to be some mental or physical database of previous behaviors, techniques, and procedures. This is the sum total of prescribed and exhibited behaviors in conflict situations. This is neither simple nor fast, but over time the patterns can be built. In developing the database, the use of techniques by the opponent is important—has the opponent typically remained in one conceptual element or has he altered conceptual models? Understanding how the opponent utilizes resources and opportunities can shape the created template so that it is more and more accurate over time. This highlights the point that all elements of identification are living and adjust over time.

Cultural

The fourth subcomponent of identification is cultural. The difficulty of identifying cultural templates is that it requires cultural expertise that is not gained quickly or without investment of resources and effort. In essence, the goal here is to be able to overlay the cultural worldview and conflict understanding of the opponent over his doctrinal set of previous actions. Not only does the database reflect what he has done, but, to some degree, it reflects what has shaped the reasoning behind the actions. This allows an identification of some fundamental motivations. Is the opponent from a culture based on obedience to the state or sovereign? Is the will of the individual placed above all else? Are they a tribal society? Are they a religiously motivated culture? If so, how does their religion shape their worldview and their concept of the law of war?

The answers to these questions and numerous other unlisted questions help to shape an understanding of the foundational base of the opponent. This understanding, in turn, affects the view of legitimate targets, the opportunity and possibility of a negotiated settlement, what holds symbolic value, and what may be considered a position of advantage. Not all similar cultures are equal, and the importance of nuance is crucial, hence the need for investment of resources to achieve this understanding.

In the case of legitimate targets among a population, personal experience has demonstrated interesting views. I have spoken with officers and citizens from opposing cultures and countries who have voiced similar views in reference to civilians; both sides viewed all opposing citizens as combatants. They viewed the children and women of villages as current or future combatants and, therefore, legitimate targets. Only when we understand the current existing culture we are fighting rather than the academic classical culture will we be truly effective in identifying the nuances our opponent will use.

Empathy

The final component of identification is empathy. This is a difficult trait to categorize, but its importance is so paramount to accurate identification that it is placed here. Empathy is not the same as moral equivalence. This is not the process through which all actions are viewed as the same when using the appropriate perspective. Empathy is the ability to understand the opponent on his or her own terms, to see the world through the opponent's eyes, so to speak. This is the pinnacle. When this can be achieved, then identification is simple. The challenge is to get to this point.

This is much easier when opponents come from similar training, culture, worldview, etc. In many of the most well-known conflicts where the U.S. military participated, this was the case. U.S. revolutionary leaders understood the British military and political decision makers because they were, for the most part, products of British colonial education, service, and culture. The U.S. Civil War was a similar example, as is true of many civil wars. World War I and World War II, with the exception of the Pacific Theater in World War II, also demonstrated the attendant benefits of fighting an opponent we understood. The conflicts that have provided the greatest level of difficulty and challenge have been those where U.S. opponents have not been from similar backgrounds and this empathy did not exist. The conflicts with the Native Americans posed significant challenges for the U.S. government and military until they were able to force the Native Americans into smaller and smaller areas where they had to fight something like Europeans. It is possible that the use of nuclear weapons on Japan was a result of U.S. inability to empathize with their opponents and understand the apparently fanatical defense of seemingly unimportant islands on the way to the Japanese homeland. This is a current and long-term problem in dealing with cultures in parts of the world that are foreign to American culture. The Middle East poses such problems, as does the ongoing Global War on Terrorism. Is there empathy with U.S. opponents such that those responsible for engaging them in this conflict can truly understand them?

The goal is to identify the opponent, as did Hannibal at Cannae. He knew where Varro and Paullus had their army, and what the size and composition was. He also knew that they would fight him symmetrically and spread their forces in an attempt to envelop him at the same time they focused on penetrating his center and that they would perceive themselves stronger and would rapidly seek to exploit any identified weakness. He also knew that once he had driven the leaders from the field and had the force surrounded with all of the standards overthrown, the army would surrender. In addition, he had the ability to see the battlefield from his opponent's perspective. Hannibal's complete mastery of the principle of identification in conflict allowed his numerically inferior force to achieve one of the greatest victories in military history.

Isolation

The next element is *isolation*. This principle is like identification in that the subcomponents begin with the most common and end with the least common and most challenging. Isolation is to deny the opponent the benefit of outside support.

Physical

In the instance of the physical subcomponent, assistance is denied from outside forces in terms of supporting fire, maneuver, or logistical support. A recent and telling example can be seen in the Chechen rebels and their ability to effectively isolate the Russian army 131st Independent Motorized Rifle Brigade during the Russian attack into Grozny of 31 December 1994. The irony of the event was that the Russians were seeking to isolate Grozny, but instead they were the ones isolated. This example is presented in detail in chapter 9.

The ability to separate opponents from outside support is ancient in its application. The most extreme version of this is the siege, where the intent is to deny the community any outside support and to starve it into submission, or at the least, to drive the community to weakness and inability to mount a successful defense. This ancient concept of isolation was performed most effectively when the siege was most complete. The Assyrian army in 721 BC laid siege to the city of Samaria, the capital of the Kingdom of Israel for three years. The siege inflicted enormous sacrifices on the citizens to the point where cannibalism became a necessity of survival. This is complete physical isolation.

Emotional

The next subcomponent of isolation is emotional. This is terribly important because the ability to attack the will of an opponent is more critical than attacking him physically. This proved very effective in the Crusades when Muslim forces encircled the Crac des Chevaliers, a famous castle in modern Syria. The position was deemed impregnable, and the current remains are still formidable. The crusaders had enough food for five years, but they succumbed after only one month because they perceived their situation as being without hope of relief. The typical tactics for withstanding a siege included holding out and hoping that your opponents would be less able to survive the elements than you, receiving assistance from the outside in military forces attacking the besiegers, or conducting a series of attacks from within your position to weaken your opponent through numerous small losses. In the case of the defense of the Crac de Chevaliers, there were only about two hundred knights present. This did not provide for the ability to sally out and attack without risking the majority of the garrison in the process. Most of the neighboring fortifications had already been taken or surrendered, and there was no perceived possibility of relief. Finally, the surrounding countryside was more amenable to the Muslim army surrounding the castle than to the Frankish knights inside it. The garrison's perception of their situation as hopeless caused the surrender of a fortification that would probably not have been successfully taken by assault for a significant time.

Communicational

In many ways, isolating the opponent emotionally will probably be preceded by isolation of communication. The opponent must not be able to communicate his plight or receive any communication from the outside for this to be truly effective. From ancient to modern times this has been relatively easy to accomplish, though there are many instances of failures to do this. However, in the current period, this is tremendously challenging, given the complexity of the modern electromagnetic spectrum.

Financial

The final aspect of isolation is one of financial isolation. This could be viewed as a form of logistical or physical isolation, but in the current era, and to a lesser degree in previous periods, there is a difference that makes it worthy of a separate category. The ability of crusaders during the first Crusade to replenish lost horses was essential to maintaining status within the group. A knight without a horse became a simple foot soldier. Those lords with sufficient funds kept their vassals and retainers on mounts as long as possible, as a sign of prestige and position. The difference is that there were some horses available, so logistically or physically it was possible to get mounts, but without money it was improbable, unless the mount was captured during combat.

In the present period, this, in combination with cultural motivations, is the lifeblood of conflict. Without money there are no modern weapons. People may resist without weapons, as demonstrated by throwing rocks and Molotov cocktails, but weapons are necessary at some point in any conflict. Unlike previous eras where the control of money could be accomplished by capturing a fleet bearing the treasury or stopping the tax collector on the road, the challenge is to electronically sift and prevent the transfer of money from seemingly legitimate businesses to illegitimate activities.

The ability to isolate an opponent through denying funds, preventing the ability to express a message or receive supportive communication, thereby breaking their emotional will, is certain to result in a complete physical isolation from outside assistance.

Suppression

Once the opponent has been identified and isolated, it is essential to deny him the ability to move and maneuver. A great example of failure in suppression is at the Battle of Gettysburg where Robert E.

Lee planned to attack the Union forces at multiple locations nearly simultaneously; however, the plan failed. Each attack was made hours apart from the others. This failure allowed George Meade to reposition his reserves and newly arriving forces to counter every attack, one at a time, by movements within his defensive perimeter.

The second element is to establish a foundation for gaining the initiative. Initiative is not simply determined by who fires first, but by who is able to adjust to the circumstances and place his opponent at a disadvantage and himself at an advantage. This was seen during the 1973 Arab-Israeli War when the Israeli Army was initially surprised by the Suez Canal crossing and placed on the defensive. They were able to halt the attacks and stabilize their positions, which they used to prepare for a counterattack to regain the initiative. When the Egyptian forces attacked beyond their initial foothold and the protection of their air defense umbrella close to the canal, they were defeated. This defeat was used as the impetus for the counterattack and the opportunity for the Israelis to gain the initiative.

At higher levels of strategy, the dynamic of suppression is embodied in preemption, where suppression and maneuver are combined. Preemption seeks to prevent enemy maneuver by attacking the opponent prior to their preparation for conflict. At Agincourt, Henry V used this technique when the French Army refused to march onto the muddy field and attack him. Henry ordered his soldiers forward, where they established a defense within longbow range of the French and Henry V attacked through missile fire, forcing the French into a disorganized and hurried assault that ended in overwhelming defeat. In this case, preemption denied organized maneuver and turned French order into chaotic defeat.

Maneuver

The next element is *maneuver*. This is a common term. The purpose of maneuver is to achieve a position of advantage from which the enemy can be destroyed. The very definition leads one to a spatial rather than a holistic understanding of the concept.

Maneuver in the physical world is only one means to achieve the maneuver aim. Sun Tzu implied this when he said that the best commanders are able to win a battle without fighting.[1] This cuts to the heart of the concept that perception is more important than reality. Most of the battles in history have not been simple mathematical formulae but rather a contest of will and perception where, at some point, one commander perceived that another had an advantage and subsequently made a series of poor decisions that eventually lead to defeat. As mentioned earlier, Alexander the Great was the dominant and ideal military leader. He clearly was able to understand the position of advantage and used that to create the perception of defeat in his opponents. At the time when he commanded on the battlefield, leaders tended to experience the chaos of conflict firsthand. If their person could be threatened, then it was more likely to create the perception of defeat. Alexander did this over and over again, causing opposing commanders to flee the battlefield. This was not his only technique of victory, but it was one that allowed his typically outnumbered army to win many times.

The real challenge of maneuver is first to identify what the position of advantage is. This is directly linked to identification of the opponent. Once a commander fully understands all aspects of his opponent, he will be able to identify clearly what will give him advantage in both perception and reality.

It is within the principle of maneuver that the existing principle of surprise best belongs. Hannibal, the Carthaginian commander in the Second Punic War, was a master of maneuver and of surprise, since he was able to seize positions of advantage in a variety of ways and a variety of locations and times of the battle. He could start the battle at a time of his choosing or through his leadership be able to change the course of a battle and hold the position of advantage later.

The position of advantage, as stated previously, is not necessarily a physical location. It can be a time, place, idea, or simple perception. Alexander's victories achieved by attacking an opposing commander and threatening him personally created a perceived position of advantage. As will be discussed in chapter 8, George Washington was able to use time as his position of advantage in the Battle of Trenton. Freedom and liberty have been used in a variety of conflicts to create a position of advantage based on an idea. This allowed numerous peoples to rally around a cause that the opposition could not defeat. In chapter 6, the Battle of Yarmouk demonstrates the position of advantage through idea in the form of a new religion and the zeal associated with it. Chapter 7 offers a clear example at the Horns of Hattin, where Saladin is able to deny his opponent access to water. By controlling this essential resource, he held the physical position of advantage.

Destruction

The final element of conflict is *destruction*. The standard method of conflict in Western civilization has been physical destruction. Two armies have faced off on a designated battlefield and then fought. The one who controlled the field of battle at the end was the victor. In many ways, this is still the prevalent view among the American military community, media, and general populace. The quest for a clear-cut and easy-to-understand conflict with a well-defined end is an example of this thinking. Another view has been to target the will of the opponent.

In several national security monograms and papers, these competing views have been termed *attrition* and *disintegration*. Terminology purists might advocate one over the other, but the point of having the two concepts as subcomponents of the destruction principle is that they both play a role, and neither will be executed in its purest form.

I have used the example of the Battle of Cannae before, and it serves as an ideal example of the classic Western/American view of warfare and destruction. The statistics below (see Figure 2.2) show the overwhelming victory enjoyed by the Carthaginians.

	Battle of Cannae	Vietnam
Engaged	~80,000 Romans ~50,000 Carthagainians	~3.3 Million (US) ~2 Million (NVN)
Loss	56,300 casualties (R) 8,000 casualties (C)	57,719 KIA (US) 303,700, WIA (US) 5,011 MIA (US) ~600,000 N. Vietnamese

Fig. 2.2 Casualty figure comparison for the Battle of Cannae and the Vietnam War.

The alternate view was expressed in recent times by Ho Chi Minh in the U.S. war in Vietnam. Many times it has been quoted that the American army never lost a battle, but it was the American army that left the field of battle without victory. The principle of destruction in this case was directed at Americans and American politicians, rather than soldiers, units, or tactical leaders. Even with this direction and focus, the North Vietnamese and the Viet Cong suffered larger casualties than did the U.S. forces.

In this case we can see the ability of Ho Chi Minh and Hannibal to understand their opponents; to isolate them from outside support; to prevent their movement and maneuver at a variety of levels, or at least negate their superiority in maneuver with effective higher strategy preemption; and to use their understanding to achieve a position of advantage from which they achieved either a destruction of the force or of the will of their opponent.

GREAT COMMANDERS—PAST, PRESENT, AND FUTURE—have utilized and will utilize these five principles. The effective use of them has meant the difference between success and failure on the battlefield and, at times, the difference between survival and extinction of cultures and civilizations. The five principles of conflict are written in such a way as to make them relevant, whether you are studying the conflicts between the Romans and the Parthians to gain vicarious lessons learned or seeking to understand the current trend of unconventional counterinsurgency. It is critical to understand that though destruction is the ultimate goal of every military engagement, battle, or war, it is not the first principle that must be applied. Only through a thorough identification of the opponent in all five of the subcomponent areas will a commander be empowered to isolate, suppress, understand the position of advantage and then gain it, and, finally, destroy the opponent's will and, as necessary, his physical material and men.

Chapter 3

Case Study: Empathy and the Suicide Terrorist

During the crusader period in the Levant, King Henry of Jerusalem was invited by the leader of the Ismaili sect of Shi'ite Islam to a banquet. This sect was and is known by its corrupted English name—Assassins. The Assassins were famous in the period before the Mongol invasions for the ability to make their way through any security and commit murder of high-level officials and rulers. Sometimes the preparation for the actual event took years of infiltration before the assassin could get the right opportunity. The fact that the assassin had every expectation of dying in the act made fear of this group significant in most palaces in the region. The primary targets of the Assassins were their Sunni Muslim opponents and not the crusader Christians. However, because of the complex shifting alliances, the Assassins also attacked Christian leaders.

The leader of the Assassins wanted the new ruler to understand the benefits of association with the sect. As the story goes, at the end of the meal, the Assassin leader indicated to a group of men standing on top of a tall tower. The Assassin leader gestured with his hand and one of the men jumped from the tower to his death on the rocky ground below. Another man moved forward to take the recent jumper's place, the leader gestured again, and the second man also jumped to his death. Another man took up the position. King Henry begged for the assassin leader to stop.

As King Henry rode away, he was shaken by what he considered the insane commitment he had just witnessed, and he considered himself lucky to have escaped the fortress with his life. The Assassin leader probably thought that he had made a clear display of the commitment and courage of his followers and that the display of strength of character and control was what had overwhelmed Henry.[1]

There may be doubts about the validity of this story, though it has been told in both medieval and modern periods. Regardless of the truth of the actual events described, the ideas represented are more important and have direct application to the case study in this chapter.

In discussions with associates, friends, and coworkers in the Middle East, I have been reminded numerous times of the dangerous aspects of this topic. The word *terrorism*, like *jihad* or *crusade*, is filled with connotations that conjure images with great variance depending on an individual's culture. Despite the pitfalls, this term is used here in a very dictionary-appropriate manner in Arabic or English.

A second area of concern with the very title of this chapter is the use of the word *suicide*. Simply put, suicide is the taking of one's own life. That said, there are numerous questions about the use of this word in terms of conflict. Is a soldier who acts audaciously to attack a machine-gun position or who leaps on a grenade in an attempt to further the advance or protect fellow soldiers committing suicide? These acts are typically admired and honored in Western cultures and militaries. In the U.S. military, many Congressional Medal of Honor recipients have committed acts that, when viewed under calm and rational circumstances, could be interpreted as suicidal. This is not to lessen the heroic nature of the acts that have been so honored but to point out that a cultural point of view is important in attaching labels. In many of the aforementioned cases, the decisions to act were made in seconds and under duress and typically not with premeditated intent. The behavior of the Assassins in the earlier related story is indicative of this debate. Were they committing suicide or following, without question, the orders of their superior? When an Assassin performed his assigned task, he typically expected to be killed. Was this a form of suicide?

Muslim associates have also informed me that in Islam, suicide is forbidden.[2] There is certainly at least one Koranic reference so condemning the act of suicide. This said, there is also a concept of martyrdom, dying for the faith, which is rich and well-developed within Islam. Depending on perspective, many acts described in this chapter and witnessed in the news could be viewed as either suicide or martyrdom.

Despite the pitfalls of the words and their incongruence or incompatibility with some basic religious teachings, we will press on with the title of this chapter and the development of empathy for suicide terrorists. The use of *suicide* in this chapter, like that of *terrorism* and *terrorist*, follows a simple dictionary-appropriate definition. Suicide is the premeditated taking of one's own life. The definition of terrorism used here is the use of terror as a tool in shaping the behavior of others or an act that has the object of creating terror in an opponent. A terrorist is one who practices terrorism. The definitions of suicide and terrorist are broad to facilitate the discussion, but arguments and questions will be raised throughout to try and perceive complexities.

Introduction

What causes someone to want to strap explosives onto his or her body and kill him or herself and numerous other people?[3] This is a common question generated by the numerous suicide bombings reported in the news. Answers to this question from the typical Western commentator or pundit seem to focus on one primary reason: they are crazy. Their insanity is most often attributed to one or more of the following reasons: religious frenzy, severe deprivation of resources and opportunity, anger over Western (American) interventions and policies, or desire to force the withdrawal of an occupying force. In general, Americans view suicide in any form as an act of insanity, temporary or otherwise.

In the case of individuals who commit acts of suicide terrorism, this chapter takes a different view. The view is one of tactical use rather than mental instability. The intent here is to offer an opportunity for Americans to develop the empathy discussed in the previous chapter and to present a theory on the forces that cause sane and committed people to perform suicide with the intent of killing as many other people as possible.

It is important to remember that in developing empathy, it is not essential that the individual establish moral equivalency. To understand a different perspective does not mean acceptance of that perspective as equal or valid. That said, there is no desire on the part of the author to communicate that there are irrevocable differences between cultures that will lead to an inevitable clash of civilizations. On the contrary, once the differences are clearly understood and empathy is developed, then many of the greatest differences can begin to be mitigated. If we can see through each others' eyes, then we may truly be able to prevent conflict in the first place. Until that paradise is reached, the utility argued here is that empathy helps to create a better environment for a successful conclusion of events. The presentation of this chapter is from one point of view to gain the understanding of that perspective. It is not intended to be balanced between competing visions.

Before continuing, it is essential to note that the experience of the author is not as a psychologist or a sociologist but rather as a soldier and historian. The views expressed here are based on anecdotal experience gleaned from numerous observations of behavior in and conversations with people in the Middle East and the Arab world; newspaper and magazine reports dealing with suicide bombers[4]; and personal reading on Middle Eastern culture, history, and social psychology. As in any work that seeks to paint a common picture of a group of people, there are inaccuracies. It is certain that specific examples can serve as refutations of the premises here provided. In the case of this chapter, the attempt in general is to explain an understanding of the mindset in question and assist others in an attempt to reduce the cultural divide. There will be inaccuracies, and this chapter seeks to challenge readers to point them out and enhance this critical discussion. As most, though not all, suicide terrorists are male, and Arab–Muslim culture places greater emphasis on the male role, the descriptions use the masculine gender.

There are many books and articles addressing terrorism and the thinking behind the actions. This chapter will not summarize all of those ideas, since this is essentially a utilitarian document—existing here to demonstrate how a reader can develop empathy for a group of people generally vilified in the Western media. The presentation of this theory is done with the hope that it will generate discussion and cause more informed people with better resource material to come forward in assisting Western minds to come to grips with this Middle Eastern mindset. It is important to make very clear in the beginning that this chapter in no way implies or states that this way of thinking applies to many, most, or all Arabs, Middle Easterners, or Muslims. In fact, it is the contention of this chapter that suicidal terrorists represent an infinitesimally small portion of these larger populations. However, there are general attitudes among the Arab, Muslim, and Middle Eastern populations, supported through numerous regionally and internationally conducted polls, that show a great deal of sympathy with those who conduct suicide attacks. Therefore, even though the people spoken of in this chapter are the extreme of minorities, there are larger cultural issues that create a seedbed for these most extreme actions.

The case study will present information in each of the categories from the general view and point out the extreme interpretations. I hope that those who are from Arab culture or from the Middle East will recognize many things with which they agree. The idea is to show the rational thought process. In many cases, the information has broad applicability. In some cases, it only applies to the most extreme elements. To use the opening example, the intent is to reconcile the views of King Henry and the Assassin leader—to prevent the disparate impressions of insanity versus commitment. When the reader closes the book at the end of the chapter he or she should see with a broader vision that will include some of what the suicide terrorist sees. This is a bold and demanding task.

Because this chapter proposes an understanding of a group of people who are currently opponents or enemies of the U.S., it is phrased in a military context. The nature of asymmetric warfare is best explained as the use of strength against an opponent's weakness. This statement will be elaborated on later. It is also important to remember the Chinese military theorist Sun Tzu's dictum that success in war is based on an understanding of three things: the terrain upon which the battle is to be fought, oneself, and one's opponent.[5] The rest of this chapter is framed by describing an understanding of the suicidal attacker's perceptions of these three critical areas.

So, what causes a young man or young woman literally to sacrifice everything with the intent of causing maximum destruction and damage? It is a combination of three major interrelated areas: culture, or a person's social terrain; perception of situation or of oneself; and perception of the target or opponent (see figure 3.1). It is important to emphasize that these areas are interrelated in a complex web of concepts, ideas, teachings, cultures, etc. Many of the items influence others. Despite this complication, it is not impossible to untangle the web and come to a more accurate understanding of the motivations leading to the confusing actions.

Cultural Terrain

Hospitality was essential, for the desert is ruthless, and if the human residents of the desert did not support each other in times of need, they would all die. With hospitality goes generosity. It is not enough simply to provide the barest of necessities and meet the letter of the request, but one must provide abundance. This almost universal attribute ensures that if anyone falls victim to the brutalities of the terrain and climate, then they have a claim on their fellow man for succor and critical assistance.

Honor is the only thing that an individual truly possesses. A man's honor is what makes him "self" and allows him to struggle against nature, which he can never completely conquer. A man

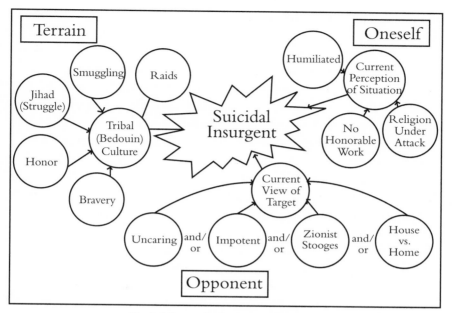

Fig. 3.1 Factors shaping insurgent propensity

can lose everything to the conquering elements, but only he can surrender his honor. This is an essential element of understanding offense and the concept of retribution. If the honor is damaged, it is necessary to repair it in the eyes of the individual and the eyes of the community.

Bravery is closely associated with honor, since it is one of the most significant vehicles for building the perception of honor among the community. If a man can protect his family, regardless of the challenge, then he builds honor while in the process of demonstrating bravery. The emphasis on bravery makes a Bedouin a warrior rather than a soldier. Bedouins fought for many reasons, some of which will be discussed later in this chapter, but high among them were the desire to display the bravery and courage of a warrior and the desire to be recognized as such. These are not professionals trained to fight under bureaucratic direction in the defense of ideals, rather they fought for personal and collective honor.

For the average American citizen, the word *tribe* might bring to mind western movies, Native Americans, chiefs, and warriors.

Sadly, the perception of Native Americans and the sociopolitical structure of their tribes is nearly as filled with mistakes as is our understanding of Bedouin tribes. The Bedouin tribe is built on the concept of extended family. In fact, in several dialects of Arabic, one accepted translation of the word for tribe could be family. The tribal culture was and is built around the concept of family. Though this discussion is about the older cultural tradition, there are still Bedouin tribes living and following many of the family-based cultural patterns today.

The family unit lives and works together. The size of each family element varies considerably, depending on the wealth of the tribe. It was, and is, essential that this unit protect its resources and gain more resources. These resources could include water sources; animals, typically sheep, goats, and camels; or control of trade routes. The necessity of protecting the current resources and gaining more meant that bravery and honor were essential to the survival of the tribe or family. Men and women had to risk their lives to protect these precious assets.

The men were primarily charged with this responsibility. They also took it upon themselves to increase the family holdings by acquiring more assets through raids of neighboring tribes. The focus of the raids was to capture useful booty—animals, control of water sources, key terrain-controlling trade routes, women, slaves, etc.— not on battles of annihilation. The raid was designed to capture and return with little or no loss of life on either side. The emphasis of the activity was honor through risk and accomplishment, not slaughter.

Even in battles fought between large tribes involving hundreds or thousands of warriors, casualties were low in comparison to European battles of a similar size and period. The decisive point of a tribal battle was to demonstrate dominance and thereby force capitulation. The tribes did not fight to erase one another completely but to gain access to trade routes or other resources. This was accomplished when one of the opponents acknowledged the dominance of the other, rather than by killing everyone.

The emphasis on dominance rather than annihilation is further demonstrated by the nature of Bedouin fortifications. Unlike

European or Levantine fortifications of comparable periods, the Arab-Bedouin fortifications were almost entirely defensive in nature, with little opportunity to mount offensive action from the fort itself. Sometimes the protection of a city might simply have been that the outside houses were built immediately adjacent to each other, providing a continuous wall around the village. Typically, fortifications were built over a water source and were not designed to withstand sieges consisting of sophisticated siege engines. This is an example of the intent—to deter aggression or annihilation and prevent capitulation.

Raids were honorable affairs. They were an opportunity for the men to demonstrate their bravery and courage by risking injury and, potentially, death. The difference between the ancient example of raids and the modern performance where casualties are the ideal is a change in view of the opponent. When the opponent was perceived as a peer tribe from the same culture, then these rules applied, but, as will be elaborated later, the opponent is no longer a peer. The casualties, like in the raids, are not the goal *per se*, but the resources gained are the goal. The aspect of the raid that has direct application is the emphasis on proving oneself and bringing in resources to help the larger collective.

Along with raids went the closely associated concept of caravans. Moving goods from one part of the region and selling them in another has been a recurring form of legitimate commerce. This was one of the most significant means of gaining additional resources—trading. Along with caravans went the raids on the caravans. Along the paths of these caravans, local tribal leaders would offer assistance with securing the caravan by requiring tolls, or tolls would be demanded as a payment to prevent raids from the tribe against the caravan.

The tolls exacted were typically not legal from a large-perspective bureaucratic approach. The empires who claimed suzerainty over the caravan routes would state that only they had the authority to levy taxes on commerce within their empire. The concept of legality was dependent upon a person or group's ability to enforce the law. If you could force people to pay the toll, then it was a legal or ethical act. It is important to note here a different view of the concept of rule of law. The law followed was mostly religious or socially accepted, since these were the laws enforced. There was, and to some degree still is, little regard for the concept of adherence to abstract legal principles without practical enforcement—driving in any Middle Eastern city reveals this perspective of rule of law. This meant there was nothing illegal about working to avoid payment of the tolls. In fact, it was incumbent on every caravan leader to guide his train on the safest and least expensive route possible. The process of avoiding tolls was also linked to raiding parties sent to find the caravans and exact tolls. Toll collection and raids against caravans served as a significant source of income for all of the tribes along the major routes of commerce and pilgrimage. The potential for disruption of the lucrative tolls from the Hajj pilgrims caused by the Hijaz railway was one reason that incited the Arab tribes to revolt against the Ottoman Sultan just prior to and during World War I.

In the modern world, where borders are drawn across barren landscapes to define physically the span of control of a state, the view of toll requirement and toll avoidance has changed. Now, the actions conducted at an official border crossing have the weight of legal support behind them, but to many, they are little different than the ancient toll collector. Today, Westerners refer to the avoidance of border fees and import taxes as smuggling. In the Middle East, it was, and in some locations still is, a part of the culture, and there is no dishonor in successfully avoiding paying a toll.

The tribal emphasis on bravery and honor through physical endeavors like raids, successful arrival with a caravan bypassing tolls, or the acquiring of tolls from caravans leads to a romantic view of bravery and honor. This is not unlike the American view of the nineteenth-century cowboy as a man defying the odds and living life on his own terms. Seldom is there an emphasis on the poor health conditions and severely hard life these men lived. As a result, most Americans do not really know what it means to be a cowboy, but he is still an icon of American culture, just as the Bedouin tribesman is for most Middle Eastern peoples, whether they draw their roots from Bedouin tribes or from village agrarian families.

On top of this ancient Bedouin-Arab culture was added the all-encompassing culture of Islam. There are many ways that Islam affects the lives of the average person in the Near East. First this chapter presents a broad way and then a narrow one that directly relates to suicidal terrorism.

In general, Islam affects all aspects of a Muslim's life. It impacts the dress, diet, sleep cycle, daily actions, finances, and general worldview of each Muslim. To many in America, this complete devotion to a religion that affects all aspects of life is extreme. It is not just a Friday-only religion. Islam is religion, law, government, mores, and social standards. It is life in the Middle East. To separate Islam from the Arab culture is to separate the heart from the body. Islamic and Arab cultures are so tightly intertwined that they are inseparable in the modern world. Certainly this was not always so, and others have suggested various theories about which one influenced the other more. The point is moot, since they have become one culture to the contemporary Arab-Muslim.

In specific, the concept of *jihad* within the Arab-Muslim culture is particularly important. Jihad is a verbal noun derived from the verb *jahada*. There are a variety of meanings for this word in most Arabic-English dictionaries—endeavor, strive, struggle, fight, to wage holy war against the infidels.[6] It is typically this last definition that Americans think of when they hear the word jihad, since this is the common definition used by the media. For most Muslims, the word has one of the former meanings. Their struggles to control their physical appetites during Ramadan are an example of a jihad. Striving toward moral purity and focus is a jihad as well. The word commonly means an inward struggle to cleanse self from impurity. Hence the final use of the word. A jihad, or Holy War, is usually declared to defend Islam from invasion by infidels. A jihad is typically not offensive in nature, meaning that it does not go outside Islam to wage the war, but it wages war to cleanse the house, once it has been invaded. It is also generally accepted that armed struggle against injustice, persecution, occupation, and oppression will always be considered jihad.

An interesting spin on the use of this word in the world of Internet connections is that there are those who view Islam as being invaded through the temptations of Western decadence and capitalist materialism. Therefore, to fight this invasion, it is necessary to strike outside the traditional geographic boundaries of Islam. Those who wage jihad are rewarded socially by praise and respect, and spiritually with promises of eternal rewards. The title of *shaheed*, which means martyr, is attached to those who die in jihad. Those who wage jihad, or *mujahid*—*mujahideen* is the plural—and die will be recognized as dying in the service and for the cause of God.

Those who are tempted toward the role of suicidal terrorist function within an ancient cultural terrain that holds in high esteem, among other things, the demonstration of bravery and honor through actions. These actions are in support of the individual's unit of association—tribe, community, family, terrorist cell, organization—and these actions may be perceived by outsiders as going beyond the accepted bounds of the legal framework. This is not unlike the stories of the Bedouin raider who captures sheep from a neighboring tribe. There are those who call him hero, while others call him thief. It is entirely dependent on from which side of the action your perspective is derived. All of this is encompassed in a culture that encourages a purging of the inner vessel from foreign invasion and promises social and spiritual rewards for those who do so.

In summary, the suicidal terrorist from the Middle East or Middle Eastern cultures has a series of cultural icons and concepts that lead toward a physical response to a negative situation. The emphasis on bravery and honor, the tradition of aggressive actions in the ancient form of raids, and the concept of legal ambiguity or situational legality extend from the Bedouin traditions and stories. Additionally, the emphasis on collective well-being over personal safety, especially in the context of waging an aggressive campaign to cleanse the vessel of the House of Islam, is all important in the decision to become a suicide terrorist.

Seeing Oneself

On top of the cultural terrain is laid the perception of self. The modern Arab man, first and foremost, perceives himself as being a strong and independent individual, but most also view themselves as being constantly humiliated. This humiliation is an extension of the treatment of Arab men throughout the region by occupying powers. This is not a new perception, since many Arabs espoused similar feelings during the rise of Turkish nationalism in the Ottoman Empire of the early twentieth century. This feeling grew as the domination by Turkish Muslims changed to domination by European Christians. The European dominance of the region began in Egypt and, following World War I, extended to the rest of the region. In many cases, policies of resource concessions that sent the majority of money to the Europeans and left a small percentage for the local populace further aggravated this dominant humiliation.

In addition to all of this, European and American Christian governments imposed, through a sense of collective guilt, the homeland of Judaism on the region, displacing hundreds of thousands of Arabs in the process. Adding further insult to this situation is the fact that the nation of Israel has grown from a perception of the Jews as a group requiring protection of Islam and Muslims to being a dominator of Muslims. This growth and change of fortune is typically attributed to the support of America and, to a lesser degree, Europe. This is also attributed to reliance on technology rather than on personal valor or capability. This becomes an important point later when discussing the perception of the opponent.

The feeling of humiliation is further enhanced through frustration about internal corruption, ineffective governments, and failure to provide a living standard equal to the West. However, religious purists argue that the West's living standards are a result of capitalist materialism and are not worthy of emulation.

This religious purist view is important because it is central to the view that Islam is under attack from the Christian West. The assault on Islam is physical, social, and cultural. Physically, the domination of the House of Islam by Western Christianity began in the eighteenth century and continued with the Israeli victories, the Serbian aggressions against Bosnian Muslims in the Balkans, and the American invasions of Afghanistan and Iraq. The social assault began with the infiltration of Western-inspired ideas of nationalism, which separated the House of Islam[7] into competing calls for Turkish,

Arabic, Kurdish, Berber, and a host of other ethnic group identities. This social assault continues with emphasis on other Western ideals dealing with women, governance, economic reform, materialism, capitalism, voting rights, political participation, etc.

Cultural assaults are viewed in many ways as the most damaging because they provide the most appeal. These are cultural temptations— the emphasis on connectivity, consumerism, and material acquisition. Each of these strikes at core cultural beliefs of simplicity, generosity, dialogue, and individual worth within a family or tribal framework. Western culture emphasizes the individual separate from and over the group.

The attacks and humiliation lead to a perception that the work available in their home countries—whether occupational or vocational—is not of honorable quality. The individual works to provide things for the family rather than the family striving to provide resources for each other. Raiding and trade (smuggling), as a result of the cultural and social attacks of the West, are viewed as illegal and unacceptable. The view of raiding and trading tends to be localized both geographically and culturally. Those people closest to their Bedouin roots in geography and history are the most inclined to be so motivated. The opportunity to demonstrate honor and bravery can only come through opposition to those who provide the humiliation and attacks.

Seeing the Opponent

In understanding the difference of perspective, the 2006 conflict between Israel and Hezbollah is instructive. Early in the conflict, most U.S. television broadcasts seemed to lay the blame for the fighting on the capture of Israeli soldiers by Hezbollah. The Arab media blamed Israel for the conflict based on the occupation of Palestine and the holding of thousands of Palestinian prisoners. The difference in perspective dictates where to draw the starting line for the question of who is to blame. If, in answering this question, the beginning of the timeline is summer 2006, then the blame rests on Hezbollah. If the beginning of the timeline is 1967, 1973, 1980, or 2000, then the blame is placed on Israel. Many of the differences in perception between the U.S. and the Arab media revolve around this issue of when the discussion begins.

It is a nearly universal belief within the Near East that the opponent of the Arab people in general, and the Arab-Muslim people specifically, is Israel, and the U.S. as an extension of U.S. foreign policy. This is irrespective of education, experience abroad, or relationships with Americans and Israelis. This view can be supported by nearly everyone, again regardless of education level, being able to recite a series of foreign policies dating back, typically, to the Balfour Declaration.[8] The list continues with the agreement of European powers to divide the Near East following World War I, rather than establishing an Arab state, in contradiction to promises made to Arab leaders in order to gain their support.

The discovery of oil and the forcing of oil concessions that granted enormous profits to U.S. and European oil companies, while keeping the local people and nations poor, further exacerbated issues in the region. This would ultimately lead to conflict over the nationalization of the oil industries in all of the countries in the region and, in an associated way, the nationalization of the Suez Canal. The list of offenses continues and includes those directly attributed to the U.S., with the establishment of Israel. Additional problems followed as the Cold War caused the U.S. to support corrupt and abusive regimes against the legitimate protests of those oppressed. The ideals of the U.S. are now seen as hypocritical statements that the U.S. expects others to follow under threat of war but that the country itself sets in abeyance when they do not meet the financial or geopolitical desires of whatever administration is currently in power in Washington, D.C. The uneven emphasis on the potential weapons of mass destruction in Iraq and Iran, as opposed to the expected, though never disclosed, weapons of mass destruction in Israel, is further evidence of duplicity and hypocrisy in policy. What Americans see as liberation in Afghanistan and Iraq is typically viewed by Arabs as invasion and occupation. American-style economic success has not followed the military actions, but a perceived increase in misery and suffering has. Another recent and contemporary example of perceived hypocrisy and duplicity is the 2006 election of the Hamas government in Palestine and the U.S. reaction to it. The U.S. government made great efforts to emphasize the importance of supporting democracy, then, when a democratically elected government came to power that was not approved by the U.S., the U.S. administration cut off all funding and supported what is seen among Arabs as rampant human rights abuses by Israel. All of this can be recited by the average man on the street in any Arab capital, city, or village.

It is this image among the vast majority of Arab-Muslims that is then taken by the extreme elements of the society to be crafted into a call to arms. The perception of the *opponent* is derived from the previous two understandings of cultural terrain and self. The opponent is the one attacking the House of Islam—the culture, social structure, or physical entity. The opponent is weak because his foundation is based on imperfect—not Islamic—principles and culture. The only reason the opponent is successful is because of his technology or outside support. In many editorials and commentaries discussing Israel, this is a common theme. Israel won because of American support and the technologically advanced weaponry they possess. The events of the conflict between Israel and Hezbollah in the summer of 2006 further support this view, since the Hezbollah fighters appeared heroically to withstand Israel's technology and achieve tremendous success in fighting in a non-Western fashion.

The view of *opponent* is not limited by Western mores or even older Islamic ones. In both cases, there are prohibitions against attacks on noncombatants, women, and children. In the extreme view, the opponent employs women in combat, and they have people of nearly all ages in the service, therefore, everyone can be construed as a current or potential target. No one is considered a noncombatant. This is specifically true with relation to Israel, but in a looser way, it also applies to the European nations and the U.S.

There are four ways the suicidal terrorist perceives the West, and particularly America. First is the assumption of many (maybe most) people from the Near East that America can do anything. Quite literally, there is no limit to American technology and power. The television programs and movies that show government officials instantly locating people and targeting a satellite to follow a subject continually fuel this perception, as does a regional propensity toward acceptance of outlandish conspiracy-theory explanations for events.

If America is so powerful and has unlimited resources, why doesn't it make the Israelis come to a settlement? Why doesn't it control the corrupt regimes and stop the corruption and evil perpetrated by those America claims as friends? The answer is simple—America does not care about the Arabs and the Muslims. This view is very prevalent. Virtually no editorial or opinion piece in a popular newspaper in the region will emphasize America's support to Muslims in Bosnia, the liberation of Muslims in Afghanistan, the support of Egypt against Western Imperialism in 1956, or any other way America has assisted and advanced the Arab-Muslim cause. Much of this is a result of the different perspectives identified previously. When the U.S. does provide assistance and help, it is perceived as self-serving and promoting a culturally or physically imperialist agenda, rather than altruistically beneficial. America does not support the Arabs (in the extreme view) because America does not care.

The second view, which seems to be at odds with the first, is one of American impotence. If America has all this power and knowledge, how can Osama bin Ladin continue to run free? It is certain that America knows where he is. Why has the U.S. not captured him? Because the U.S. lacks the will to use the power it has. The U.S. is impotent. For example, many within Iraq question why America allows the turmoil within Iraq to continue. They do not understand that government officials mean what they say about free elections and the Iraqi government taking charge, especially in light of the 2006 elections of the Hamas-led government. They believe the U.S. does not do this either because of a lack of concern for Iraqis, or because it lacks the will to use its power to enforce a policy of security against sectarian attacks and reprisals.

The third view of the opponent relates more to the first view than the second. This is the view of America as a Zionist stooge. Conspiracy theorists on websites began some of these rumors within a day of the September 11th attacks. The theory was that the Israeli

Mossad (the Israeli Intelligence Agency), in an attempt to start a war between Christians and Muslims, conducted the attacks on New York City and Washington, D.C. In the attacks on Iraq, America is accused of being a Zionist stooge and attacking Iraq because Iraq posed a threat to Israel and not America. America is also charged with stooging for the Zionists when the U.S. tries to get Iran to stop its nuclear aspirations but does not require Israel to do the same. The list of proposed reasons in support of the theory that the U.S. is a Zionist stooge is much longer than those given here, but in brief, the U.S. does not care about the plight of the Arab-Muslims because it is in the interest of the Zionists to have the Arab-Muslim nations weak, corrupt, and fighting among themselves, rather than allowing them to be strong and united, which they would certainly be under the extremist banner.

It is a common perception in the West that if someone from a developing country would only live in America or Europe for a short while, they would become co-opted, see the light of Western civilization and tolerance, and accept it. The train bombings in Madrid and the attacks on London's transportation infrastructure by men who had lived, some of them, their entire lives among these civilizations and were still willing to sacrifice their lives to attack them proved that to be a myth. How can this be? It is because of the fourth view that many extremists from the Middle East have. They do not view Europe and the U.S. as an educational or economic home but rather as a house. The house is a building where you reside, but a home is a place of emotional attachment with a sense of belonging. The house versus home view is neither permanent nor fixed at a specific time. There are those who may have chosen to go to the West to make it a home but became disillusioned by what they saw or how they were received. Others may have viewed it from the beginning as a necessary but temporary arrangement (the house) though their attachments always remained with their region of origin (the home).

In the case of Moroccans involved in the Madrid train bombings, some of these men lived in Spain or Europe for years. They attended school there and worked there. Some had European passports.

Despite this association, they were not Europeans. They were not a part of the fabric of the society. This disassociation allowed them to distance themselves emotionally from the people and cultures they attacked. It is not clear from the reports when this happened or what triggered it. As previously stated, this analogy is not time specific and recognizes the fact that events, reactions, and previous illusions can all affect the time when people no longer view their current residence as a home but simply a house, a utilitarian necessity, and a means to an end. The economic opportunities are greater than in the individual's home country, and the education is also perceived as better. Once the view is one of a house rather than a home, there is no longer an attempt to adopt the local culture or the local values—Bill of Rights, Declaration of Independence, Rights of Man—rather the drive can change, and does change for those who become suicide terrorists, to gain the benefits available and then use that knowledge to punish the house nation for its perceived failures.

Tactical and Strategic Result

It is essential to emphasize again that this chapter seeks to describe the general attitudes that create a fertile ground for those of the extreme minority who view suicidal terrorism as acceptable and, indeed, ideal for their struggle. The purpose is to try and see the world from their perspective and, in a small way, gain empathy for them. This is not a broad generalization of Arabs or Muslims but that very small element within the broader culture and society that garners so much of the world's attention.

This understanding of the opponent leads directly to an asymmetric tactical approach. The opponent believes that if the technology cannot be overcome, then do not fight the technology. The fight is against the people—the people and their will or spirit. Their will and spirit are weak because they do not have the strength of Islam. The West fears the media and harsh images, which leads to another tactic of conducting attacks or murders that provide the most gruesome and heinous results. The most heinous of attacks are those against civilians because civilians are not protected, nor are they trained to react to such events. Attacks against masses of civilians are not possible by means of overt military forces, given the perception of the opponent as technologically superior; therefore, the way to attack them is with civilian–appearing assailants.

The tactic of suicide bombing further enhances each of the four areas of perception just described. First, it cleanses Islam from the association with the house and returns the individual spiritually and physically to his home. The Arab–Muslim casualties are irrelevant to the attacker as a source of guilt, since a merciful God, who will recognize their innocence, will bless them. The casualties are very relevant as a resource that brings the images and reactions desired. The inability of the Western or Israeli governments to stop the attacks further emphasizes their impotence. The fact that civilians, many of whom are Arab–Muslims, are dying is a testimony of the West's lack of concern. If they truly cared and were truly powerful, they would stop this. They do not stop the attacks because they are impotent, do not care, or want a weak and divided Arab–Muslim people.

Suicide terrorists are not insane; in fact, they would and do characterize themselves as warriors in a holy war, feeling that they are attacking their opponents in the smartest and most effective way possible. It is worthy of repetition to say that those who perform these acts see themselves as warriors from a warrior culture. They also see that they are in a war and must take actions necessary to win this war. By dying in the act of committing the carnage, thus testifying of their opponents' weakness or complicity, the terrorist demonstrates that he is cleansed and that his commitment will cleanse the region from the stain of evil temptation and association. He cannot gain honor through a raid on horseback or camel with a rifle because of the technology of the opponent. He cannot demonstrate his bravery, though many try and succeed, through smuggling, since either the technology prevents it or another group already controls the smuggling. He must fight and struggle to cleanse the inner vessel of the House of Islam. This can only happen through direct attacks on the opponent.

The opponent is a concept rather than specific individuals or organizations. The attack at the highest conceptual levels is on the

West, more specifically America and its Western-leaning allies in the region. At the tactical level, it is not just government or military but also the people and their weak, poorly supported wills. The will of the populace is targeted; the perception is that this is the weakness of the West and its institutions.

The best way to attack this will is through *terror*. The best way to generate terror is through random acts that remove any sense of security in time or place. Attacks are on transportation, where people are trapped and cannot flee; they are at restaurants, where people are seated and captive; they are on churches and mosques, where people are in communion or have just finished communion with deity. If a person is not safe talking with God, how can there be safety?

When looked at rationally, from the perspective of one who views this as a war of cultures, this is the smartest and most appropriate technique available. The groups who have collectively developed and improved this technique have created the most successful stealth smart bomb in military history. Because, unlike the American version, which is only a success if it hits a precise target, the suicide individual or car bomber is a success anytime someone dies.

The understanding is easy; the struggle against it is difficult. How can you stop this? How do you clean the seedbed from the poisonous seeds planted therein? That is a separate topic all together. The purpose here was to put forward an explanation of how a rational mind comes to a rational conclusion to conduct a rational act of war viewed by so many in the West as irrational and insane.

The acts of the Assassins briefly mentioned at the beginning of this chapter show that similar techniques have been used by religious extremists for hundreds of years. The Assassins of the thirteenth century would have used explosive belts if they had had that technology. They would have targeted civilians if they had also had a media to spread the images for them and if the leaders they targeted actually cared about the reactions of the people. This technique is not new, nor has it been limited to the Arab-Muslim culture. It is a relatively common thread of previous eras for extremely committed individuals to use their lives as tools to generate specific reactions and behaviors in their targets. The assassination of a leader hundreds of years ago typically caused the successor to change their policies to those more favorable to the sect, just as the goal is to use the carnage of the modern events to cause a change in policy.

This concludes where it began. While this is an opinion and perspective of the author, and is quite possibly flawed, the hope is to generate discussion and disagreement. The intent is to gain empathy and a sense of why these things are happening and to encourage those with alternate viewpoints to provide different, and hopefully better, explanations for why very rational people can perform what, to the West, appear to be acts of insanity. This conversation, conducted in the right forum, may generate further productive discussion on how best to fight and win against this threatening technique.

Chapter 4

Case Study: The Battle of Little Bighorn (25 June 1876)

It is a rare occurrence in Indian warfare that gives a commander the opportunity to reconnoiter the enemy's position in daylight. This is particularly true if the Indians have a knowledge of the presence of troops in the country. . . . When the "signs" indicate a "hot trail," i.e., near approach, the commander judges his distance and by a forced march, usually in the night-time, tries to reach the Indian village at night and make his disposition for a surprise attack at daylight. At all events his attack must be made with celerity, and generally without other knowledge of the numbers of the opposing force than that discovered or conjectured while following the trail.

—E. S. Godfrey, Commander, K Troop, 7th U.S. Cavalry (1892)[1]

The army brought to the task no new strategy. In fact, there had never been any formal strategy for fighting Indians, and there never would be. The generals looked on Indian warfare as a momentary distraction from their principal concern—preparing for the next foreign war.

—Robert M. Utley, historian (1988)[2]

Strategies Emphasized:

1. Introspection
2. Empathetic Appreciation
3. Empathetic Expectation
5. Study of History

6. Study of Culture
7. Multiple Reserves
8. Initiative

As with most famous events, controversy swirls around the Battle of Little Bighorn. The historical interpretation of the battle has experienced significant transformation over the decades since the first reports of the losses suffered by the 7th U.S. Cavalry. A pendulum has swung from the initial interpretation of heroic gallantry ambushed by barbaric savages to European imperialist expansion bravely faced by native warriors defending families, a way of life, and nature. The pendulum now sits on an interpretation that emphasizes the roles and efforts of the individuals on both sides of the battle rather than on the large-scale history of decades past.

The opinions of this battle from a military history standpoint tend to be polarized around the author's opinion of the controversial character of the commander of the 7th U.S. Cavalry—George Armstrong Custer. Those who view Custer as a competent commander seek for reasons why this battle went so horribly wrong for his command. Those who see him as a reckless and irresponsible waster of human life see this battle as proof of his flawed leadership and tactical perceptions. In this brief treatment of the battle the perspective is that of the period itself rather than through historical eyes. The benefit of understanding this battle is to see it as it was viewed at the time it was fought.

The Little Bighorn battle is one of the best examples of aberrational conflict. It is the battle that inspired this philosophical view of seeing aberrations in conflict. For this reason this battle is one of the two most detailed accounts included in this book. How and why this aberrational event occurred are instructive for those seeking to understand ways to foresee and prevent such events.

Throughout this chapter the Native Americans will be referred to as Indians. Though there are numerous issues with this term, it is probably the best word. One particular reason for using the label stands out—this was the word used by the U.S. Cavalry soldiers in talking about their opponents. It is also the word most commonly used by the current descendants of the Indian tribes who fought in the battle to refer to themselves. In general, the Indians tended to refer to themselves in their own languages as something like "the people," but for the purposes of this book, such a label will not work.

In addition to the use of the word Indian, there is a more problematic assumption that such a word denotes hostility toward the U.S. government of the time period or toward the U.S. Army. This is not the case. Within the U.S. Army there was a division of hostile and non-hostile Indians. Such a division was of limited value because at various times the same group could change from one to the other. An example of this comes from the battle itself in that there were Indians participating on both sides with numerous Indians serving as scouts and warriors for the U.S. Army. Some of the Indian scouts for the 7th U.S. Cavalry were from the Crow nation. This same tribe had been deemed hostile in earlier conflicts, but at the time of the battle they were nonhostile. Since the focus of this chapter is to see things as much as possible as they were seen in the period, then the terms *hostile, nonhostile,* and *Indian* will be used as they were applied in 1876.

The nineteenth century was an era of significant military change and transition in the West. The military was evolving from the feudal-style armies and small yet professional militaries of earlier eras to armies of mass conscription and large-scale battles. Within the United States, the century included three large-scale conflicts against England (War of 1812), Spain (Mexican War), and itself (U.S. Civil War). Each war created a rush for recruitment and expansion followed by a reduction of forces and disbanding of military units.

The U.S. Army saw the greatest level of expansion for the U.S. Civil War, where battles were fought with Napoleonic tactics despite ever-increasing levels of lethality that resulted in horrendous casualties. The army then went through a similarly precipitous decline as it was reduced to prewar levels. The army went from Napoleonic contest to fighting what we would now call an unconventional opponent in unconventional tactics and styles of battles. It was a dramatic shock for those responsible for leading the conduct of conflict. Custer himself struggled with the transition, as did many of his superiors and subordinates. Numerous senior-ranking officers during the U.S. Civil War returned to their prewar ranks. The personal challenge of reduced rank coupled with the military-social challenge of a complete transformation of opponent and style of fighting provided pre-existing complications to which were added the challenges of the campaign.

Geographical Setting

Location

Indian camp movements were dependent on resources—water and food. The Indians moved to maintain contact with game animals and to ensure there was always a ready supply of water. As a result of the water imperative, the U.S. Army campaign against the Sioux nation in the late winter, spring, and early summer of 1876 was essentially a campaign of rivers. The Yellowstone River was the *de facto* northern boundary of the campaign, since the river runs in a generally southwest to northeast direction of current. Into the Yellowstone River flowed a series of other rivers in a generally south to north direction. From the east to the west the most important of these rivers are as follows: Powder River, Tongue River, Rosebud River, and Bighorn River. Several miles up (south) the Bighorn River, from its confluence with the Yellowstone, there is a fork where it divides and the Little Bighorn enters the stream. The Little Bighorn River extends from this point to the southeast and then due south. It is along this branch that the battle itself occurred. It was between the Little Bighorn and the Rosebud that most of the decisions were made.

In a geopolitical setting, most of this area was in what was typically referred to as Unceded Territory, or within the Crow Reservation. These areas were designated as a result of the treaty of 1868, which also identified the great Sioux reservation that took up most of the modern state of South Dakota.

Terrain and Vegetation

The terrain in this part of the modern state of Montana is one of rolling ground. The significance of rivers identified above means that the terrain really is a sequence of river valleys and intervening higher terrain separating the rivers. Some of the intervening terrain was of dramatic relief, providing long-range observation. River valleys tended to be relatively broad plains of grassland with dense softwood trees and undergrowth along the water course.

The valley of the Little Bighorn River needs specific attention. On the eastern side of the river were significant bluffs that in some areas rose almost in a sheer cliff from the riverbank. The portion of the valley featured in the battle was about five miles in length and about a half mile wide. Along this five miles there was one crossing in the south and two more crossings more than four miles to the north and beyond. The rest of the riverbank featured no good ford sites, and much of the riverbank was covered with softwood trees throughout. On the western side of the valley was a slightly higher plateau of land that served to funnel movement into the lower valley, but it was also used for grazing the enormous Indian pony herd.

The bluffs rising on the eastern side prevented observation of the Indian camp for most of the battle for Custer and the elements of the command moving with him. Within the river valley itself, the trees and vegetation along the riverbank in concert with the meandering nature of the river made observation of the camp difficult until the soldiers were nearly on top of the encampment. The rolling terrain, deep coulees[3], and ridges made sound travel problematic and observation nearly impossible. Once the 7th U.S. Cavalry separated, the entire regiment was not again in observation of all elements. The same challenges faced the Indian warriors, since they never had a full understanding of the battle, nor could they see the entire battlefield at any time because the battle was fought over more than three miles of river valley, bluffs, and coulees.

The vegetation played an important role in the battle. The ridges had little vegetation other than low prairie grasses. Down in the river valley the trees and shrubs clogged the riverbed, and these were used by the soldiers of the 7th U.S. Cavalry for cover and concealment early in the engagement. Trees and shrubs were also in several of the coulees that descended to the river valley.

Weather

Weather was significant in the campaign and in the battle. The intent of conducting a semi-coordinated winter campaign was defeated by the severely cold weather. Later, as the snow and ice began to melt, the northern prairie became a morass of mud that further delayed the beginning of the expedition and slowed early movement from the various military bases. By the time the campaign reached the critical places of decision, the weather was hot and dry. Fatigue, combined with weather, also played a key role in the battle. Because of decisions and changes in decisions based on a seemingly rapidly changing situation, the soldiers of the U.S. Army went from a night march right into a movement and then a battle with little opportunity to fill or refill canteens. The soldiers suffered throughout the battle from a lack of water. The heat of the summer sun on the northern plains made the suffering of wounded and nonwounded horrible. Outside of the river valley there was no access to water.

Units Involved

U.S. Army

Operationally speaking, the U.S. Army employed three columns, two of which operated in concert, and the third functioned on its own. The three columns (with points of departure) were commanded by Brig. Gen. Alfred Terry (Fort Abraham Lincoln, near present-day Bismarck, North Dakota), traveling along the Yellowstone River from east to west; Col. John Gibbon (Fort Ellis, present-day Bozeman, Montana), traveling along the Yellowstone River from west to east; and Brig. Gen. George Crook (Fort Fetterman, present-day Douglas, Wyoming), traveling from the south toward the Rosebud River to the north. Each column consisted of hundreds of soldiers from a variety of units. In some measure, they all included cavalry and infantry forces. For the purpose of this chapter the focus is on the column led by Brigadier General Terry, which included the 7th U.S. Cavalry regiment.

The 7th U.S. Cavalry consisted of twelve troops or companies. The original intent was that each cavalry troop was supposed to include 100 men.[4] This was rarely the case in the frontier army. Typically, each company consisted of about 50–60 soldiers. The entire regiment consisted of 597 soldiers with 35 Indian scouts from the Crow and Arikara tribes.[5] Additionally there were civilian scouts and civilian packers who were responsible for the mules in the pack train.

The troops had been spread out over the previous months (and, in a few instances, years), conducting various missions—national border security and securing infrastructure against Indian attacks—with only six of the troops collocated in the regiment's largest concentration. The regiment was gathered for the purposes of the campaign, and they were only united in the months immediately preceding the campaign. For the most part, the soldiers who left Fort Abraham Lincoln were foreign born, typically coming from Ireland or Germany, with others recently immigrating from Italy, Scandinavia, or other western European countries. Many of the soldiers were new to the army and only had the experience of constabulary duty or, at most, the campaigns into the Yellowstone River valley (1873) or the Black Hills (1874). Though many of the officers had combat experience both in the U.S. Civil War and in fighting Indians, most of the enlisted soldiers did not.

The soldiers carried the Springfield trapdoor carbine and a revolver. The Springfield fired a single bullet about a half an inch in diameter. After each firing the trapdoor needed to be lifted, ejecting the spent cartridge, and another cartridge needed to be loaded. The Springfield had long-range accuracy, in excess of four hundred yards, but the rate of fire was slow because each firing required the reloading process. Cavalry soldiers typically carried sabers into battle, but Lieutenant Colonel Custer felt that sabers were an unnecessary burden and would only weigh the troopers down. The sabers spent the campaign boxed up on the steamboat *Far West*.

The U.S. cavalry force of the nineteenth century fought according to drill. The drill was designed to control the soldiers and their firing while maintaining discipline. Most of the soldiers were uneducated, and many were illiterate, thus the officers considered significant control to be essential to mission success. The soldiers rode to battle on their large, grain-fed horses, dismounted, and then fought in a skirmish line. One trooper out of four would serve as a horse-holder for the other three firers. Typically, the horse holder was the senior person in the group of four, but at the Little Bighorn the lack of junior soldier experience meant that the experienced noncommissioned officers were mostly on the line. The person holding the horses was probably a private facing his first experience fighting Indians. The skirmish line could be ordered to volley fire (all or portions of the line firing simultaneously) or fire at will (each soldier firing as he was ready and he identified a target).

Between the regiment and the troop/company was the squadron/ battalion. In theory, a regiment of twelve troops could be formed into three squadron/battalions of four companies each. Typically this division was based on the nature of the campaign and made only as situations required. In the years preceding the campaign the regiment was located at four locations, Fort Abraham Lincoln with six troops and three other locations with two troops each.

The 7th U.S. Cavalry had several unique personality issues worthy of note. The regiment was divided into two primary factions—"the Royal Family" and the outsiders. The Royal Family was an appellation given by officers outside the group, and it consisted of officers related to Lieutenant Colonel Custer by blood or by marriage and their close associates. The outsiders were those excluded either through personality conflicts or through possessing negative views of the commanding officer. The letters and material of the period show that a majority of the officers moved freely within the Royal Family, but there were many others who excluded themselves or who were excluded by the group. Both Maj. Marcus Reno and Capt. Frederick Benteen were among those excluded.

The history of the expansion and contraction of the U.S. Army as a result of the U.S. Civil War and the unit's history of campaigns and engagements had significant bearing on the emotions within the regiment. Lieutenant Colonel Custer was a brevet major general of volunteers and enjoyed a spectacular career throughout the U.S. Civil War. After the war he returned, as did many other officers, to his prewar rank. though in Custer's case this included a promotion— he became a captain. Custer fought to get the command of a unit, and he was able to gain the position of second in command of the 7th U.S. Cavalry when it was formed in 1867 with a permanent rank of lieutenant colonel. Many of his subordinates had also held higher ranks during the previous war and were much senior to him in overall service—Custer graduated the U.S. Military Academy at West Point in 1861. Captain Benteen was a brevet colonel, and he deeply resented Custer's flamboyant style and connections that allowed him to leapfrog so many others. The campaign of 1867, the 7th U.S. Cavalry's first campaign, was one that did not feature the best leadership of Lieutenant Colonel Custer, and this affected the opinions of several officers for the remainder of Custer's career.

Additionally, the unit fought in a winter campaign in 1868, and during that campaign the regiment attacked an Indian camp at the Washita River. During the fighting, one officer charged off in pursuit of fleeing Indians only to be surrounded and his entire element of fifteen soldiers killed. The regiment came under heavy counterattack during the same period, and Lieutenant Colonel Custer ordered the regiment to withdraw without determining the situation of the officer and his men. Captain Benteen held Custer personally responsible for the death of the detail and held a pent-up grudge until the battle under examination—over eight years. The bitter feelings harbored by Captain Benteen were shared by some other officers in lesser measure, and the regiment was somewhat divided into those who liked Custer and those who did not. Despite the division, it was clear that most of the officers respected the commander and recognized his success and luck, even if they did not give him full credit for brilliance. Benteen was not the next most senior officer in the regiment at the time of the campaign. That position belonged to Major Reno. This campaign was Reno's first against the Sioux and his first real campaign against any hostile Indians. The personality issues and inexperience played a significant part in the post-battle criticisms of decisions and actions during the battle.

Indian Forces

Most of the Indian opponents were from the Sioux Nation. Sioux is a word that is common but often misunderstood. It has numerous meanings depending on who uses it. In this case, the word applies to a large group of tribes and families that generally speak the same type of language. In the case of the Sioux campaign of 1876, the Sioux in question were the Teton Sioux, who were a combination of five tribal groups—Uncpapas, Blackfeet, Sans Arc, Minneconjou, and Oglalla—with the addition of the Northern Cheyenne. The Teton Sioux in 1876 were an angry and united group—initially united by grievances against the U.S. government and then physically united in a gigantic camp that may have included as many as twenty thousand inhabitants.

There were two primary issues against the U.S. government. Both of these issues were related to the 1868 Treaty of Fort Laramie in which the Great Sioux Reservation was created and the areas designated for the Sioux and other Indian free hunting grounds—typically known as the Unceded Territory. The first issue was the continued expansion west of the whites. This was clearly demonstrated by the 1873 Yellowstone River expedition to survey the future line of the Northern Pacific Railroad. The Indians knew that where the railroad went, the white settlers followed. The route of the railroad could be argued as both violating the treaty and not violating the treaty, depending on the interpretation of the specifics. The second issue dealt with the Black Hills region. This was a beautiful area that was in the heart of the Great Sioux Reservation. The rumors of gold in the region were confirmed by an expedition in 1874. The U.S. government sought to buy the land from the Sioux, but there was no agreement. The U.S. government grew frustrated by Sioux intransigence, and the Sioux were angry by the insatiable appetite of the whites for Indian lands.

In a related issue, the reservations served to both support the Indian militancy and to provide fuel for the anger with the whites. Those opposed to accommodation with the whites could go to a reservation and there trade for a repeating rifle, ammunition, and supplies. It was also there that Indians were regularly degraded and their way of life insulted and denigrated. At the same time, the reservations and the U.S. government agents who operated there provided the fuel for anger and for effective resistance in the spring and summer of 1876.

Indian tribes were not unified groups of people with official leaders and political systems. Rather, the tribe was typically an informal grouping that expanded and contracted as smaller family groups moved freely in and out of the circle. As the expansion of the U.S. moved further and further west and Indians were increasingly moved onto reservations, many families began a cycle of using the reservation in the winter for provisions and protection and then leaving for the Unceded Territory in the late spring and early summer. By 1876 this was common and expected.

In addition to the five Sioux tribes, the Indians encamped on the Little Bighorn River included the Northern Cheyenne and Arapahoe. All of these groups came together in response to a general sense of anger and frustration that gave the impression of no other choice but military resistance.

The Plains Indians of the nineteenth century were a tribal people who viewed armed conflict as a means to demonstrate the virtues of bravery, valor, courage, and strength. Combat was a way of life. In combination with hunting, it was the primary means of demonstrating individual worth and valor. The young men needed to fight to prove themselves to the society. Even when the older men of the tribe counseled for peace, the younger men would fight. This distinction is critical to appreciate the fact that there was no way to ensure 100 percent compliance with any treaty where nonaggression was a stipulation. The same was true of the U.S. Army's ability to control civilian actions. By 1876, the old men in the Unceded Territory were counseling for war as much as the young men, and the unification of the culture was important to the tactics used throughout the campaign.

Typically, a battle with Indians was one of chaos, since the Indians did not fight like Europeans armies. War was for individuals, and they fought accordingly. Each warrior sought to demonstrate his ability individually. This allowed for both significant amounts of individual initiative and unpredictable actions. This style of warfare led to an emphasis on the raid. The culture and experience of the average Indian warrior did not lend itself to protracted or static defense. Plains Indians did not and would not seek to defend a trench or a ditch. They sought their protection through mobility, and they would either attack an enemy who outnumbered them in a manner committed to death in battle or they would flee. The biggest weakness lay in attacks on their villages, in which case the warriors could not simply flee but were forced to remain and protect their families. Here was the instance where the Indian warrior was most easily overwhelmed because he was forced to think not only of fighting but also of protection.

Key Leaders in the Battle

These are brief sketches to familiarize readers with those personality aspects most important to this battle. Given the nature of the battle and the fact that the U.S. Army fought in a more hierarchical and bureaucratic system, it is easier to define those individuals of significance. The Indian leaders are based off of the best known men and those who were recognized as leaders by the U.S. government. It is certain that there were many notable Indian leaders who are not mentioned here but probably should have been. Space and the focus of the chapter have limited those referenced.

U.S. Army

Brigadier General George Crook—Commander, Department of the Platte. He had successfully fought Indians in Oregon and Arizona and for this was rewarded with his promotion to Brigadier General. He had revolutionized the way to support U.S. Army columns in pursuit of Indians. He commanded the southern column, headquartered in Fort Fettermen (Douglas, Wyoming), and during the campaign demonstrated initial aggressiveness and then an uncharacteristic sense of timidity.

Brigadier General Alfred Terry—Commander, Department of Dakota. Originally, he was to command the eastern portion of the campaign from his headquarters in modern-day North Dakota while Custer acted as the field commander. When Custer was removed from command of his regiment, Terry was forced to become a field commander with no experience in commanding field forces against Indians. His orders to Custer prior to the battle are at the center of much of the controversy concerning fault and blame for the battle.

Colonel John Gibbon—Commander, District of Montana. He led the western column from Fort Ellis (Bozeman, Montana).

Lieutenant Colonel George Armstrong Custer—the most controversial figure in nineteenth-century America and possibly one of the most controversial in all of American history. Year for year of military service, Custer has more books written about him than any other U.S. military figure. It is difficult to identify clearly the personality of Custer. He was the central figure of this battle, and he decided the time, location, and manner in which the battle would be fought. To understand these decisions, it would be useful to understand the character of the person who made them.

Custer was a complex person with two very distinct parts to his military career—the U.S. Civil War and the frontier. The U.S. Civil War featured an officer who rarely made a mistake and who had the ability seemingly to make the right decision at the right time regardless of the odds of the engagement. Custer demonstrated himself to be a competent staff officer and battlefield commander. He earned the loyalty and adoration of those who served under him and the respect of his peers and superiors. He became the youngest general officer in U.S. history, achieved the rank of major general, and commanded a cavalry brigade and division with great distinction for the last two years of the war.

The frontier Custer was a different man. Still young and facing a very different set of circumstances, he showed an immature leadership style and a poor ability to generate loyalty and respect from subordinates during times of inactivity. Most of the work was constabulary in nature and featured days, weeks, and months of tedious garrison duties with very little chance for the glories of the battlefield or the environment of engagement for which Custer had showed himself to be a natural. He earned a reputation among officers and enlisted soldiers quite the opposite from those of his Civil War units. He was feared and hated. Later (in 1866) he was given a different unit, the 7th U.S. Cavalry Regiment, where he gained the opportunities to conduct campaigns against the Indians.

Through the battlefield experience he was able to regain some of his luster, though the 1868 Washita battle provided both glory and harsh criticism for leaving Maj. Joel Elliot's fate unknown and leaving the battlefield. The Washita battle was the frontier Custer in microcosm. He was audacious, and he understood the Indians enough to seize victory, but he was not thorough, nor did he empathize with the opponent sufficiently to truly understand them. Washita provided glory—battlefield victory publicized in the east— and criticism. No longer was fighting clear cut and victory simple to define. The fact that fighting Indians meant killing women and children and that the enemy would mutilate those that fell into their hands meant that the victories were never above reproach, and mistakes were never simply passed over by evaluating the greater good achieved.

Custer also used this period of engagement to develop his personal conceptualization of his opponent.

Within the regiment he had created a separation among the officers. In some circles it was referred to as the Royal Court. Custer himself sometimes used this term. He surrounded himself with likeminded and loyal officers. Those who did not agree with the commander or who were singled out were relegated to the units not stationed at Fort Abraham Lincoln.

Captain Frederick Benteen—third most senior officer in the 7th U.S. Cavalry at the time of the battle. He was a brevet colonel and had commanded a regiment in the U.S. Civil War. He wrote negative comments about nearly every officer in the regiment, especially Custer. He referred to Custer's book *My Life on the Plains* as *My Lie on the Plains*. The relationship between the two was barely professional, and Benteen's opinion of the commander was clearly one of disdain and contempt. Despite Benteen's issues as a follower and loyal subordinate, no one doubted his ability as an Indian fighter. He was almost unanimously praised for his performance after arriving at the Reno-Benteen entrenchment and credited with making possible the survival of the remainder of the regiment. This comment exceeds the bounds of understanding the leaders at the time of the battle, but it is indicative of his ability to lead men in times of crisis and also demonstrative of the dual nature of his character—irascible and courageous.

Major Marcus Reno—second in command of the regiment. This was Reno's first major Indian fight. He was generally not considered that capable by his superiors and most of the regimental officers. He was to command the regiment while Custer was detained in Washington, D.C. His behavior while Custer was away caused Custer to question his loyalty.

Indian Forces
Command among the Indians was not defined by a rigid hierarchical relationship. Rather, it was one of influence. The few Indians identified here were considered to be the most influential in the battle.

Sitting Bull—one of the most well known and influential of the Teton Sioux. He was probably the closest thing to a universal Indian leader. He was generally respected by members of all of the tribes of the Northern Plains. Sitting Bull was a political and a religious leader. He shared his visions and premonitions given him by the Great Spirit, and this was, at least in some measure, a source of his influence and ability to lead. He was the closest thing to a leader of the nonreservation Indians and advocated separation from the whites and rejection of all things associated with them, especially the reservation system and reservation life.

Crazy Horse—Like Custer, this is a man who is difficult to characterize. He was certainly a great Indian war leader and could command the respect and the obedience of hundreds of warriors in battle. He did not seem to seek political leadership as did Sitting Bull.

Gall—one of the tribal leaders of the Teton Sioux. His family was killed at the beginning of the battle, and as a result, he fought with total commitment and abandon throughout the battle.

Historical and Grand Strategy Context

In the past few decades the characterization of the westward expansion of white Americans has gone through significant revision, and the corresponding characterization of the U.S. Army soldiers who enforced the movement has been equally criticized. The Indians faced challenges in their struggle with the white Europeans (and later white Americans) and endured a series of expansions and related clashes. The U.S. Civil War served as a watershed event in that the events and relations between the two groups dramatically transformed after the end of the war, and the U.S. government looked west with greater commitment and a greater appreciation for the concept of total war. In addition, they now had leaders with the experience, understanding, and commitment to enforce such a doctrine. They also had an army with the technology to overcome the historical weakness of the U.S. Army vis-à-vis the Indians on the Great American Plains—mobility. The expansion of the railroads brought to the west the same operational mobility it had brought to the campaigns in the war in the east.

There is neither space nor intent to express all of the military history between the two cultures involved in this engagement. The priority here is to address those events that had direct relation to the decisions leading to the 1876 Sioux Campaign.

Much of the U.S. Army that was led onto the plains following the end of the war in the east had the impression that the Indians would be easily defeated. The four years of slaughter on the European-style battlefields of the east gave the impression that an enemy armed with arrows and spears would quickly fall. A relatively young officer made the quip that, given sixty soldiers, he could conquer the entire Sioux nation. In one of the great ironies of American military history, he was lured into an ambush where he and sixty other U.S. soldiers were killed by the same Sioux warriors he had threatened. The event that was misnamed "The Fetterman Massacre" began two years of war that ended with a treaty with the Sioux Chief Red Cloud and other Indian leaders. This gave the Great Sioux Reservation to the Sioux and designated the Unceded Territory as open range for Indian hunting and free movement.

Though the treaty redefined geographical boundaries, it did not redefine cultures. The whites would continue to expand and run into direct competition with the Sioux for land and resources. The Sioux continued to hunt and raid without concern for boundaries or signatures on paper. As previously identified, the expansion of the Northern Pacific Railroad and the hint and later discovery of gold in the Black Hills were two of the most contested issues between the Sioux and the whites. The continued raids, murders, and thefts by the Sioux were issues that concerned white settlers and Indian agents. On both sides there was no trust and little to no understanding. The issues that developed continued to fester until finally the administration of President Ulysses Grant developed a plan to force the issue and make it an issue of war.

Between the Fetterman Massacre and the Grant administration's dramatic change in policy were the campaigns of 1868 (in which Custer and the 7th U.S. Cavalry fought the Battle of the Washita) and the Red River Campaign of 1872–1874. The two campaigns demonstrated the effectiveness of winter campaigns and the ability of separated but loosely associated columns to effectively fight Indians. It is important to understand that in neither campaign, nor in the specific campaign of 1876, was there intent to control the columns closely. Not only was this impossible with the technology of the day, it was also not deemed prudent, given the fluid nature of Indian fighting of the nineteenth century.

In both of these critical campaigns the fundamental principle of Indian fighting was established—to defeat the Indians you must first catch them. Winter campaigns facilitated this because the Indians were more significantly hampered by the weather than the more logistically reliant U.S. Army soldiers. Based on this principle, the operational concept of loosely associated columns was designed to give the maximum opportunity to bring the tribes to a fight. Not at any time did the U.S. Army officers consider that the Indians would seek major engagements or that they would stand and fight when faced with a determined opponent. Both of these behaviors were contrary to the sum total of U.S. Army experience in fighting Indians. It was also contrary to the nature of tribal warfare that existed on the plains for the known history of the Indians. They did not seek out European-style decisive battles. Warfare was a modification of the hunt, and animals never sought a decisive engagement.

The Grant administration wanted the Black Hills, and the Sioux were not interested in or willing to negotiate its sale in a manner agreeable to the U.S. government. In November 1875, key members of the administration used the pretext of a recent Indian agent report to issue an ultimatum that all Indian groups must return to their reservations by 30 January 1876 or be deemed hostile and therefore turned over to the U.S. Army for military action.

The limited response time and the vastness of the territory combined with the limited media technology of the period made the demand ludicrous. It would have been impossible for all of the bands to return to the reservation even if they had been informed and if they had an inclination. The fact that very few of the bands and tribes currently off the reservation had any real desire to obey such a demand from a government generally viewed as treacherous only served to provide support for the administration's claim. The timing of the demand gives credence to those who claim that this was a fabricated pretext to generate a way to nearly steal the Black Hills through the manufacturing of an excuse for a winter campaign.

Thoughts Before the Battle

The U.S. Army had two imperatives—first, find the concentrations of Indians, and second, force their capitulation. The movement of families, bands, and tribes back to the reservations would happen once they were shown that they did not have unlimited mobility in the Unceded Territory. The primary concern of all commanders from Custer in the field up to William Tecumseh Sherman, the army's commanding general, was to prevent the flight of the main camp and thereby make this a rapid campaign rather than the feared fruitless pursuit that so many of the Indian campaigns seemed to become.

The Indians only had to maintain their freedom of mobility. If they remained away from the U.S. Army and undiscoverable, then force would prove irrelevant.

Operational Context

The campaign only started in the winter in the technical sense, since the earliest columns departed in mid- to late March. Neither of the columns who left in March achieved any success. A portion of Crook's column came in contact with a small Indian village and attacked it. The initial engagement went well, but as they were withdrawing the soldiers lost the captured ponies to an Indian counterattack. Crook ended up relieving the officer in charge when the entire column returned to Fort Fetterman. The column started out again in May, and Crook pushed them north toward the Rosebud. Gibbon started and marched to and then along the Yellowstone River to link up with Brigadier General Terry. Terry's column was the last to start. This was mostly due to weather constraints and partially to political issues with Lieutenant Colonel Custer.

The weather is important to note now. The idea and success of earlier winter campaigns was very valid, but it was difficult simply to move the concept north. The northern Great Plains were different in climate than those of Oklahoma and Texas. The winters were generally more severe in cold and length. This lesson was not learned until the campaign was delayed until March, and then all of the columns who departed were forced to return to their home bases. The weather was always a challenge, and even when Col. Nelson A. Miles conducted his successful campaign in late 1876 and 1877, there were numerous weather-related casualties among the soldiers in his command.

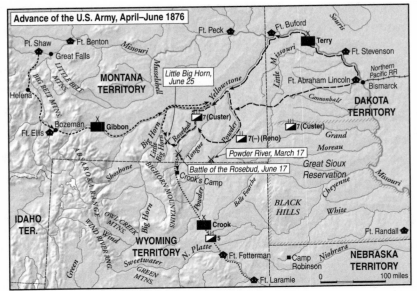

Fig. 4.1

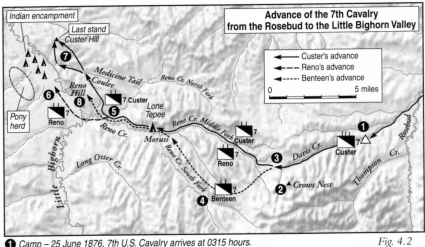

Fig. 4.2

❶ Camp – 25 June 1876, 7th U.S. Cavalry arrives at 0315 hours.

❷ Crow's Nest – Hostile Indians seen at 0540 hours.

❸ Custer divides his column, he sends Benteen to scout to the south, 1212 hours.

❹ Benteen turns to rejoin Custer, 1315 hours.

❺ Custer and Reno separate, Custer heads north to flank the village, 1435 hours.

❻ Reno charges, then forms skirmish line; he reforms in the woodline and then retreats to the bluff.

❼ Custer moves north, then fights final battle.

❽ Benteen joins Reno.

Custer had been recalled to testify before the U.S. Congress on charges of corruption within the Grant administration. He was relieved of command of the column departing from Fort Abraham Lincoln as a result of his leaving Washington, D.C., without permission, and he was barely able to argue himself back into command of his regiment in the field. He succeeded in regaining the position through the direct intervention of Brigadier General Terry, who pleaded with General Sherman and President Ulysses S. Grant. Grant relented, and Custer was able to march out of the fort as his unit's commander. This entire series of incidents is often blamed for creating a greater desire in Custer to achieve something brilliant to overcome the political cloud and once again place himself favorably in the limelight. This supposition may be accurate, since he did make statements about his desire to break free of Terry, but Custer always preferred to be free of oversight regardless of the circumstances. Terry's lack of experience in fighting Indians also played a key role in this desire to break free, since it would be certain that Terry would be more cautious and slower than Custer felt necessary.

It was Crook who first encountered the Indians on 17 June 1876. He did so not based on the U.S. Army finding them, but on the Indians finding the U.S. Army. This was a radical shift in behavior. The Indians actually identified the army column through scouts and then conducted an offensive operation at the level of hundreds of warriors—possibly eight hundred. This may not have been the first time such a thing happened, but it was a very rare occurrence and completely outside the experience of the U.S. Army officers involved. The level of surprise experienced by the army was demonstrated by the fact that Crook sent a column to find and attack the expected nearby Indian village, but there was no such place close by. The battle that is known as the Battle of the Rosebud is not the focus of this chapter, so the details will not be included here, but the important aspects must be mentioned because many of them were repeated or in some way present at the Little Bighorn two weeks later. First, it is important to note the aggressive nature of the warriors as they conducted an offensive operation with hundreds of warriors tens of miles from their camp against an equal-size U.S. Army force. Second, the fact that the warriors continually used flanking maneuvers to try and find the sides and the rear of the enemy was previously unheard of in frontier battle. Third, the Indians revealed themselves to have a large number of rifles and the ability to stand and fight a pitched battle for hours. This was not a hit-and-run raid but a stand-up fight—exactly the type of battle for which the U.S. Army would have asked.

Crook maintained the field at the end of the battle—the U.S. Civil War definition of battlefield victory. Despite this, Crook withdrew back to a supply camp tens of miles to the south and did not again move from that site until after the defeat at the Little Bighorn. This meant that the Indians faced one column at a time rather than receiving pressure from two columns nearly simultaneously. Though Crook never admitted it, it seemed as if the aggressive nature of the Indians spooked him into a much more cautious decision cycle. This would be true of all the commanders after the Battle of the Little Bighorn. Once the Indians demonstrated the ability to mass and aggressively engage the army, they were viewed as an omnipresent threat, and columns reduced their movement rates and their attendant risk in significant measure.

Crook was never expected to coordinate his movements with Custer, Terry, or Gibbon, and, therefore, the previous comments about Crook's decision not to press forward are not designed to question obedience to or violation of orders, but simply to be a statement of historical fact.

Terry and his column departed and headed along the Yellowstone, with Terry using the river and the 7th U.S. Cavalry marching cross-country. Much of the regiment was sent on a reconnaissance under the command of Marcus Reno shortly after the river-borne portion and the regiment reunited. Reno disobeyed orders and pursued a trail beyond where he was directed, and, in the process, he risked spooking the enemy earlier than the command was ready to react. He was criticized, but the behavior did not seem to present any warning to Terry that once a command was sent off on its own there was no further way to control them. Instead, Terry issued very loose language and orders to Custer as he departed with the entire regiment on 21 June 1876.

Throughout the period of the U.S. Army campaign the designated hostiles were in a camp that was consistently increasing in size and moving every few days from one river valley to the next as it tended toward the west. Prior to departing Fort Abraham Lincoln, Brigadier General Terry received information on the expected size of the hostiles—roughly two thousand with an estimated eight hundred warriors. The intelligence of two thousand people and eight hundred warriors was approximately true when Crook encountered the Indian warriors, but by the time Custer did, the camp had more than doubled in size and was one of the largest cities west of the Mississippi River on the American continent.[6]

Custer took his command, refusing the additional support of more cavalry and the Gatling guns. He intended to move quickly with only a mule train and no wagons at all. The intent was to find the Indian camp and prevent them from escaping to the south and away from the rest of the Terry and Gibbon columns—now united and moving west along the Yellowstone River valley. The Yellowstone River was the northern edge of the search area, and Custer was expected to fight the Indians or make them flee north. The idea of a coordinated attack on a specific date was not a certainty. The concept of a date certain for a coordinated link-up in the valley of the Little Bighorn River was given to fix a general movement table and not a fighting schedule, since everyone accepted that the Indians would play a critical role in the decisions of where and when to fight.

The primary concern of Terry and all of the column commanders was the desire to bring the Indians to battle and prevent them from scattering and escaping, thus necessitating a campaign all summer long to get the U.S. military's arms again around the camp. The guidance given to Custer directly conveyed the fear and uncertainty of the Indians getting away.

Technical Context

The nature of fighting Indians in the Great Plains was not directly related to doctrine, since there was never any doctrine for Indian fighting created. The U.S. Army fought with the Springfield trapdoor carbine, which fired a single shot and took several seconds, sometimes tens of seconds, to load or reload. The fielding of a slow-loading weapon was a decision to limit ammunition expenditures and waste. The repeating rifle was viewed as logistically wasteful. This was probably true from an accounting perspective, but the soldiers in the field certainly would have preferred a quicker-firing weapon. The Springfield was much more accurate than the repeating rifles and certainly more accurate at greater ranges. The long-range nature of the weapon should not be exaggerated, since a human being at four hundred yards using iron sights is little more than a dark dot. Additionally, long-range marksmanship is as much an issue of training as it is of weaponry. Soldiers have to be trained extensively to be able to engage targets effectively at ranges in excess of two hundred yards. One would think that the Great Plains would provide opportunity for long-range marksmanship, but in this battle the various undulations of the terrain and the mastery of the individuals and small groups of Indian warriors allowed them to close well within a hundred yards before they presented suitable targets.

The Indian warrior tended to fight with either traditional weapons or a wide variety of firearms—from repeating rifles to muzzle loaders. Indians brought hundreds of firearms to the battle, and in every engagement within the battle the Indians actually outgunned the U.S. Army in terms of numbers, with a significant percentage of warriors having better-quality firearms—repeating rifles that offered a rate of fire vastly superior to that of the cavalry troopers with which they were engaged.

This is the single most significant technical aspect of this battle—the Indians were not some primitive fighting force with archaic weapons defeating a heavily armed military with the proverbial sling. The Indians had quality modern firearms in a quantity that was significant and powerful on a contemporary battlefield. In each of the separate engagements—Reno's Attack and Custer's Last Stand—the Indians probably outgunned the U.S. Army. The outgunning mentioned was both in terms of numbers of firearms present and in the ability of the Indians to put more bullets down range in a given time period—volume of weapons and volume of fire. The nature of the fighting in this battle was well within the range of the Indian firearms rather than at distances that favored the Springfield rifles of the cavalry. The close fighting as a result of a wise use of terrain played very clearly into the tactics and weapons of the Indians.

Why no Gatling guns? This issue is commonly referred to in the decision cycle of this battle. Custer was offered a platoon of guns, but he refused to take them with him and the regiment. It is crucial to recall that Custer had Gatling guns in his trains during the 1874 Black Hills expedition. He knew of the challenges of the guns, with their carriages regularly tipping and slowing the column to re-right the system and allow the horse-pulled guns to maintain the pace. Additionally, the guns had a known history of jams, anecdotally as often as once every six rounds fired. In general, in a race to find and prevent the flight of the Indians, the idea of taking a weapon that was designed to face a determined attacking opponent was unnecessary.

Tactical Chronology

The battle fought at the Little Bighorn River has significant detail and numerous books about the details. For the sake of space, the information here deals with the major decisions made by the commander and the information provided to the subordinate commanders. The 7th U.S. Cavalry rode for several days up the Rosebud River valley until they reached the Indian trail previously identified by the reconnaissance led by Major Reno. As part of the movement, the scouts identified signs pointing to a much more recent movement of the village to the west. The decision was made to follow the trail rather than continue up the Rosebud as Custer was originally directed. In considering the decision, it is critical to note that Custer now had recent information and could be reasonably certain that the Indian camp was to the west and not further to the south.

Custer's scouts had identified the general location of the Indian camp early on the morning of 25 June. There was some issue over the identification because the Indian scouts were adamant that they saw the horse herd, but none of the white scouts or officers could say they did. Custer himself looked, and he did not see the movement, since the light was significantly different by the time he arrived at the Crow's Nest. Despite the fact that he could not see the camp himself, Custer decided to change the existing plan—to spend the day in recovery and reconnaissance. The regiment had conducted a night move, and the men were functioning on only a few hours of sleep. Custer ordered the regiment forward and into a more concealed position. He still wanted to conduct more reconnaissance, but he soon learned that men who had gone back to find some lost supplies on the trail had encountered Indian warriors, who fled toward the suspected location of the camp.

This report caused Custer to change the plan again and order an attack on the village on that day. Custer task-organized the regiment into four battalions plus the trains. Major Reno and Captain Benteen each were given command of three companies. The two other battalions of three and two companies were with Custer, so he effectively controlled five companies. The last company was escorting the pack train with augmentation from each company.

The Indian scouts were clear that they saw evidence of a village larger than any they had known. They warned Custer that this was a large group, much larger than expected. Custer did not accept their warnings as given but considered them to be the voice of fear rather than experience. In fact, history has shown the Indian scouts to be correct. The village had grown from the size it was when the warriors had gone off to fight at the Battle of the Rosebud. No longer did the village have only 800 warriors, but it most probably had something like 2,000. The numbers in the sources range from 1,500 to as many as 4,000, but the mid-range number is probably close. That means it was a village with a thousand lodges or maybe many more. This was a city of as many as 20,000 men, women, and children.[7]

As the regiment marched toward the Little Bighorn River valley, they encountered more and more signs of movement and some abandoned teepees. Custer ordered Benteen to take his battalion and

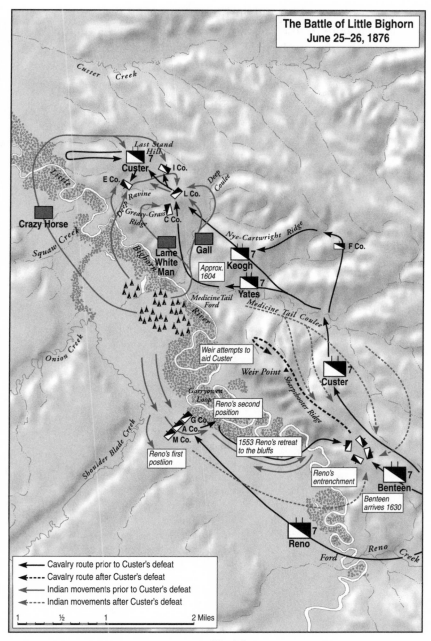

The Battle of Little Bighorn
June 25–26, 1876

Custer Creek

Little

Last Stand Hill

7

Custer

E Co.

I Co.

Deep Coulee

L Co.

Deep Ravine

Greasy Grass Ridge

C Co.

Crazy Horse

Squaw Creek

Nye-Cartwright Ridge

F Co.

Bighorn River

Lame White Man

Gall

Approx. 1604

7

Keogh

7

Yates

Medicine Tail Ford

Medicine Tail Coulee

Onion Creek

Weir attempts to aid Custer

Weir Point

7

Custer

Sharpshooter Ridge

Garryowen Loop

Reno's second position

G Co.

A Co.

M Co.

1553 Reno's retreat to the bluffs

7

Reno's first postiion

Reno's entrenchment

7

Benteen

Benteen arrives 1630

Shoulder Blade Creek

7

Reno

Ford

Reno Creek

→ Cavalry route prior to Custer's defeat
◄- - - Cavalry route after Custer's defeat
← Indian movements prior to Custer's defeat
◄- - - Indian movements after Custer's defeat

1   ½   1   2 Miles

Fig. 4.3

scout to the south with the purpose of ensuring that the regiment would be able to hit the village from the south and not on the north end or in the middle. Fear of escape was once again a preeminent concern and driving force for this reasoning. This order was given at about 1145 hours, and an hour later Custer was sending a messenger to Benteen to tell him to rejoin the regiment. This was close to the time when some Indians were spotted riding toward the camp.

Date	Time	Timeline Event
17 June 1876		Battle of the Rosebud.
20 June 1876		Conference on the *Far West* at the mouth of the Rosebud River. Custer receives his orders from Brigadier General Terry.
21 June 1876		7th U.S. Cavalry departs with 652 men.
21–24 June 1876		7th identifies signs of abandoned camps as it moves south.
25 June 1876		7th conducts a night movement.
	0805	Hostile Indians spotted fleeing west.
	0805	Hostile Indians spotted fleeing west.
	0900	Custer at the Crow's Nest—sees valley.
	1050	Custer gives final guidance.
	1145	Benteen sent south to secure flank and prevent escape.
	1245	Benteen ordered to come forward and rejoin the regiment.
	Est. 1500	Custer sends for Benteen to join him.
	1503	Reno attacks into the valley.
	1515	Final message sent to the trains to hurry forward.
	1553	Reno begins retreat to the bluffs.
	1604	Custer attacks down Medicine Tail Coulee.
	Est. 1630	Benteen joins Reno at the entrenchment.
	1646	Last Stand—defense of Reno-Benteen.
26 June 1876		Reno-Benteen entrenchment continues to fight all day.
27 June 1876		Brigadier General Terry arrives in the valley.

Fig. 4.4

At about 1500 hours Custer ordered Reno and his battalion into the valley. Dust clouds had been seen, and the fear was the village had been warned and was breaking up and departing. Custer gave Reno the order to attack the village from the south, indicating that he would be supported by the regiment. Reno crossed the river, spread his battalion out, and attacked up the valley toward the village. Several hundred yards from the southern portions of the encampment, Reno dismounted his men and formed a skirmish line. Custer observed this from the ridgeline east of the river as he moved his portion of the command supposedly to find the other end of the village.

Reno was unable to hold the skirmish line for very long because he was being flanked on his left (west). He ordered his men to fall back to the wood line that ran along the riverbank. Reno only held the wood line for fifteen or so minutes when he ordered a withdrawal across the river and to the bluffs on the east side. The order to withdraw came immediately after Reno had witnessed the death of one of the civilian scouts whose head had been exploded by a bullet, causing blood, gore, and bone fragments to impact Reno's face. Most of the casualties suffered by the troops who survived the battle came as this withdrawal happened and soldiers were caught by warriors as they hastily forded the river and scrambled up the steep slopes on the far side. The entire efforts of Reno lasted less than an hour—from the crossing of the river to the charge and skirmish line to the withdrawal to the wood line and then the withdrawal from the wood line.

As this was occurring, Custer sent another and final message to Benteen to hurry up and a message to the packs to bring the ammunition up. When Benteen received the directives from the commander, rather than immediately order his battalion to trot or gallop to the support of Custer, he initially maintained his unit at a walk and only increased that pace with the subsequent and final directive. Even then, he did not gallop to the rescue, but maintained a very conservative pace.

This last message was sent from a position just south of the Medicine Tail Coulee. From archaeological evidence it is expected that Custer moved down the coulee and may have tried to ford at the end of it. The command did not ford but rather moved toward the heights to the northeast, and there they met their fates in small groups and company skirmish lines. It is unclear what exactly happened, though Indian accounts explain that the soldiers did approach the ford and that a small engagement occurred. The soldiers then moved away toward the high ground. Several companies fought as integrated units, but many soldiers fought and were killed as individuals or in small groups. The largest concentration of soldiers was at the hill commonly known as Last Stand Hill, where the white monument stands today.

The Indian warriors swarmed out of the village against Custer when Reno was no longer a threat to the south. Warriors attacked from the Medicine Tail Coulee ford and also from the north with relatively long-range marksmanship. Custer's command was destroyed in a relatively short engagement of probably less than an hour.

Benteen reached Reno's position at about the same time as the pack train, and he was entreated by Reno to assist his command. The two battalion commanders settled in to a defense with a brief foray toward the sound of the fighting to the north. The foray proved fruitless, and the soldiers returned and began to assume a defensive position. The defensive position was improved with the limited digging implements available as well as makeshift digging tools. The soldiers all suffered from thirst, and most especially the wounded. Benteen mostly commanded the defense, and he organized several counterattacks that drove off sharpshooters and attempts by the Indians to conduct mounted attacks. This defense lasted all of the night and throughout the following day—26 June 1876.

The Indians celebrated their great victory on the night of 25–26 June and conducted fixing attacks throughout the day on 26 June to ensure that the soldiers could not hamper the movement of the village. The village departed on the afternoon of 26 June.

By mid-morning of 27 June the scouts of Brigadier General Terry's column had entered the valley, and they were the first ones to identify the dead bodies of Custer and his men. The village was gone, and only a few lodges were left to house the dead.

Battlefield Leadership

On the morning of 25 June 1876, there was no given for the conclusion of the battle to come. There was the great possibility that the 7th U.S. Cavalry could have achieved what it needed to do even though it was outmanned and, in each of the separate engagements, probably outgunned. Throughout the battle discussed here there was a series of decisions made by the leaders on both sides but primarily by George Armstrong Custer. The record on this battle details many of Custer's decisions, and like almost no other battle, these decisions have been scrutinized, criticized, and picked apart. The intent here is to identify those that were most critical to the larger issues. The most important influencing factor is that Custer felt he had to prevent the escape of the Indian camp. All of the other decisions derived from this primary imperative.

Custer's decision to attack on 25 June has been criticized as disobeying orders from Brigadier General Terry. Given the nature of orders in the era and the nature of the opponent, the idea that there was a strict plan of attack and control of subordinate elements was just not true. Most of this was derived as a result of the fallout after the defeat. This is not to say that Brigadier General Terry did not have an idea of a coordinated attack, but he would never had concurred with a delay that lost contact with the Indians by simply waiting for the right day either.

As Custer moved the 7th U.S. Cavalry forward, he divided the command into three major subordinate elements and then gave each a separate and unsupported mission. Though there may have been good and sound reasons for this series of decisions and task assignments, the reality is that regardless of the possible soundness, this led directly to the defeat because it allowed the Indians to face three engagements, separated in time and space, and mass their weapons and dedicated warriors against the soldiers.

The manner of issuing orders in this era was not as specific and directive as it is today. Commanders used respectful language, and it seemed as if they gave great freedom to subordinates about whether or not to obey. This perception is incorrect. The polite wording was simply the way of speaking in an era where the commander's wish was his command. When Custer extended his respects in requesting that Benteen come, this was an order as strong as those issued in any era. Though the wording was different, one thing was clear; Custer was unclear in communicating his intent to his two key subordinates. Reno thought that Custer would follow him into the valley when he was told that he would be supported by the regiment. The failure of the regiment to materialize played at least some part in Reno's difficulty in decision making during the valley fight. Benteen did not understand his role or the urgency of the commands he received. Part of the decision to maintain a walk rather than move his battalion faster was due to his personality conflicts with Custer, but part was also a failure of communication between commander and subordinate. No subordinate who survived understood the scheme of maneuver for the regiment or the plan beyond his very narrow view of the battlefield.

As just noted, personality conflicts played a key role in the swiftness to respond and the decisions made. Neither Reno nor Benteen perceived that he had Custer's confidence, and in some measure neither respected the judgment of their commander. Benteen clearly had less respect for Custer than Reno, but neither viewed Custer equal to his Civil War reputation. This must have played a role in the decisions made by each of the commanders—Custer's selection of who to send on certain missions and the rapidity, decisiveness, and commitment each subordinate had in fulfilling the orders received. No student of this battle can claim that Reno or Benteen acted as Custer would have if the roles were reversed, and this is at the heart of command influence and battlefield leadership.

The final point is one of large scope, since it deals with perceptions and the ability of leaders to see "the box" as it really is, as opposed to some other way. The challenge of command when the box is perceived to have collapsed is overwhelming—Reno's reaction versus Benteen's is one excellent example of this principle. When Benteen arrived, he saw a situation that was desperate but well within his box. Reno had gone through a previous emotionally disturbing and box-shattering experience that caused his perceptions to become completely overwhelmed. To Reno, the world had changed, and the box was collapsing on him. He did not reassert effective leadership again in the battle, and history showed that he rarely did again in his career.

Significance

The Battle of Little Bighorn was arguably the single most significant battle in the wars with the Indians of the nineteenth century, not because of the casualties on either side, but because the event shocked the nation and galvanized an already antagonistic administration and congress into a unified policy that saw the Indians as the enemy. The U.S. Army suffered 262 killed in the battle, with 14 officers, which represented a significant percentage of officers in a small peace-time constabulary-focused army. The Indians lost an unconfirmed number, but the estimates range from 30 to as many as 300.

The fact that most major cities received the news in the midst of large centennial celebrations meant that the word was spread in the best way to galvanize large amounts of public sentiment very quickly. Some of the most important results follow:

*   The U.S. Army generated and executed relentless pursuit throughout the rest of 1876 and into 1877, either returning all major Native American groups to the reservations or driving them into Canada. The army was enlarged through congressional action, and the force directed against the Indians in the west increased to meet the new policy of total war against the Sioux.
*   The American people were shocked and angered by the initial reports. This led to legislation supporting strict action against Native Americans on and off the reservations. This also led to a tacit acceptance of atrocities during engagements against perceived renegades.
*   There was a sea change in cultural dominance in the west. There was an increase in the influx of settlement, development, and resource exploitation as a result of the pacification of the Sioux nation. This is a direct result of the aftermath of the battle. The Native American tactical

victory at Little Bighorn directly resulted in their own strategic defeat. Sherman would give credit for much of his ultimate success against the Sioux in 1883 to the expansion of the railroads, and in an operational and tactical sense he was right, but the unification of the nation against the Indians after the Battle of Little Bighorn was the catalyst that turned an apathetic nation to action at the level of total war.

Lessons Learned: Principles of Conflict

The most critical lesson from the battle has to do with identification. The simple lessons from this battle have lasting value because so many of the failures were a direct result of the failure to recognize the aberrational nature of the event prior to lethal contact with the opponent.

- **Identification:** There is a need to empathize with the opponent on the day they are the enemy. Custer saw in the information he received shades of past battles, and he empathized with an enemy he had previously fought and not the one he was fighting. There are many clichés in this battle about reconnaissance and physical, conceptual, doctrinal, and cultural identification. Despite the fact that they are clichés, they are true. It is necessary to know where and how large the opponent is, to know how and why they will fight, and to see how their culture is shaping their decisions in the present.

- **Isolation:** In an unknown environment against an unclear enemy, it is difficult, if not impossible, to isolate them. Division of forces in the face of an unknown, but suspected to be larger, enemy is foolhardy. If the enemy of the past were present, Custer's plan might have worked, but he was facing a different enemy. At a larger level, the policies of the Indian Bureau to sell weapons to Indians who would later participate in battles against the U.S. Army denied any opportunity for the army to conduct an effective campaign to prevent the support of their opponent.

- **Suppression:** The ability of disciplined soldiers to defend reasonable terrain with capable weapons is another cliché important from this battle. New and untested soldiers fought well under physically demanding circumstances to survive and remain a cohesive unit. This ensured that the Indians could not maneuver without interdiction from U.S. Army rifle fire. Though the cavalry soldiers could not prevent the Indian warriors from dominating the field of battle, they did prevent total freedom of maneuver.

- **Maneuver:** What defines the position of advantage is much more important than its physical location. The effort to get to a place, which was expected but yet unknown, rather than to achieve an effect created the series of poor decisions made by Custer.
- **Destruction:** Clear and decisive defeat is the result of failure to adhere to the principles of conflict. The confusion of orders, separation of forces, and lack of understanding caused many in Reno's command, and specifically Reno, to be destroyed in spirit, despite the survival of their portion of the command.

Conclusion

The following comments tend to focus on what happened and why—within the U.S. Army, since they were the ones facing the aberration. Before this begins, the simplest explanation for the events on 25 June 1876 is that the Indians won the battle. They achieved victory. Anything else is arguing about historical possibilities.

> Never before or after were the northern Plains tribes better prepared for war. They were numerous, united, confident, superbly led, emotionally charged to defend their homeland and freedom, and able, through design or good fortune, to catch their adversary in unfavorable tactical situations. Even flawless generalship might not have prevailed over Sitting Bull's mighty coalition that summer. In large part the generals lost the war because the Indians won it.[8]

Classic failures throughout all levels in identifying the opponent led first to inaccurate assumptions of size, quality, and intent, which in turn led to poor decisions. The decisions of commanders based on these assumptions led to one of the most publicized defeats in U.S. military history. Much criticism can be heaped on a variety of people. Brigadier General Crook, for one, deserves criticism for his failure either to advance or to inform the other commands of his battle and the change in Indian tactics and behavior in battle. Though this criticism is justified, it is doubtful whether it would have resulted in any change in conceptualization of the enemy. Custer, his peers, and his superiors had an ethnocentric view of the Indian that would probably not have allowed them to perceive the Indians to be capable of a significant cultural shift in warfare. The fact that the battles fought by the Indians after Little Bighorn were like those before it and the Rosebud support that general prejudice.

The reaction of the military and then the public to the results of the path of failed assumptions was extreme. This is to be expected, since strong reactions come from unexpected events. The reaction caused the stronger nation to use more of its power to achieve a result that was then perceived as necessary—total domination of the west, no compromise. The moral debate about treating the Indians as equivalents either faded or was completely shouted down by the shrill voices for revenge.

Here was a box constructed from previous and very valid experiences. The box had become rigid, and the perception of the opponent as a savage meant he could not reshape that box but must stay inside of it. No empathy means no understanding and, therefore, defeat.

How Does It Fit Inside the Box?

- This battle featured warriors, soldiers, leaders, and commanders who had faced each other and similar opponents numerous times previously. There were many preconceptions that shaped the decisions and thinking of leaders and, subsequently, the conduct and outcome of the battle.

- The Indian people and warriors understood the stakes of this campaign—returning to the reservation versus staying in their ancestral lands. The overall objective of the campaign of the U.S. Army was clear to both sides.
- The U.S. soldiers and leaders expected to see a common pattern followed. They expected that when faced by a large body of U.S. Army soldiers, the Native Americans would try to use their greater operational mobility and escape the encirclement to another location. There were plans for dealing with a large number of Native Americans who might chose to fight, but the expectation was flight rather than fight.

Why Is It an Aberration?

- **Means:** The Indians possessed better-quality weapons in larger numbers and with more ammunition than previously experienced by the U.S. soldiers. Their typical experience with Indian marksmanship was that it was questionable, and typically the warrior had to get very close for him to be effective with the weapon. In this battle, the Indian warriors had weapons of comparable quality with their opponent, with a faster rate of fire, and in similar to greater quantity than the 7th U.S. Cavalry. Additionally, there were accomplished Indian sharpshooters who added to the advantage.
- **Means:** The weapons were important, but it is still critical to note that the Indians had an advantage in numbers. Not only did they outnumber their opponent at each engagement by more than four to one, but they had more total warriors than there were soldiers in the regiment attacking them. Even if Custer had massed all of his troopers, the battle would still have been in question.
- **Means:** The Indians used basic elements of the principles of conflict to achieve victory. Partly this was made possible by the deployment of the U.S. soldiers by Custer, but the Native Americans were able to isolate, suppress, and destroy their opponents effectively through simple commands and tribal controls.

105

- **Understanding:** The U.S. military entered this battle with respect for their opponent as a competent savage, but the idea of their opponent as a tactical and strategic equal was nonexistent. Soldiers and leaders did not conceive of an enemy who could outfight them. Throughout their lives, the survivors of the 7th U.S. Cavalry, and of the campaign as a whole, tended to believe the U.S. soldiers and leaders lost the battle more than that it was won by the savage. This manner of thinking had direct impact on the thought process and tactical decisions going into the fight.

- **Understanding:** No officer conceived of an enemy who would stay and fight once the approaching U.S. Army column was detected. It was an axiom in fighting the Native Americans that they would flee rather than fight a large U.S. Army force. In this case, there was no Indian attempt to flee the scene of the battle until after the discovery of the northern column.

- **Understanding:** The size of the Native American encampment was beyond any soldier's experience. Not in the history of U.S. Army–Native American conflict had a Native American encampment held this many warriors. Even though there was intelligence on the size of the encampment, even that was typically smaller than the actual force.

- **Leader:** Custer was under a cloud of discipline for leaving hearings in Washington, D.C., without receiving appropriate permission. He had had to argue to be able to even accompany his unit and had lost command of the column to the department commander, Brigadier General Terry. This led to Custer being more inclined to prove himself and overcome the criticism.

- **Target:** This battle and the larger campaign were seen by the older Native American leaders as a last opportunity to confirm their way of life and remain independent. The fact that this was not a simple roundup of the usual suspects for return to the reservation but a determined attempt to define and protect a way of life transcended basic conflict and elevated the battle to a religious struggle for the definition of freedom among peoples.

Strategies (numbered based on the nine strategies for victory)

1. **Introspection:** Custer did not see his unit clearly in comparison with his opponent. His conception of his regiment was that no Indian force could defeat it. Custer also did not understand how he saw his opponent. He viewed himself as the ideal Indian-fighter and, therefore, was not questioning his own conceptualizations of the campaign.

2. **Empathetic Appreciation:** As previously stated, Custer thought he knew the Indian. He did not. No U.S. Army officer of comparable command position had any better empathetic appreciation of the Indian. They all looked at their opponent through very ethnocentric and judgmental eyes— savage versus civilized.

3. **Empathetic Expectation:** Custer did not expect, nor did any other commander at any level, the Indians to fight with such aggression and determination as they did. The Battle of the Rosebud should have been a warning, but Crook did not inform anyone of the change because he probably did not perceive the change in behavior for what it was. Even with his failings, Custer did understand enough of his opponent seemingly to continue to seek for a position of advantage that would shock them into flight. He knew that the possibility existed.

5. **Study of History:** It was uncommon for officers to be students of other's tactics or new techniques. One cause of this was the difficulty in disseminating information among the various geographic areas. Another was the officer culture that did not encourage such intellectual assessments, especially not about engagements with savages. If someone was studying military strategies, it was probably based on European battles.

6. **Study of Culture:** Custer used an Indian woman to assist him in his 1868 campaign, and there were historical rumors of his having a relationship with the woman. Despite what could have been an opportunity for understanding the Indian, it seems that Custer never truly sought to study the culture of his opponent. He was able to communicate at some level with his Indian scouts, but he missed the deeper and nuanced aspects of the culture.

7. **Multiple Reserves:** Custer divided his element into a configuration that might have allowed for meeting this strategy, but the elements were never in a position to support each other while the outcome was in debate. His seeming intent to find a way to shock his opponent into flight was in line with many of the premises presented here, but he did not position his forces in such a way as to make that a reality.

8. **Initiative:** Custer began the battle feeling that the enemy was in the process of breaking camp after they had been informed of his column's presence. His initial decisions were designed to regain what he perceived to be the initiative lost. As a result, he began with the initiative, but Reno's unsupported attack and relatively quick retreat soon turned the initiative to his opponent. His effort to find an assailable flank without understanding the size of the village meant he could not have regained the initiative.

So much of what has been said is critical of Custer as if he were alone in this manner of thinking or behavior. Custer was considered to be one of the best, most knowledgeable, and competent Indian-fighters of his era by most of his peers and superiors. He was not markedly worse in these areas than his peers but was better than most. What is important is to appreciate both the fact that Custer was aberrationally shocked and that any other officer from that era and social-military training would have been just as shocked or even more so.

Chapter 5

Case Study:
The Battle of Cannae
(2 August 216 BC)

He said that at the time when his father was about to start with his army on his expedition to Spain, he himself, then nine years of age, was standing by the altar, while Hamilcar was sacrificing to Zeus. When, on the omens being favourable, Hamilcar had poured a libation to the gods and performed all the customary rites, he ordered the others who were attending the sacrifice to withdraw to a slight distance and calling Hannibal to him asked him kindly if he wished to accompany him on the expedition. On his accepting with delight, and, like a boy, even begging to do it besides, his father took him by the hand, led him up to the altar, and bade him lay his hand on the victim and swear never to be the friend of the Romans.

—Polybius, Greek historian (203–120 BC)[1]

One general point is worth emphasizing, namely that each society and culture tends to have a unique view of warfare that affects how they fight and as a result how they may be beaten. This can be seen in most periods of history, but the difference between two philosophies of war has rarely been as clearly illustrated as it was during the Punic War.

—Adrian Goldsworthy, historian (2000)[2]

Strategies Emphasized:

1. Introspection
2. Empathetic Appreciation
3. Empathetic Expectation
5. Study of History
6. Study of Culture
7. Multiple Reserves
8. Initiative

Many of the battles included here have a romantic historiography. It may be the nature of aberrations that they catch the imagination of people throughout history and thereby attain places of near idols for historians and readers. Cannae certainly fits well in this genre. It contains one of the most famous battlefield commanders of all time—Hannibal Barca. The Carthaginian commander held a position of mythological significance even in his own lifetime, something achieved by few humans in history. Roman mothers would use the threat of Hannibal to scare obedience from their children, much as the boogeyman of later eras. Hannibal was able to lead an army in accomplishing that which no reasonable and objective commander could have ever imagined—he accomplished a double envelopment of a superior-sized opponent on an open plain with no terrain obstructions. The double envelopment then evolved into a complete encirclement. This was tactical genius.

Hannibal accomplished the feat of Cannae through a very thorough understanding of himself and his opponent. There was no question in his mind about the way he arranged his forces, who he placed in command, and how each element would fight to accomplish a design. Hannibal sought to create an aberration by staging all of the pieces in a precise way.

Geographical Setting

Location

Cannae was a small Latin village situated on the eastern side and the southern portion of the Italian peninsula in the modern region of Puglia. The village was itself of little significance, since it had been previously destroyed. The citadel had been used for grain storage, and that was why Hannibal went there. As Hannibal and his army were encamped around a critical store of provisions, the Roman army came to him. The river Aufidus flowed through the plain from generally west (or southwest) to the Adriatic Sea to the east (or slightly northeast). The river divided the plain into north and south, and the Romans had a camp on either side. Hannibal's camp was on the south side of the river, where Cannae was located. Whether the battle occurred on the north or south of the river is open for scholarly debate, but in this telling it occurred on the northern side of the river.

Terrain and Vegetation

The plain of the Aufidus River was generally flat and treeless. There was no significant role played by vegetation or by the terrain throughout the battle other than in the position of the camps and the battlefield in relation to the river.

Weather

This was an August battle in the Mediterranean world, and as such the weather was hot and dry. The battle lasted for some hours, and heat and thirst must have played a role in the general weakening of the losing side over time.

Units Involved

Carthaginian Forces

Hannibal brought into Italy a heterogeneous force composed of warriors from numerous cultures, nationalities, and languages. The fact that the warriors came from a variety of locations meant that they also carried a variety of weapons and armor and fought using different techniques. The single most significant unifying force was that they were winning, and in 216 BC they were deep in Roman–Latin territory where they could only survive through unified action. The truth was that victory was not just a unifier in spirit, but it was also a unifier in equipment, since the two previous large-scale wins over the Roman army meant that much of Hannibal's

111

army wore Roman armor and carried Roman weapons. This was especially true of his African units. The Gauls and Spaniards tended to retain their weapons and culturally unique styles of fighting. The army was a combination of North African infantry and cavalry, Numidian cavalry, Spanish tribal infantry, and the recently recruited Gallic tribesmen of the Po River valley. The numbers given in ancient sources tend to be conveniently round, but that is all we have—roughly ten thousand cavalry and forty thousand infantry.

One of Hannibal's innovative strengths was his use of cavalry as a decisive arm in his battles. He had both the light, very mobile, and elusive Numidian cavalry, as well as heavier and shock-producing Spanish and Gallic cavalry. The Romans believed in the strength of infantry, and their cavalry component was comparably weak. Not only did Hannibal emphasize his strength in terms of his cavalry, but this strength directly opposed a Roman weakness. In this way he mirrored Alexander the Great and his use of his Companion Cavalry to win battles. Though cavalry was important, unlike Alexander, Hannibal rarely rode with them in battle. He tended to remain in the center or in whichever position he considered most vital. He commanded the battlefield much more like a modern military commander than one of the ancient world. He managed battles rather than led them. This was especially true of large battles or engagements.

Roman Forces

The emergency represented by Hannibal operating on Italian soil led to the focus of both consular armies against Hannibal. The two consuls brought with them eight Roman Legions and an equal number of Latin ally legions. The legions fought in a triple line with subordinate units called maniples forming the basic unit of action within the army. Given that this was one of the greatest emergencies in Roman history, it can be safely assumed that the legions were at the maximum capacities of 5,200 or so, which make the suggested numbers of about 90,000 plausible, though still large for a Roman army of the period—the largest ever assembled at this point. In general the Romans brought about eighty thousand infantry and roughly six thousand cavalry.

Romans had cavalry, but their primary arm was the infantry. The majority of the cavalry was provided by their Latin allies. The Roman infantryman was designed to fight in a triple-line system with his compatriots. He used a short stabbing and slashing weapon and javelins.

Leaders in the Battle

Only the most senior leaders are discussed here. Leadership and personality of commanders are paramount for understanding both the events and the myths that surrounded the events.

Carthaginian Forces

Hannibal Barca—Hannibal was born into a family that played an important role in Carthaginian military and politics. As stated in the first opening quote, legend has it that his father made him swear an oath on a temple altar that he would not rest until he had destroyed Rome. He was the Carthaginian military governor of Spain, and he effectively built a military there, as well as making Spain a beneficial part of the Carthaginian economic empire. Legend has it that Hannibal led an unprovoked attack on a Roman ally on the Iberian Peninsula—Saguntum. The attack on this city was the pretext for the Second Punic War. The reason for the attack is unclear, though it was ascribed to Hannibal wishing to manufacture a reason to go to war with his lifetime enemy. Hannibal was one of the most impressive tactical-level leaders in the ancient world and maybe throughout history. He developed the strengths of his army while mitigating its weaknesses. He commanded an army that was almost always outnumbered, drawn from a variety of peoples and languages, motivated mostly as mercenaries, and he made that army the most feared combat force in his time or almost any other. Hannibal would later lose at Zama and eventually be driven out of Carthage by Roman political pressure, forced to flee from one kingdom to another until finally he reportedly killed himself in Asia Minor.

Hasdrubal Barca—the second in command of the army and Hannibal's brother. He commanded the Carthaginian left and the Celtic and Spanish cavalry.

Roman Forces

The Roman system of combat leadership of such an army was that the two consuls alternated command daily. There were also numerous military tribunes—men who functioned as officers of the legion. Most of these men came from the Senatorial and equestrian classes—Roman nobles. There were former consuls in these positions as well as future greats—Publius Cornelius Scipio was one such future great serving as a military tribune in the 2nd Legion. He would go on to be the greatest Roman general of the war by the time he defeated Hannibal at Zama.

Lucius Aemilius Paullus—One of two consuls responsible for leading the combined Roman army. Paullus was an older Roman senator with combat experience. He was more cautious, and he realized the importance of preserving the state and maintaining Roman power. He was an associate of Fabius, the dictator of the previous year whose tactics had frustrated Hannibal and the Roman populace by harassing rather than fighting the Carthaginian. Though he intended to fight with the enormous army he had, he did not want to do so rashly. He commanded the Roman right wing, which meant he was with the Roman cavalry, though he was reported to have moved to and fought in the center, as well. He died during the fighting.

Gaius Terentius Varro—One of two consuls responsible for leading the combined Roman army. He was much younger than his associate commander. He was also a demagogue and one who had raised the expectations of the average Roman, as well as the soldiers in the army for complete destruction of Hannibal and his army. Varro is attributed with being impetuous to the point of being foolhardy. He commanded on the Roman left, meaning he was with the allied cavalry. He survived the battle.

Historical and Grand Strategy Context

Rome and Carthage faced off in two major wars and a third lesser war that was mostly a siege. These two competing cities represented different political models and different cultural and military models. They also represented two different and expanding economic models. The two expanding models almost ensured collision between the two cities. The initial competition was mostly fought over the island of Sicily and on the ocean. In this first war Rome displayed elements of its national character that would be further demonstrated in the Second Punic War. In one telling series of events, the Roman fleet, representing nearly 75 percent of the total Roman warships, was lost in a combination of storm and battle. Within a year the Romans had completely replaced all of these ships and built even more. The tenacity and ability to absorb punishment was again demonstrated in the Second Punic War as the Romans absorbed huge losses at both Trebia and Lake Trasimene and went on to field the largest army in their history within a year and a half of the last loss. The ability for Rome to again endure the losses of Cannae and continue and eventually win was yet another example of tenacity.

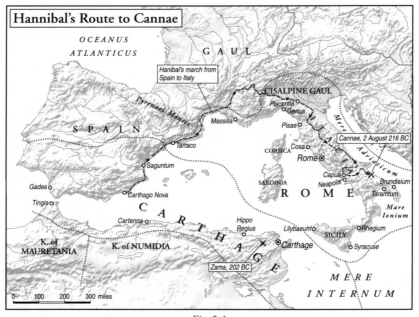

Fig. 5.1

The Second Punic War began with the assault on Saguntum on the east coast of the Iberian Peninsula. Hannibal then took his army and marched toward the Italian Peninsula. His decision was tremendously audacious. He fought several battles en route and was able to avoid contact with a large Roman army sent to stop him. Then he continued on toward Italy by way of the Alps. The crossing of the Alps was fraught with conflict and was arguably one of the most logistically impressive feats in the ancient world. The losses sustained in the crossing reflected a greater percentage of loss than any of the subsequent three great battles fought between the Carthaginian commander and his directly opposing Roman commanders.

He began with an enormous army that was slowly whittled down over time, various tasks, and casualties. He crossed the Ebro River in the Iberian Peninsula with about ninety thousand infantry and more than twelve thousand cavalry. He crossed the Rhone River and began his ascent of the Alps with thirty-eight thousand infantry and eight thousand cavalry. He completed the crossing of the Alps with about twenty thousand infantry and six thousand cavalry. Of the thirty-seven elephants that had crossed the Rhone, almost all were dead and none would survive to fight at Cannae.[3]

The Romans made a critical decision, too, in the war when the army sent to intercept Hannibal missed him in what is now southern France. Rather than pursue Hannibal on his path back toward Italy, the army continued on toward Spain where they had expected to meet Hannibal. An associated decision was to raise an additional consular army to operate within Italy. This decision allowed Rome to wage, at significant resource expense, a multi-front war against the Carthaginians. Throughout the war the Romans made quality operational and grand strategy decisions that would ultimately lead to victory, whereas Hannibal seemed to make better tactical decisions but poor grand strategy ones. This statement is one made with the certitude of historic hindsight. When the Roman consul made the decision to continue with the movement to Spain and Hannibal arrived in northern Italy, there was significant second-guessing and concern over the policies.

In addition to the key decisions associated with the direct confrontation with Hannibal, the other recent historic event of importance was the consolidation of alliance with the Gallic tribes in the northern portion of the Italian peninsula in the Po River valley. These were peoples who had crossed the Alps within a few previous generations and had settled in the agriculturally rich river valley. They represented a present threat to Roman interests. They were not of the same linguistic and cultural heritage of most of the peninsula, which consisted of a variety of Latins, Romans, and smaller ethnic groups. The Gauls were from north of the Alps and had their cultural roots associated with those living in the current country of France.

The cultural divisions and political dealings of the Romans were at the heart of Hannibal's audacious plan to move into Italy and take the fight directly against Rome. The assumption of the great commander was that if the war could be successfully brought onto the Italian peninsula, then Carthage might be able to separate the Latin allies from Rome and turn the surrounding polities and nations of the peninsula against their Roman overlords. Hannibal seemed to recognize that the best hope for Carthage to defeat Rome was to create a situation that would allow Carthage to face Rome directly, rather than to continue fighting Rome and its allies.

Rome's policies toward the Latin allies were an evolving process over time. At some point, Rome was as at war with each of the Latin groups as they now were with Carthage. Over time, Rome had established treaties with each of these groups and then brought them into alliance status such that they provided a significant portion of the military might of the Roman state—every consular army was 50 percent allies. The association with Rome had proved to be a benefit for most of the Latin states, and this benefit would be put to the test by Hannibal and his premise of war on the peninsula taking allies away from Rome.

Thoughts Before the Battle

It is unclear how many of these large-scale imperatives were clearly understood by the decision makers before or even during the fighting involved in 216 BC. These can be clear from historical observation.

Hannibal had to accomplish three things in his campaign. First, he had to survive on the Italian peninsula. It was not enough just to get there; he had to demonstrate to the Roman allies that Carthage had the power to protect them against Rome. Second, he needed to defeat Roman armies and weaken Roman might on the peninsula sufficient to eventually destroy Roman power. Third, his threat to Rome had to be so great as to focus all of Rome's military activities against him, leaving the rest of the Carthaginian merchant interests safe and viable and allowing Carthage to grow economically while threatening the heart of the Roman economy.

Rome had to deny Hannibal a permanent base within the peninsula. It was imperative that he and his army always feel like an army at war and not in a secure enclave. Destruction of Hannibal was not imperative, since time without a secure home would wear away at the army much more effectively than direct attacks. Despite this assertion, the three major battles all greatly contributed to Hannibal's ultimate failure because he was not able to replace the losses sustained.

Operational Context

For the sake of this chapter, the operational campaign began when Hannibal crossed the Alps and arrived in Cisalpine Gaul (a Roman term for Gaul on *this* side of the Alps). The Roman Senate had authorized the raising of another army in addition to the one currently en route to Spain. The new army was led by a consul to Gaul, and there it confronted Hannibal. Hannibal had been unable to convince the Gallic tribes to come over to his side, and his army was physically still suffering from a contentious and deadly alpine crossing. The Roman army was sucked into an ill-conceived attack. Hannibal took advantage of poor Roman generalship and destroyed the opposing army, inflicting heavy casualties. The Battle of Trebia, as it is known, resulted in the winning of support from several Gallic tribes, allowing Hannibal to strengthen his army. Once he incorporated the new recruits, he moved south.

On the move toward the heart of Italy, Hannibal confused the consul waiting to confront him by deceiving him as to the mountain pass he was to take; he crossed from the Po River valley to Italy proper and camped his army close by Lake Trasimene. Another large Roman army came to confront him, and Hannibal again inflicted a staggering defeat as he ambushed the Roman columns as they marched along the lakeshore, forcing the Roman commander and his army to fight or drown. The Romans lost fifteen thousand dead in this battle and more than fifteen thousand as prisoners.[4]

The defeat at Trasimene brought Quintus Fabius Maximus to be named dictator. He employed a completely different vision in fighting the Carthaginian. He employed delay and attrition tactics that came to be called, with some derision, "Fabian tactics" against the Carthaginian. He attacked foraging parties, reconnaissance groups, and any separate elements, but he did not offer a full-scale battle to Hannibal. He nibbled at the edges rather than taking a bite. Fabius did not lose large numbers of men, but he did not gain great victories. For this he was derided, especially by populist demagogues like Varro. In 216 BC the frustration was great enough for Varro to be selected as consul, and he took his and the collective Roman frustration with him into battle.

Technical Context

Ancient battle meant no modern communications. This may seem obvious and unnecessary, but it is clear that most people are so inundated with modern communications that it is extremely difficult to imagine an era in which the only way to deliver a message was to take it there by person, and the message could only move as fast as a horse could run. For this reason it is important to note.

Roman consuls were expected to be leaders rather than commanders. This is in direct contrast to the fact that Hannibal was a commander more than a leader. The difference is that leaders are expected to lead others into battle physically. They are to be at or near the front, and others follow their example. A commander makes decisions from a place of importance, and this allows him to make adjustments throughout the engagement. Hannibal placed himself in the center of his army where the greatest risk was to his plan. Both Varro and Paullus were with the cavalry elements on the two flanks, and both elements were quickly engaged so that neither man was able to effect any subsequent decisions after the initial decision to attack. The consuls of the previous year were with the center of the army, but the press of the battle and the attendant dust and sound prevented them from being able to effect battlefield decisions. Varro did ride into the fray, and he himself led attacks against the Carthaginian center. Hannibal also was reported to have engaged in the hard fighting in the center.[5]

The nature of ancient warfare, especially in a battlefield that featured more than one hundred and fifty thousand combatants, meant that control was nearly impossible once forces engaged in combat. As a result, small unit leaders—centurions—made the key and costly decisions in this battle. By the end of the Second Punic War, the Roman general Scipio Africanus was commanding armies and no longer leading them.

The Romans typically fought in three-layered formations with the ability to reinforce, replace, and retrograde without causing harm to the formation. This was very much unlike the relatively static spear-based formations of the Carthaginians. The Carthaginians attacked in large groups without specific patterns or mutual support between nationalities or other formations. Hannibal mitigated this somewhat by staggering formations of Gauls and Spaniards so that their units and the capabilities they represented were intermixed, but linguistic and cultural barriers made truly combined operations nearly impossible. In many ways, the Roman system was superior and offered greater flexibility. Varro changed this when he ordered his army essentially to form a single phalanx-like formation and attack much more like the Carthaginians than the Romans. In one way this made sense, since he intended to overwhelm the inferior force with his numbers.

Varro made the key mistake of discounting two aspects of human nature and violating the fundamental rule of command in the attack. The two aspects of human nature are first, that any but the most disciplined soldiers will follow a fleeing enemy, and second, that once the formation loses cohesion human beings move toward each other rather than maintaining formation-prescribed distances when faced with the threat of physical harm. This meant that a pursuing army would tend to form a wedge shape rather than a line in pursuit, since the warriors or soldiers in closest contact with the fleeing opponent would pursue the fastest and all of the others would move forward and toward the pursuit as if pulled by a magnet. Varro did plan for the penetration and intended it to happen, feeling that this had been the failing in the previous large-scale battles with Hannibal—break the center and break the army.

The fundamental rule of command in the attack is that once the attack is launched the only real decision a commander has is when and how to commit his reserve or reserves. This is especially true on the ancient battlefield where the dust, debris, and noise of the battlefield shrouded command decisions and the ability to control those elements in the greatest contact. Varro did not have a reserve, and therefore once his army moved forward, he had no ability to influence the battle through his role as commander.

Tactical Chronology

The battle was a direct result of several previous smaller engagements. In one engagement Paullus was instrumental in preventing the Romans from pursuing the Carthaginians, even though Varro loudly proclaimed a pursuit necessary. Paullus also displayed mature restraint when Hannibal tried to lure the Romans into attacking their recently abandoned camp. Hannibal was able to deduce from these two events that Paullus was a more cautious and mature commander and that Varro could be lured into an attack. Hannibal chose to precipitate such a battle on a day when Varro was in command.

Hannibal organized his forces with his Gauls and Spaniards in the center and their lines slightly convex in shape, extending toward the Roman lines. He put his African soldiers on the two flanks, made their frontage more narrow, and added depth to their lines instead. He placed his strongest cavalry on the left against the river and the Roman cavalry and he placed his Numidian cavalry on the

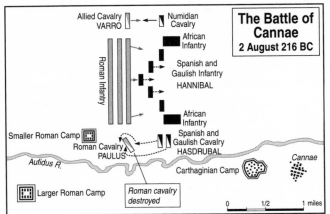

Allied Cavalry
VARRO

Numidian
Cavalry

African
Infantry

Spanish and
Gaulish Infantry
HANNIBAL

**The Battle of
Cannae**
2 August 216 BC

Roman Infantry

African
Infantry

Smaller Roman Camp

Spanish and
Gaulish Cavalry
HASDRUBAL

Roman Cavalry
PAULUS

Aufidus R.

Cannae

Carthaginian Camp

Larger Roman Camp

*Roman cavalry
destroyed*

0   1/2   1 miles

Fig. 5.2

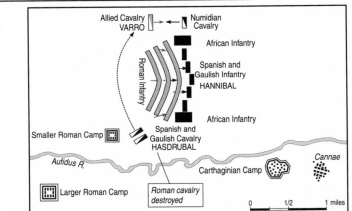

Fig. 5.3

Allied Cavalry
VARRO

Numidian
Cavalry

African Infantry

Spanish and
Gaulish Infantry
HANNIBAL

Roman Infantry

African Infantry

Smaller Roman Camp

Spanish and
Gaulish Cavalry
HASDRUBAL

Aufidus R.

Cannae

Carthaginian Camp

Larger Roman Camp

*Roman cavalry
destroyed*

0   1/2   1 miles

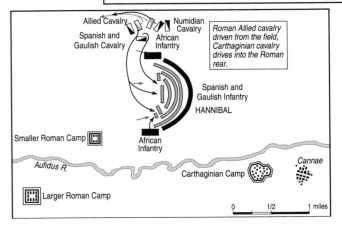

Allied Cavalry

Numidian
Cavalry

Spanish and
Gaulish Cavalry

African
Infantry

*Roman Allied cavalry
driven from the field,
Carthaginian cavalry
drives into the Roman
rear.*

Spanish and
Gaulish Infantry
HANNIBAL

Smaller Roman Camp

African
Infantry

Aufidus R.

Cannae

Carthaginian Camp

Larger Roman Camp

0   1/2   1 miles

Fig. 5.4

right where they would have more maneuver space against the Latin cavalry. The Romans formed up in a generally large phalanx with Roman cavalry on the right between the army and the river and Latin allied cavalry on the left facing the Numidians. The infantry was in ranks, but each rank could not move through the ones in front or behind because they each formed a continuous line.

The two armies advanced, and the initial collision went well for Hannibal's warriors, but soon the Romans began to win the day and force the Gauls and Spaniards back. As the press of numbers became greater and greater, the Carthaginian lines became more and more concave, though they never broke. The Romans filled the ever-deepening bowl like a pursuing wedge, and this gave room for the African troops on the flanks to begin to attack the Roman flanks in force, flanks that may never have been at risk if the Romans had remained in a line, since their line was much longer than that of their opponents.

The cavalry exchange did not last long. The Carthaginian horse was able to overwhelm the Roman cavalry with an aggressive charge and dismounted fighting. Once they fought their way through the Romans and forced their flight, Hasdrubal led his cavalry against the allied cavalry who were being harassed by the Numidian light cavalry. Once both cavalry groups engaged the allies, they fled from the field with Numidians in pursuit. Hasdrubal brought his cavalry in a series of repeated charges against the rear of the Romans and in direct support of the attacking African infantry.

Timeline	
Date	**Event**
Summer 218 BC	Crossing of the Alps
November 218 BC	Battle of Ticinus
Late December 218	BC Battle of Trebia
21 June 217 BC	Battle of Lake Trasimene
July 216 BC	Hannibal takes Cannae
2 August 216 BC	Battle of Cannae

Fig. 5.5

Earlier in the battle, a group of the Numidian cavalry surrendered to the Romans and offered to fight for them. When the battle's rage took the guards away, those who had surrendered took up their weapons from the ground and began to attack the unsuspecting Roman lines from the rear.

The Romans were now fighting in the front, on both flanks, and in the rear. They were completely surrounded, though this was not evident for most of the soldiers; the noise and dust was so great that they did not realize they were surrounded until they themselves suffered from an attack that originated from an unexpected angle. The press of bodies in the center also became a debilitating event as the Roman lines collapsed on each other, denying each individual the necessary room to operate his own weapon. The carnage and terror of those caught in the trap were horrific; ancient sources talk of soldiers burying their own heads in the ground to suffocate themselves rather than suffer any longer the anguish of the packed encirclement.[6]

The losses for the Romans were in the tens of thousands (see figure 5.2). Ancient sources vary between about forty-eight thousand to seventy thousand and are typically rounded to the nearest ten thousand. Regardless of the specifics, the realities were that the vast majority of the eight legions engaged were killed or captured. This was a loss of staggering numerical proportions for a modern country with tens of millions of people. The effect on an agrarian ancient culture must have been completely transformative.

Hannibal's forces suffered something like eight thousand losses. Though this is small in comparison, it still represents about 12 percent of the Carthaginian force—a large number for an ancient victorious army. This is especially large when considering these were all men who could not be replaced through local recruiting.

Battlefield Leadership

Hannibal created one of the greatest pre-battle plans in ancient history. He placed strength against weakness(his heavy cavalry against the Roman cavalry and the African infantry on the flanks), as well as weakness against strength (the Gauls and Spaniards against the center of the Roman line). He placed quality subordinate commanders in charge of the decisive elements and himself in the position of most danger where a commander/leader's inspiration was most needed—the center. It is probable that Hannibal's presence directly resulted in the fact that the center bent but did not break.

Hannibal chose the day and instigated the battle at his desire. He sought to do so on consecutive days, but one consul would not accept while the other did. The Romans alternated command between the two consuls present. Hannibal's choice and that of the Romans placed the younger and less-experienced commander as his opponent. It also placed the most audacious and biggest risk-taker in the position of command.

Hannibal chose the site of the battle to be on the far side of the river from his camp. This meant that his soldiers knew that a simple retreat was not possible and that their best chance for survival was in cohesion and will to win. This was certainly a strengthening factor in the minds of his recently recruited Gallic and Spanish warriors.

The placement of his forces in a very specific order is almost chess-like in its methodical manner. This specific placement of units allowed Hannibal to execute his maneuver plan to perfection. The location and responsibilities of subordinate commanders were also crucial decisions. All of this was necessary because he, like his opposing commander, lost the ability to give directions in the noise and confusion of the combat—the system had to be created such that it would function even without his personal commands.

The organization of the Roman army meant that there was no reserve available to a commander. Varro's position with the Roman cavalry and then among the center of the fighting meant he could not have made a key decision about reserve commitment even if he had had one. No reserve meant that initiative was conceded to the Carthaginians from the very beginning of the battle.

Significance

Cannae was a great tactical victory—the greatest defeat of a superior force by an inferior one in the ancient world. It was staggering in its immediate achievement and equally staggering in its operational and strategic failure. The failure to seize the initiative immediately and bring Rome to its knees and the ability of the Romans to come back from such a loss speaks a great deal about both Hannibal and Rome's policies and people.

In many ways Cannae can be linked to Operation Desert Storm. Both achieved great and unprecedented tactical success but failed to reshape the region or achieve greater operational or strategic gains. The criticisms of both battles are probably ill-founded because they tend to ignore the present realities in favor of historic hindsight. Hannibal's army was exhausted, in a foreign land, and seemingly surrounded by an inexhaustible supply of Roman soldiers. Rome had wasted the lives of tens of thousands of its men, yet it always came up with more. Hannibal did not have a siege train, and he would have been hard pressed to blockade Rome and lay effective siege to it all while defending his army from allied or Roman attack. Though revisionists point to Desert Storm's failure to remove Saddam Hussein, they rarely point out that world opinion would not have supported such a bold and unauthorized action, nor would the coalition have been likely to withstand a dramatic re-envisioning of the mission.

Some of the other key significant results are as follows:

- The loss at Cannae was the single largest defeat and loss of life for Roman soldiery. As a result of the enormous casualties, the Roman government returned to the Fabian tactics used before the battle to maintain contact with Hannibal but to deny him another large and decisive battle.
- Hannibal did not follow this victory with an assault of Rome. It is probable that he could not have done so, but the failure to gain any strategic success from the brilliant tactical maneuver resulted in eventual Carthaginian defeat.
- Rome developed leaders who took the aberration and created from it a norm of competence. The aberration was the inspiration of a military machine. One of the military

tribunes present at Cannae would later develop into the general who would defeat Hannibal approximately fourteen years later—Scipio Africanus.

- There was no sea change in culture or behavior—despite the loss, Italian allies of Rome generally did not abandon Rome. This was the main objective of taking the campaign into the Italian peninsula, and it failed to occur. Hannibal's brilliance was tactical, and that was where he achieved victory. In many ways this was as much an aberration as the victory itself. What other ancient or modern state could have inspired or compelled such loyalty after such a catastrophic defeat?

Lessons Learmed: Principles of Conflict

Hannibal dominated in every aspect of the principles of conflict. In no other instance in this book and in few instances in history did one commander identify his opponent as well as Hannibal did Varro. This level of identification was achieved without any reciprocal identification because Varro really had no understanding of Hannibal's way of thinking or fighting.

- **Identification:** This is the ideal battle of identification. Hannibal saw, understood, and had empathy for his opponent in a way few other commanders have ever equaled.
- **Isolation:** Success of the Carthaginian cavalry in driving the Roman cavalry from the field was critical in preventing commanders from having flexibility and denying any outside assistance or escape, since the Carthaginian cavalry would complete the encirclement.
- **Suppression:** The Roman army was completely surrounded. There is no better form of suppression.
- **Maneuver:** The position of advantage was the success of the cavalry. This allowed Hannibal to conduct actions at his pace and without interruption. The ability of the Carthaginian center to hold despite significant pressure was also critical to the overall success.

- **Destruction:** This was complete physical destruction. The will of the Roman soldiers was also destroyed as the encirclement became apparent.

Conclusion

The ability to clearly see, understand, and empathize with the opponent, in combination with tactical aptitude, makes such victories possible. Hannibal shaped the battle through placement of his varied forces and with the instructions issued to each subordinate commander. His understanding of the reactions of inexperienced soldiers and commanders allowed him to plan and place his various organizational elements so carefully and effectively. Hannibal knew what box to fashion for his opponent, and he kept his opponent within that box throughout the battle.

Despite Hannibal's tactical success, the Second Punic War was lost to Rome because Hannibal could not bring Rome to her knees through military or political success. He completely underestimated the strength of the alliance of the Italians with Rome.

How Does It Fit Inside the Box?

- The Roman armies and the Carthaginian mercenaries had faced off in the Italian peninsula on two previous occasions, resulting in disastrous defeats for the Romans. The Fabian tactics of the preceding years were successful in keeping Hannibal and his army under control and from causing significant harm, but they did not result in a perception of victory in the Senate. The enormous army the Romans fielded that met Hannibal on the plain outside of Cannae was confident that there was an understanding of how to defeat Hannibal. They had removed the possibilities of surprise and terrain that Hannibal had used so effectively in the two previous battles.
- Both armies, from the commanders down to the soldiers, understood that this battle had the potential to decide the fate of empires. This common perception of result assisted the soldiers in entering the battle with the conviction necessary

to remain in formation and fight.

- Expectation was for a frontal clash with the understanding that both armies would either seek to penetrate the center or to turn the flank of the opponent.

Why Is It an Aberration?

- **Means:** The soldiers in each army were very different. Hannibal's army consisted mostly of foreign-born allied warriors and mercenaries who had traveled all the way from Spain to Italy and had fought and defeated numerous opponents en route to Cannae. Despite suffering heavy losses, the Carthaginians had supreme confidence in their abilities and in their commander. The Romans were new recruits, drafted after two previous Roman armies had been destroyed. The soldiers entered the battle viewing Hannibal as a nearly mythical figure.

- **Means:** Hannibal accomplished something in this battle that most ancient and modern commanders have sought to achieve—a double envelopment and complete encirclement. This means that his army surrounded the opponent from both sides nearly simultaneously. This is extremely difficult, and the fact that Hannibal achieved it on an open plain in sight of his opposing commander makes the tactical achievement that much more amazing. Though many commanders since have enveloped and even encircled their opponents, no one has equaled Hannibal in the way and the terrain upon which he achieved this feat.

- **Understanding:** Hannibal was able to execute his tactical genius because not only could he perceive the physical movement of his own forces, but he effectively planned for the reactions of the enemy. He understood his Roman opponents to such a degree that he was able to execute the ideal tactical maneuver.

- **Leader:** Hannibal saw what he could do and was not afraid to do it. There was significant risk in Hannibal's plan because he placed weakness against strength, but he was willing to risk it and was also able to convince his subordinates and soldiers to execute the plan.

Strategies (numbered based on the nine strategies for victory)

1. **Introspection:** Cannae presents both sides of this strategy. Hannibal is an excellent example of seeing the strengths and weaknesses of each of his subordinate elements and then using them within their sphere of capability. Varro did not see the dangers in his thinking or his plan. Simplicity—breaking through the center—was without flaw in his mind.

2. **Empathetic Appreciation:** Hannibal found an opposing commander that he could bring to battle on terrain that favored him. He also perceived Varro's aggressive nature and the general frustration of the Romans with bringing about a major battle.

3. **Empathetic Expectation:** This knowledge of the opponent gave Hannibal the ability to see how he might react to withdrawal—aggressive pursuit. The previous smaller engagements and skirmishes provided the information on commander personality that Hannibal needed, and he used that to craft his plan.

6. **Study of Culture:** The quote at the beginning of the chapter expresses the differences between the opposing cultures and the probability for problems as a result. The Romans perceived in the mercenary army of Hannibal simple barbarians who could be overwhelmed with Roman superiority. They did not see the capability of their opponent through their cultural fog. Hannibal also struggled with his cultural perceptions. He perceived the alliances between Rome and her allies as being similar to those between Carthage and her allies. The formulation of his strategic plan hinged on this being true. His ultimate failure was a direct result of failure to grasp the Roman culture and the political agreements cemented through that culture.

7. **Multiple Reserves:** Varro had no reserve. He did not even

use legionaries to reinforce his cavalry, who were outnumbered. His entire focus was on penetration of the center. Hannibal did not have a specifically designated reserve either, but his plan was about creating reserves through maneuver. His African-heavy infantry was not engaged until later in the battle, and, therefore, when they crashed into the flanks of the Roman line they carried an effect similar to that of an employed reserve. The second created reserve was accomplished through Hasdrubal's success on the battlefield. As both Hannibal and Hasdrubal expected him to be successful in defeating the opposing Roman cavalry, it was a way to create a reserve in the middle of the fight—defeat the opponent and become available for additional missions— defeating the other cavalry then attacking the infantry in the rear.

8. **Initiative:** Hannibal had and maintained the initiative from the moment of deployment until the end of the battle. He executed his plan, and Varro only thought he was executing his own. It is uncertain but could be supposed that Varro never really knew what was happening as it happened. Hannibal's means of engaging with a partially thrust forward line meant that he drew the Romans to attack him where he wanted to be attacked. He determined the place of contact and then drew the Romans into the trap as he withdrew. All of the subsequent steps were further means of dominating the battle of initiative. The Romans always reacted to Hannibal's decisions.

Chapter 6

Case Study: The Battle of Yarmouk (15–20 August 636)

Since desert life no doubt is the source of bravery, savage groups are braver than others. They are, therefore, better able to achieve superiority and to take away the things that are in the hands of other nations.
— Ibn Khaldun, Arab historian (1377)[1]

The Battle of Kariun [July 641], like so many of the greatest Muslim victories lasted several days, a fact which seems to prove that the Arabs made use of attrition rather than shock tactics, as more suited to their character. The successful use of the mass attack depends on training and discipline, qualities in which they were still inferior to their enemies. The Arabs, however, greatly excelled all their adversaries in spirit and initiative. We may perhaps conjecture that they first engaged the enemy everywhere in exploratory actions, until they found a weak point. As soon as any success was achieved, it was boldly exploited by the initiative of the men on the spot, without awaiting orders from above.
— John Bagot Glubb, soldier and historian (1954)[2]

Strategies Emphasized:

1. Introspection
2. Empathetic Appreciation
3. Empathetic Expectation
5. Study of History

6. Study of Culture
7. Multiple Reserves
8. Initiative

The battles fought on the plateaus around the Yarmouk River canyon occurred within slightly more than a decade from the time that Muhammad made his famous immigration from the city of Mecca to Yathrib, later to be named Medina. The impact of this dynamic leader and the religious movement for which he was prophet, teacher, disciple, and political leader were to fundamentally reshape the Near East and completely surprise two of the oldest existing empires in the ancient world—Sassanid Persia and Byzantine Rome. It is clear that no one foresaw what Muhammad was able to accomplish—the unification of a historically divided people who had remained on the fringes of history throughout the ancient world and then propel this people forward to conquer most of the ancient imperial heartlands of the great Mesopotamian and Mediterranean empires.

Yarmouk is one of the true turning points in history. The failure of either side would have had dramatic cultural and political consequences for historically significant areas of the globe. The victory of the Muslim-Arabs over the Christian-Romans meant that the Near East, Middle East, and North Africa were now Muslim and typically Eastern oriented in traditions and means of governance and business rather than European and Western.

The primary aspect of this battle is one of understanding the change in culture and motivation. This period of history is one of true change and arguably large-scale aberrational change. The conversion to Islam of millions of people and the religious zeal with which those people exploded from the Arabian Peninsula were unlike any other event in history. The only conquest that is similar in terms of size and speed was that of Alexander the Great. Unlike Alexander, Muhammad preached a religion and way of life that transcended his own life and united a historically disunited people for more than half a century—long enough to establish a bureaucracy and begin dynastic succession.

Alexander's conquests were spectacular, but they did not last beyond his death, and though his efforts expanded Hellenic culture over huge areas of the Near and Middle East, they did not fundamentally change the way people thought and saw the world as did the teachings of Muhammad.

Several notes are important prior to continuing. First, I use the term Roman rather than Byzantine. This is done because that is how the Romans described and saw themselves, and this is also the term used by the Muslims in describing their opponent. The use of the word Rome is done to denote the ruling organization rather than the city in Italy. In many ways Constantinople had become the "new Rome," and the use of Rome could also be replaced with Constantinople. Second, the spelling of names will follow a pattern of easiest to pronounce. This is especially true for Arabic names that do not easily transliterate into English. Third, the sources for this battle are primarily Muslim because the Roman sources are very limited. Since this is an important battle and has been seen as such for centuries, there are numerous secondary accounts. I will generally follow the account given by John Bagot Glubb where he differs with the other scholars.

The reason for this is important and will be addressed here rather than in a note because it cuts to some of the key points of this book. Glubb served as a British officer seconded to both the Iraqi and the Jordanian armies for a period of approximately thirty years. He spoke, read, wrote, and studied Arabic. He served among and knew the Bedouin culture better than any Western authority on this battle. He also fought on this same ground in leading the Arab Legion (original British name of the current Jordanian Army) during World War II against the Vichy French government located in Damascus, Syria. His interpretations of the historical record and original source material come from scholarship and practical experience in a way that no other author on this battle comes close to matching. Those who argue with Glubb's conclusions do so with the perspective of the library over the battlefield, and as far as this book is concerned, the battlefield wins.

Geographical Setting

Location

The greatest controversies surrounding this battle concern location and timing. For the purposes of this book, the battle took place in 636 AD. As for the location, this book follows John Bagot Glubb's assertion of operational and tactical setting. This battle occurred at or near a place he refers to as the Dera'a Gap.[3] This is an area of relatively maneuverable rolling terrain that sits between the eastern end of the Yarmouk River canyon and the western end of the Al Harra area. Al Harra is a term in Arabic that literally translates as "the hot area." This is an area of significant relief and basaltic rock with few water sources. It is only passable by foot or mounted on animals. Even in modern times this area requires improved roads for vehicular movement. Those who patrol the area now still use the methods of the ancients—camels.

The gap between these two areas served anciently and today as an operational corridor between the lands of Jordan and Syria. It sits on the edge of the Syrian Desert and at the point where desert and arable lands meet. In thinking of this battle as a clash of military cultures as well as religious and social cultures, the location of the battle is metaphorical. The Roman army of this era was one that fought mostly for position and preferred to occupy a location and force the enemy to attack it. The Muslim army wanted to keep the desert at its back as a means of escape. The location of the battle where both types of land met in many ways allowed both groups to fight at or close to their preferred terrain.

The area to the west of the Dera'a Gap and into the Golan Heights was the homeland of an Arab-Christian tribe—the Ghassanids—who were allies of Rome. They played a critical part in the defense of Roman Syria and were instrumental in the structure of the battle.

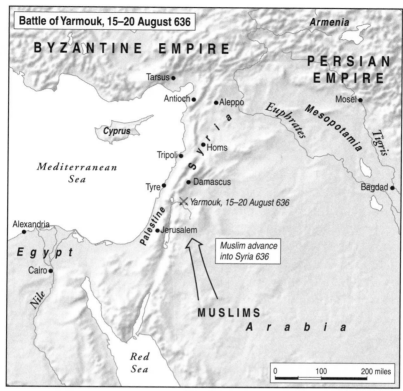

Fig. 6.1

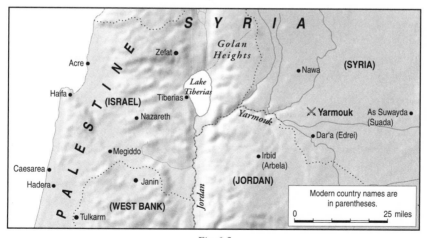

Fig. 6.2

When considering the purpose for the battle—to repel the Muslim invasion of Roman Palestine and Jordan and prevent further invasion and loss of territory in Syria—establishing an army near this mobility corridor made significant sense.

Terrain and Vegetation

The region consists of rolling hills and deep ravines with limited vegetation. The current area is home to numerous farms and a flourishing agricultural zone. Much of this modern expansion is a result of modern irrigation and water transportation rather than a reflection of the nature of the ground and the rainfall sufficient to support such efforts. In ancient times the cities and villages were smaller with less farming and cultivation. Thus vegetation was not of much significance.

In addition to the rolling hills there is also the Yarmouk River canyon. This is a steep-walled canyon with precipitous cliffs that are hundreds and sometimes more than a thousand feet high in many places. The canyon and its sheer walls were crucial at the end of the battle.

Weather

This battle took place in August, one of the two hottest months of the year. The weather can be oppressively hot and dry, with little relief from the winds that sometimes blow from the Mediterranean and off the Golan Heights. Many of the Roman soldiers fighting in this battle were from Armenia or other areas to the north. There were numerous Arab auxiliaries who lived in this area and were well acclimatized. There was reference to a sandstorm during a critical phase of the battle, and this was blowing generally from the south or southeast toward the north or northwest. This meant that the sand was blowing into the Roman faces and from behind the backs of the Muslim attackers. The limited visibility caused by the sandstorm was not the only limited-visibility operation. At least one of the attacks was made during hours of limited visibility, either at night or in the predawn dark.

Units Involved

Roman Forces

The Roman force was a conglomeration of Roman professional soldiers and numerous allied and mercenary units. In no way could it have been considered a homogenous or unified group. In this fashion it was indicative of the challenges facing the emperors of the late classical and early medieval periods. The vaunted legions that had made Rome a power in the entire Mediterranean basin were no longer in existence, and the system and bureaucracy to raise and equip such a force no longer existed.

The military weakness was made manifest in the numerous Persian successes of the later sixth and early seventh centuries. Rome still had the benefit of being the seat of eastern Christianity and was considered the protector of Christians throughout the region. This guaranteed a certain base for recruitment among the neighbors of the empire—Armenians and Arabs. At this point most Arabs in greater Syria and Palestine were Christian or polytheistic pagans.

The records of the battle vary radically in the size and composition of the Roman force. It is highly unlikely that the recorded size of the Roman armies is even remotely correct—numbers like 250,000, which included more than 120,000 killed in the battle, are absurd. The Roman Empire did not have the ability to field such a force.[4] The Arabs and Armenians did not possess warriors in the tens of thousands sufficient to make up the difference between what Rome could provide and what is suggested in Arab-Muslim sources. It is more likely that the numbers need to be reduced by a factor of five or six to get a more accurate picture of size.

Within this forty- to fifty-thousand-man force the army consisted of Romans, Armenians, Arab tribal allies, and mercenaries hired from the Balkans and western Europe. The nature of the local political climate will be discussed later, but it is worthy to note that this army did not enjoy local support and that the Roman government was only accepted in a utilitarian way—it was there and needed to be worked with as much as necessary.

The army mainly consisted of a spear-wielding, infantry-based force. The Armenians provided effective archers, and the Arabs acclimatized cavalry. There were other cavalry and missile organizations within the Roman and mercenary contingents, but these ethnic divisions are generally correct.

The Arabs from the local area had typically been used to secure the desert frontier of the empire for several centuries. It was less expensive and tended to be more effective than garrisoning Roman professional soldiers in distant and harsh locations where the land and environmental challenges were foreign and deadly. At various times the Arab allies might purposely fail in their assigned vigilance to gain greater payment or simply to demonstrate their importance to the empire. During the war between Rome and Persia, various Arab tribes changed sides regularly. This was a sign of the practical outlook of the Arabs—Constantinople and Ctesiphon were a long way away, yet the various proxy tribes were always present or in near-constant conflict. It was always better to make a deal if the protector state seemed no longer to be in a position to provide protection.

The Arab tribe most closely allied with Constantinople was the previously mentioned Ghassanids. This was a tribe that suffered greatly in the preceding war with Sassanid Persia and, like the Roman influence in the Near East, they were in the process of rebuilding their tribe and their influence as the Arab-Muslims flooded out of the desert and into their ancestral homeland.

The friction and conflict inherent in the combinations of cultures, languages, and various competing loyalties are essential when understanding the nature of change in this battle.

Muslim Forces

Though the Arab-Muslims could never be considered perfectly unified, in comparison with the Roman army they faced they enjoyed a tremendous level of unity. Specifically they had the unifying conceptualization of God and his divine message through his messenger, Muhammad. This allowed groups who could not have been relied upon to fight together to do so throughout a long and challenging series of engagements.

The Muslim army generally consisted of mounted infantry. Most of the army rode to the location of the battle, dismounted, and then fought as spear-wielding infantry. This tends to run counter to a prevailing lay view of the Arabs as an army that attacked from horseback or camelback. In general, this was a conceptualization of warfare brought from the steppes of Central Asia by the Turkomen tribes.

With the importance of infantry noted, the role of mounted maneuver was critical in this battle. The Arab-Muslim force was smaller than the Roman army they faced—maybe by as much as two-to-one. The force was divided into twenty-eight squadrons or battalions for the battle. It is of little value to make the Arab style of warfare overly schematic. Their traditional and cultural roots were tribal, and they were warriors, not soldiers—they did not fight in anything like the very disciplined ranks of spearmen in the Greek hoplite phalanxes or Roman legions of previous centuries. The divisions were not made to determine regimented movement, but more as a division of command responsibilities and general designations. The following quote provides some insight into organization and character:

> The size of units must presumably have been extremely elastic because the Arabs fought in their tribes. Accustomed as we are to reading of incidents in the past centuries in which primitive tribes have been routed by small detachments of regular forces, we are inclined to regard tribal organization as utterly inefficient from a military standpoint. Yet it may perhaps have been the lack of modern weapons rather than the tribal system which was responsible for these defeats. When, however, the lance, the sword, and the bow were the principal weapons, the tribes could be nearly as well armed as the regular armies. They, moreover, already instinctively possessed that esprit-de-corps which professional armies are at such infinite pains to inculcate in their soldiers. As long as the tribal system survived, tribesmen fought infinitely better among "the sons of their uncles" than in mixed

groups among men of other tribes whom they regarded almost as foreigners.[5]

Additionally, the importance of initiative in the Arab–Bedouin is further emphasized by Glubb when he says, "The Bedouin is characterized by one quality perhaps more than any other—his readiness to take the initiative in a tight corner, without paying any attention to anyone else."[6] The tribesmen who came from the desert were used to operating in small groups conducting small–unit raids and attacks. The divisions made by the Muslim commanders were useful in keeping a large army of tens of thousands feeling like a small tribal force of hundreds.

The Arab source material makes several notes of the ferocity of the Arab women present in the camp when it was attacked. Arab women played important combat roles in several battles, though they never stood at the lines of combat, but if a camp were attacked they would defend it vigorously.

Key Leaders in the Battle

Roman Forces

The references to specific leaders in the original source material can be very confusing because the same person may have his name spelled a variety of ways such that it is nearly impossible to determine about whom the source author is speaking. The nature of this battle, generally taken from the Arab tactical view and the Roman geo-strategic one, means that the roles or decisions of specific Roman commanders are less important. In addition to the below listed leaders there was also the son of a Sassanid Persian general who served as a commander. The very nature of the multiethnic and multilingual components of the Roman army points to difficulties in command and a common view. This was an army ruled by a usurping Roman, managed by a Roman general-bureaucrat, led by an Armenian general who had Arab, Roman, and Persian subordinate commanders.

Heraclius—Roman emperor. Heraclius was a usurper in an era of usurpers. He seized power in a period of great Roman decline and loss of prestige. The Sassanid Persians had threatened the walls of Constantinople on several occasions. Heraclius seized power and put together a force to conduct an aggressive and audacious plan of invasion and battle against the Sassanids on their own ground. This offensive-minded strategy was successful in significantly weakening the opponent and led to a negotiated settlement. Heraclius had only recently visited Jerusalem when the Muslims first came out from the Arabian Peninsula and attacked Palestine. It is certain that Heraclius did not see the Muslims as a threat equal with that of the Sassanid Persians, and this must have delayed his responses to their successful attacks.

In addition to his missing the threat, it is probable that the threat may have known of and about him. He had a record of combat command that extended for longer than a decade. It is not unlikely that some of the Arab-Muslims knew how he would try to defend and attack. Despite his history of success, he was neither feared nor avoided. Some of this may have extended from his opponent knowing about him, but most of this came from a belief of divine will and providential protection. In this vein, Heraclius and his experience paled in comparison with the knowledge and might of God.

Theodore Trithourios—commander of the Roman forces fighting in Syria. He held the title of treasurer, but he was certainly also a military commander.

Vahan—the Roman field commander and an ethnic Armenian. He was the commander at Emesa.

Jabala—the leader of the Ghassanids. He would at one point ally with the conquering Muslims only to return to Roman authority after an argument years later.

Muslim Forces

As previously noted, the Arab-Muslims enjoyed the strength of cultural, linguistic, and tribal unity at a level vastly greater than their opponents. The details of the leadership identified below come from near-contemporary Arab sources and demonstrate the homogenous nature of the command. There has been some debate on who was actually in command of the Muslim forces at this battle. Arguments about the actual date of the battle tend to revolve around this dispute. It is probable that the titular commander was Abu Ubaiydah and that the field commander was Khalid bin Walid. All of the battles were fought under the direction of the Caliph in Medina—Umar bin Al Khattab.

Umar bin Al Khattab—second Caliph (successor) to the Prophet Muhammad.

Abu Ubaiydah bin Al Jarrah—"He was one of the earliest Muslims and greatest Companions [of the Prophet Muhammad]. He played an important role in the election of Abu Bakr. Later, he governed Syria until his death of the plague at the age of fifty-eight in [639] at Amwas in Palestine. [Some sources make] him the overall commander on the Syrian front from the outset."[7]

Khalid bin Walid—one of the great commanders of this period. He was initially opposed to the message of Islam and its prophet. He converted and became a great military commander for Islam. He led the battle against the other Arab tribes during Muhammad's lifetime and was instrumental in uniting the tribes under the banner of Islam. He also commanded against those who left Islam following the death of Muhammad. Muhammad referred to him as the Sword of Allah. One of the great quotes about Khalid bin Walid is attributed to Abu Bakr in relation to the comments of Umar to relieve him: "I will not put away a sword that Allah has drawn against the unbelievers."[8] Khalid was given command of the conquest of Persia and later was directed to bring his army to the Syrian theater. He commanded in Syria until the death of the Caliph Abu Bakr. The new Caliph,

Umar bin Al Khattab, removed Khalid from his role as commander, and he became a subordinate commander for Abu Ubaiydah.

Historical and Grand Strategy Context

The success of Muhammad in approximately 628 AD of uniting the various tribes and groups on the Arabian Peninsula was, as previously stated, a work of tremendous statesmanship and leadership. Following the unification, an expedition was sent out to Roman Palestine (629 AD). This expedition was soundly defeated at a place called Mota (September 629 AD) in modern Jordan. Even though the Muslims lost, they had begun a trend of military expansionism and conquest that would not end until all the Near East, the Middle East, and North Africa were ruled by Muslims. The death of Muhammad within four years of the unification meant an inevitable internal struggle, since many believed they had pledged their loyalty to Muhammad and not to a larger conceptual entity. Additionally, there was a great deal of prejudicial treatment based on tribal and familial relationships. Those who were not of the specific families and tribes of Muhammad and his companions knew they would be denied any chance of real control and power.

The transition in motivation and focus was staggering. The Arab tribes had conducted raids into the Persian and Roman empires for generations and hundreds of years. Now an entire region was opened for the spreading of a new faith. The religious fervor of new converts was ubiquitous, and this changed the dynamic of all engagements—even when it was clearly a losing situation, the warriors of this new army of Islam fought with ferocious tenacity that meant the difference in many of their victories.

The previous movement of Arab armies into the great civilizations had been in the form of raids for limited gain and relatively limited times. Those tribes who stayed on the fringes of the empires were co-opted into the imperial defensive plans. Neither Persia nor Rome would have considered any attack, regardless of how large, as a serious threat to their existence or to the control of massive areas of their territory.

When the Arab-Muslims came out of the desert and attacked at Mota, the Roman Empire had only recently regained control of the Levant. The Persians had captured Syria and Palestine and controlled it for several decades. It was during this same period (about 602 AD) that Persia launched several attacks, taking their armies up to the walls of Constantinople. The Roman emperor came to power as a usurper, and he quickly raised a force that he took deep into Persian territory. He launched several campaigns in Persia that severally weakened the empire and soon forced a negotiated settlement that returned the entire Levant to Roman control (628 AD). The Roman efforts to reassert their control on the region resulted in significant oppression of religious heretics and taxation. The general attitude toward the Roman presence was at best neutral, and in many cases, it was viewed as negative. Rome was trying to regain control and authority. In addition to the issue of political and bureaucratic control, there was the issue of security and placing garrisons. The empire had suffered significant losses in the previous war in both personnel and treasure. They did not have the resources to face another major war.

As the Roman Empire declined in power and influence, it changed from primarily using military force to using more subtle means of coercion. It was common for the empire to use payments to buy off troublesome opponents. Another common technique was to play one group against another. Both of these techniques allowed local rulers and military commanders to adopt a less aggressive and more passive role. The idea was to allow the process to develop rather than to force conflict.

The Muslim armies following Mota enjoyed success after success in Palestine and Syria (633–636 AD). They attacked and won numerous battles in what is today southern Israel and northwestern Jordan. This campaign was conducted simultaneously with the campaign against the Persians. The Muslims defeated the Roman garrisons and marched north to take Damascus. This happened in 635 AD. This series of successes forced Heraclius to partially rethink his strategy. He needed a large army to stop the advance and force the Muslims back to the desert. He took time, nearly two years, gathering forces and building up an army that he then sent toward Damascus.

The Muslims had enjoyed greater success against the Persians, and thus the Caliph directed Khalid bin Walid to take his force from the Persian front and to bring it over to Syria. Khalid conducted a successful movement across the Syrian Desert and arrived in time to assist in the surrounding and defeat of Damascus in 635 AD. All of the key players were now on the same front.

Thoughts Before the Battle

The Romans had completed a victorious and audacious series of campaigns and regained their territory on the eastern coast of the Mediterranean Sea. The reestablishment of authority was done with significant oppression of those perceived to have been supportive of the Persians and with external diplomacy that encouraged inaction rather than aggressive response. The Romans were not fully in control of Syria at the time of the battle. Few of the inhabitants would have thought of themselves as Romans.

The Romans felt they needed only to delay until the Muslims could no longer maintain their cohesion and would therefore disband. The need was to deny them success and wait them out. In reality, the Romans needed to strengthen their local support, occupy fortifications, and force the Muslims, who were inexperienced in siege warfare, to attack the fortifications.

Into this environment appeared the Muslim armies. The Muslims needed to maintain a string of success. They could not afford to have the perception of invincibility destroyed. The last loss of note was during the lifetime of Muhammad. Any significant loss after Muhammad's death might have returned the Arab tribes to their historical disunity.

Operational Context

The Muslim armies attacked over a period of several years to cause the collapse of the Roman presence in the Levant. The attacks began with the areas geographically closer to the Arabian Peninsula—locations in modern southern Israel and the Gaza Strip. The Battle of Ajnadain (northeast of Gaza) was in July 634, along with several other battles. The victories were generally against regional Roman armies and the local garrisons. The Muslims moved north toward the prize of Damascus. The success in these earlier attacks led to greater expansion toward Damascus, the oldest and most significant city in the region. Victories were won as the Muslims marched north. Damascus fell to the Muslims in 635 but was lost to Roman efforts later that year. In 634, Khalid bin Walid was ordered to bring his army from the Persian front to the Roman front. He did so and arrived in time to support the capture of Damascus. A battle at Pella followed, which brought about the near complete collapse of the existing regional Roman military. The only recourse was from the army being raised from throughout the empire.

At the time of the battle in 636 AD, the Romans had invested nearly two years into gathering military strength and assembling an army sufficient to repel the Muslim invasion. The Romans regained all of the territory lost north of the Yarmouk River, since the Muslims simply withdrew in the face of the larger army, and were now in a position to enforce their will on the Muslims to the south of the river. The Arab allies were critical in this battle, and they were paid by the Romans to provide the expertise in matching the Arab-Muslims.

Technical Context

The Romans were not interested in fighting a large-open-field battle, but rather considered that the Muslims were like Arab raiders of earlier eras and over time would lose cohesion, return to the deserts of Arabia, and leave the empire alone. The Romans still built and used the marching forts common centuries earlier, though not as often. They built such a fort close to the strategic gap near the modern city of Dera'a and there waited for the Muslims to collapse.

The Muslims did not have siege weapons and needed an open-field battle. They relied on traditional and tribal means of combat—battles of champions and massed charges to maintain fighting esprit and cohesion. They also needed the unifying and motivating religious teachings of Islam. The Muslims fought several battles that lasted multiple days. It is unclear whether there was constant fighting during these long battles or whether the battles consisted of several

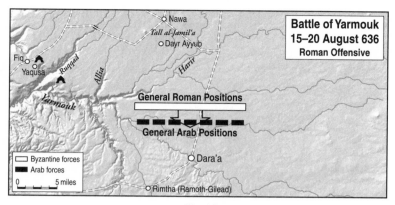

Fig. 6.3

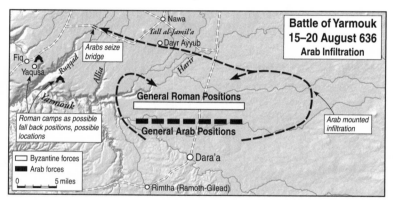

Fig. 6.4

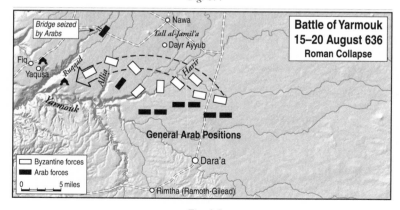

Fig. 6.5

sharp engagements interposed with periods of reconnaissance, probing, and rest and reorganization. Tribal cultures rarely fought pitched battles for days on end; instead they tended to fight, recover, and then fight again. The opening quote from Glubb is illustrative of his thinking on the reasons for the long battles and is supportive of the fighting techniques of the tribal Arabian warriors.

These elements all came into play as both armies waited for each other to change strategy. The Romans were the ones finally to relent, change strategy, and come out from their camp.

Tactical Chronology

As stated earlier in this chapter, there is debate among the ancient sources and more recent scholars and commentators about when, where, and how this battle actually happened. There are those who say it happened in 634 before the death of Caliph Abu Bakr or shortly thereafter, and there are others who place the date in 636. The original sources seem to place the battle as occurring over approximately six days with the primary engagements occurring on two of those days.

Glubb argues that a battle may have happened in both years, that the strategic nature of the terrain may have meant that the

Timeline	
Date	**Event**
February 628 AD	Peace between Rome and Persia
September 629 AD	Battle of Mota
June 632 AD	Death of Muhammad
July 634 AD	Battle of Ajnadain
23 August 634 AD	Death of Caliph Abu Bakr
August or September 634 AD	First Battle of Yarmouk
January 635 AD	Battle of Pella
September 635 AD	First capture of Damascus
20 August 636 AD	Battle of Yarmouk
September 637 AD	Capture of Jerusalem
11 February 641 AD	Death of Heraclius

Fig. 6.4

armies clashed twice in the same general area, and that this two-battle scenario answers the questions about sequence of events and how the two armies clashed to resolve the conflict. In general, as previously stated, this chapter follows Glubb, however, here it is instructive to discuss the primary events using the six-day scenario.

The Roman army came out from their camp and presented a battle order. A story exists of one of the Arab leaders for the Romans approaching Khalid bin Walid and questioning him about Islam. The Roman-allied Arab leader converted and then fought for the Muslims throughout the battle. On day two of the battle, the Romans mounted a significant attack that successfully broke through the Muslim lines, and the Romans were able to penetrate to the Muslim camp. Once at the camp, instead of encountering a soft target, fat with plunder, the soldiers were confronted by a vigorous and unexpectedly significant defense mounted by the Arab women. Many of the women fought personally to defend the camp, and they and other women mocked the Arab-Muslim men for retreating in the face of the Roman attack and shamed the men into attacking again. The efforts of the women were significant in turning the tide of the battle in favor of the Muslims.

The end of day five saw the Muslims order a mounted envelopment through the night. Khalid bin Walid was able to get cavalry behind the Romans and cut off the bridge, which was the only viable retreat option. In addition to the stealthy maneuver, a sandstorm came up from the southeast, and it blew sand in the faces of the Roman defenders. The desert-hardened Bedouins used the weather to their advantage as they closed on the Roman forces and were able to break in among the Roman lines. The loss of visibility and the chaos of the sand, sound, and wind caused the Romans to break. They could not flee to the rear because they received word that the road was cut. Instead they stumbled to the south and west. There they came upon the cliffs on the north side of the Yarmouk River canyon, and thousands fell over the cliffs to their deaths.

Much of this story is contested. There are those who criticize the weather as an after-the-fact excuse for why the Muslims were successful. Others contest the conversion story as myth, supporting the inevitability of Islam's advance in the region. All of these criticisms have validity, yet all of the elements of the story included in this brief narrative are illustrative of the challenges faced in this aberrational event.

Battlefield Leadership

Yarmouk, as all of the battles presented and referenced in this book, was not a forgone conclusion. The Muslims did not have to win this battle. They achieved victory through tremendous determination and very competent battlefield leadership. They had a culture that encouraged and rewarded bold initiative and men of vision and competence who saw opportunity and possibility and then seized it. Their collective belief in having God as an ally in this endeavor certainly allowed them to take risks that others with a lesser conviction probably would not have taken.

For the Romans, their first decision was the most costly. The failure to understand the opponent led to the decision to occupy and remain in a fortified camp for a long period and then to abandon that camp for an attack. They completely misunderstood the challenges faced by their opponents and those within their own collective organization. They also did not immediately attack a significantly inferior force, allowing the Muslims time to build morale and providing proof of Roman weakness in the face of the army of God. The Roman commander thought this tribal army could not remain together for a long period, and he waited rather than seizing the opportunity to crush their religious zeal through a rapid and overwhelming attack.

The Arab-Muslim commander (either Khalid or Abu Ubaiydah) used infiltration over time to place large numbers of forces in critical locations that would dramatically influence the battle once the Romans came out of their camp. The static nature of the Roman force made this easier. The Muslims also used the weather and darkness to facilitate the attack. The ability to do so was made possible through cultural acceptance of such hardships. The Arabs had experienced sandstorms more difficult than the one in which they fought, whereas, for most of the Romans, it was intolerable.

The Roman commander was faced with the challenge of commanding and controlling a heterogeneous ethnic force as opposed to the homogenous force of his opponent. As such, time was against him because he had the more difficult job of maintaining cohesion and a unified sense of purpose in defense of a generally unpopular empire.

Significance

The Battle of Yarmouk was a cultural watershed for much of the ancient heartland of civilization. It changed the direction of cultural development from being Western influenced to being Eastern influenced. The region had been a part of the West since Alexander the Great and his armies had crossed through and conquered it nearly a millennium earlier.

- The Arab victory meant the departure of Roman influence from the vast majority of the Levant. The cultural domination of Arabic-Islam lasts until the present.
- The loss of such a large Roman army meant that there were few resources to send to maintain Egypt, thus a logical consequence was continued military expansion of the Arab empire beyond the Levant.
- The culture in the Levant gradually changed over a period of centuries through intermarriage, conversion, and association. Nearly complete change did not occur until the crusaders were defeated.
- Islam replaced Christianity as the dominant religion in the Levant.

The role of Islam and its generally benign form of domination made acceptance of the new conquerors palatable to most of the people in the region. Islam's simplicity and emphasis on action rather than on doctrine also appealed to the people in a way that made the entire conversion and process of transition more palatable than those of previous conquests.

Lessons Learned: Principles of Conflict

The lessons from the battle of Yarmouk are focused on the identification portion of the principles of conflict.

- **Identification:** Failure of the Romans to understand their opponent—motivation, reasons, intent, goals—meant that their decisions were based on faulty premises. Coming after other battles with the Romans, the Arab commanders had learned how to fight them and, therefore, sought to surround them and make them fight on all sides. The Romans did not identify this tactic or the physical infiltration as it occurred.
- **Isolation:** The Romans became isolated by the terrain and the static position. So long as the Arabs had an open route back to the desert, they were not isolated. The movement to infiltrate cavalry to cut off the bridge to the north successfully isolated the Roman forces physically.
- **Suppression:** Static positioning accomplished suppression for the Arabs. The Roman attack, based on strength of force alone, nearly overcame the Arab army, but the fact that those in the camp were fighters as well as women effectively provided a reserve. The flexibility and positioning of the Arabs allowed them to retain the ability to maneuver.
- **Maneuver:** The unexpected attacks from the flanks and rear and the night attack all seized key perceived terrain and caused an emotional and physical collapse.
- **Destruction:** Nearly complete destruction and the pursuit of the fleeing forces denied any attempt to regain cohesion and mount any additional defense until terrain and climate prevented further Arab advance.

Conclusion

There is much about the telling of the Battle of Yarmouk that seems apocalyptic—it is almost a form of historical poetry. If this is true, there is much in the verse that helps a reader and student to see the competing leadership and dynamics. The ethnographic evidence found in the various accounts gives insight into the cultural differences and the lack of understanding between the cultures.

Some examples of this follow. First, the conversion of a non-Muslim Arab to Islam at the beginning of the battle supports a Muslim philosophy that all would join Islam if they were to see the light. This also serves to support Arab ethnocentrism and reveals the fact that information was moving among the Arab tribes and that rumors were flowing as a result of all of the contact between the various fighting groups. Second, the ferocious attack of the Arab women on the pillaging Roman soldiers is a clear example of the ignorance of the Romans about the Arab people. They were completely surprised by the ferocity and the fact that the women would fight at all. Third, the surrounding of the Romans by the flanking cavalry shows how much the Romans underestimated the Muslim understanding of the terrain and the Roman ignorance of the surrounding critical terrain. The story of the dust storm does not appear in Muslim sources, yet it bespeaks the complete loss of control of the natural world as if it were a metaphor of the impending loss of the battle. Finally, the story of the soldiers falling off the cliff serves as another demonstration of loss of control—the Romans could not see where they were going or the ground around them, and, subsequently, they plummeted to their deaths, much as the Roman leadership did not clearly see the cultural terrain around them and the army plummeted to their defeat.

Imperial exhaustion combined with new religious zeal to create one of the great underdog victories of all time. The failure of the Romans to understand what was happening on several levels of strategy caused a series of poor decisions. Failure to adopt beneficial and acceptable policies prevented many of the locals from supporting the Romans against the Arab-Muslims. Over time, and it is important to remember that the Arab-Muslims had been in this area for two years before the battle, the local populace came to accept Muslim terms for submission as much better than Roman terms of governance.

Weather, terrain, and ethnic abilities provided a significant benefit to the Arabs and blinded the Romans to better tactics. The Arabs were used to harsh climate and conditions and were able to perform in this environment.

The Roman's box for conflict with the Arabs only included raids and forays, not conquest. An aggressive attack with overwhelming forces might have made a difference, but the reality of limited resources and a weakened position in the newly reacquired provinces made the task nearly insurmountable.

How Does It Fit Inside the Box?
- The Roman army and political administration had fought Arabs before. It was expected that Arabs conducted large raids to secure materials, wealth, slaves, etc., but that they would return to the desert after a relatively short period of time in accordance with their nomadic natures.
- The Romans and Persians had completed nearly twenty years of war, and the Romans had regained much of their former Egyptian and Levantine territories. The Romans understood what was necessary for victory in a war between empires.

Why Is It an Aberration?
- **Means:** Despite their success against the Persians, the Romans were exhausted as they tried to rebuild and regain solid control of the newly reacquired provinces. The military was reduced, the treasury was spent, and religious animosities were expanded as the empire changed from war fighting to governing. Though Roman by name and occupation, the Levantine provinces were not yet again Roman by culture and control.
- **Means:** The Arab commanders and soldiers who came out of the desert in 634 to 636 AD were driven by a religious zeal unknown in that region for centuries. They possessed a commitment to the expansion of the land under their control and a willingness to sacrifice their lives as a part of the conquest, in anticipation of a religious paradise—this was not a simple raid but a determined conquest and the opening of an area for the expansion of a new faith.
- **Means:** The decisive event of the battle occurred during a sandstorm and at night. The limited visibility supported the tactics and fighting style of the Arab forces rather than those of the Romans.

- **Understanding:** Roman commanders and allied Arabs did not truly grasp the conviction and drive of their opponents. Arabs typically kept to a small tactical and operational box, and this behavioral pattern was significantly outside that behavior model. Nor did the Arab behavior fit the Persian model to which the Romans had become accustomed.
- **Leader:** The varied force of the Romans made them weaker and more difficult to control and maintain cohesion for a long period of time. The Arab conviction facilitated cohesion and commitment.
- **Target:** The Arabs were not raiding, they were conquering.

Strategies (numbered based on the nine strategies for victory)

1. **Introspection:** It is unclear what was going through Heraclius' mind as he created the strategy by which he would fight the Muslims. He gave command of a multiethnic force to a non-Roman. Whether or not Heraclius or Vahan saw the weakness of their force as an issue is unclear, but there are various accounts (mostly in the Muslim sources) of conflict within the ranks. They must have known that they would weaken over time. Garrison duty, especially the long hours of waiting for an enemy to attack, tends to grate on the discipline and cohesion of a force regardless of their quality. Vahan should have noted this dynamic and acted quickly to maintain his strength. Both Abu Ubaiydah and Khalid recognized the strength of their ethnic homogeneity and the unifying force of their religion. They perceived that they would grow stronger as time passed.
2. **Empathetic Appreciation:** It is clear that the Romans did not truly understand what had happened with the Arabs as a result of Islam. They did not see the unification and the expansion as anything like permanent.
3. **Empathetic Expectation:** The perception was that there needed to be a waiting game and the Arab raiders would go home.
6. **Study of Culture:** The Romans had Arab allies who provided a great deal of perspective on the Arab-Muslims. The biggest challenge was that though the allies understood the Muslims,

the Romans did not really understand the allies. In many ways the Ghassanids were foreign to the Romans. This played well into the hands of the Ghassanids in negotiating for protection money so that they had little incentive to educate their Roman allies in how the Bedouins thought.

7. **Multiple Reserves:** The Muslims had a nontraditional reserve in the form of those in their camp who were able to inflict a very debilitating blow on those attacking the camp. This was never intended but proved critical. The use of the Ghassanid allies in the first few days as near-shock troops meant that the primary cavalry for the Romans was expended by the time the Muslims were able to infiltrate the flanks.

   This removed any chance for a mobile reserve to assist in freeing up a line of communication to the rear.

8. **Initiative:** This was a battle of shifting initiatives, and, as such, there is a great lesson in the importance of patience. Khalid or Abu Ubaiydah allowed the battle to develop, and they continued to seek for ways to exploit their opponent. The Romans dominated the battle for initiative early in the conduct of the battle, but the counterattack from the camp defenders served as a blunt to that initiative. From that point on, the Muslims gained the initiative and began to dictate the decisions made by the Romans.

Chapter 7

Case Study: The Battle of the Horns of Hattin (3-4 July 1187)

The main and principal point in war is to secure plenty of provisions and to destroy the enemy by famine.
  —Publius Flavius Vegetius Renatus or Vegetius, military theoritician (circa 450 AD)[1]

The Horn of Hattin was believed to be the very Mount of Beatitudes where the Saviour taught the people the blessedness of peace. The Mount now bore witness to "not peace, but a sword."
  —Stanley Lane-Poole, historian (1898)[2]

Strategies Emphasized:

1. Introspection   6. Study of Culture
2. Empathetic Appreciation   7. Multiple Reserves
3. Empathetic Expectation   8. Initiative
5. Study of History

The battle fought on and around the twin hilltops named the Horns of Hattin was one that featured numerous lessons about how to prepare for aberrations. The strategies identified above are those that have direct application to this case study. The single most important feature is that of introspection. Guy of Lusignan, the king of Jerusalem, failed to understand himself, the challenges he faced in this campaign, the challenges in the way that he viewed the world around him, and the men who advised and counseled him.

In the modern world of technology and tools it sometimes gets lost how important a person and a personality really can be in shaping history and key events. The events leading up to the battle of the Horns of Hattin should force each reader to reflect on the importance of personalities more so than any of the conflict case studies discussed in this book. No decision or action in this battle can be viewed effectively without an understanding of the personality issues that revolved around the key players. As a result, this chapter features more information on those personalities than any of the others. The discussion in chapter 4 on the Battle of Little Bighorn also featured many references to potential motives and motivations, and the social dynamics in the 7th U.S. Cavalry in 1876 serve as a good baseline to launch off to the significantly more complicated issues revolving around the characters in this battle. As a result of some very significant complexities, the information presented here represents a simplified version of the relationships involved.

Several notes are important prior to continuing. First, the Latin Christian forces led by King Guy of Jerusalem will be referred to in a general sense as Franks. Most of the key players were from Frankish ancestry, spoke French, and were in some way vassals of the king of France. To call them crusaders misrepresents them and their motives. Crusaders were men who took the cross and made a religious vow to fight the *infidel* and typically to free Jerusalem. These tended to be men of a transient nature who came from Europe, fought, and then returned (if still alive) to Europe. The Frankish lords and knights who composed the army of King Guy of Jerusalem were, for the most part, not transients. Many of them had been born in the Levant or had lived there for decades with no intent of returning to Europe. The Levant was their home, and they expected to remain and leave lordships for their progeny.

Second, the spelling of names will follow a pattern of easiest to pronounce. Numerous authors have spelled the names of European and Muslim leaders a variety of ways, and in some cases there is little consensus. Saladin will be used rather than the Arabic version of Salah Al-Din (Purifier of the Faith), since it is more easily recognized by most Western-educated readers. The names of locations will tend to use the Frankish titles rather than the modern or ancient ones. This provides some challenges because spellings and use are rarely consistent.

Third, the sources are wonderful and entertaining but not very good at building a consensus. The European, mostly Frankish, sources tended to prefer one side of the intra-Frankish conflict over the other, and in general, they were supported in some conclusions by their Muslim counterparts. All of this depends on the perspective of the authors. It is important to know that most chroniclers in the medieval period worked at the largesse or patronage of a noble—this was true of both Muslims and Europeans. Therefore, what was written needs to always be filtered through the lens of intent, bias of both writer and patron, personal injuries or loyalties, and potential personal benefit from the perspective related. This is not to say that these original sources are unreliable but that like all history, they represent a perspective that is not perfectly objective. It is also important to note that the accuracy of tactical events on the battlefield does not exist in any of the original sources. The details of the battle are limited to small windows, and therefore there needs to be some effort made in piecing each of the windows together to form a complete panoramic view. Secondary-source writers have been left to piece together the events as described with their understanding of the tactics of the era and the terrain to form a complete picture of what really happened.

SALADIN IS OFTEN CREDITED AS BEING one of the greatest commanders of the crusading era. In many ways his greatness is a result of the events of this battle and those battles that immediately followed it. One of the objects of this book is to help people recognize aberrations from the perspective of the participants and not simply from the perspective of the objective armchair general. To do this, it is important to look at each person and event as they were seen, in their weaknesses and strengths, at the time and not through the long lens of historical judgment.

Geographical Setting

Location
The geography of this battle is its defining characteristic—what shaped the leadership decisions. The location of this battle plays as much a role in this battle as do the personalities. In fact, the battle of personalities, though it tended to center around the issue of whether or not to have a direct large-scale engagement, included an argument about where the battle should take place.

The terrain in the western Galilee region of what is today the State of Israel is a high plateau with few large natural water sources. The area in question is bounded on the south by the Jezreel valley, famous in ancient and medieval history for serving as the location of several battles of Megiddo in antiquity, the site of the Battle of Ein Jalut (Springs of Goliath) where the Mamluk Sultan Baibars defeated a Mongol army in 1260 AD, and the future Battle of Armageddon described in the New Testament Book of the Revelation of St. John the Divine in the Christian Bible.

Terrain and Vegetation
The region is bounded on the north by a string of higher hills that lead into the modern country of Lebanon. To the east are the Sea of Galilee and the Jordan River system, and to the west are the

highlands along the coast of the Mediterranean Sea. In general this is a plateau with a series of rolling hills and shallow valleys that provide multiple movement opportunities, both along an east–west axis and a north–south axis. Even though there are multiple mobility choices available, these are limited within the defined space between the medieval fortress of Saforie and the city/citadel of Tiberias, which is the region primarily addressed in this case study.

The medieval main road proceeded from Acre to Tiberias. It passed by Saforie and continued to the east along a valley that closely approached the foot of Mount Tur'an. A few miles after exiting the valley and arriving at a plain, the road dived and one branch ran to the southeast toward the settlement of Kafr Sabt while the other ran to the northeast and the village of Lubiyah. A few more miles on this northeastern road yet another division with a north–northeast path existed that led to the village of Meskenah and then to Arbel. The most direct route was the more or less middle road through Lubiyah and on to Tiberias.[3]

The location of water sources is always important to armies operating in the Levant, and this battle emphasized this point more than most. The most significant fresh water source in the region was, of course, the Sea of Galilee, or Tiberias. There were also large and sufficient springs at Saforie, Kafr Sabt, Tur'an, and Hattin. The location of springs and the quality and/or quantity of water present played a major role in the variety of accounts written about the battle. It was also a reality of conducting large-scale military operations that water sources had to be controlled in order to control the battlefield.

The uncultivated hills were covered with a scrub brush. The valleys were barren of significant vegetation, and there were few trees, with none near the battle site. This meant there was little shade from the sun and no concealment from opposing archers.

Weather

The physical events of this battle were in early July. This is a hot and dry period in this part of the world. There is no rain, and all of the intermittent streams are dry. The temperature tends to exceed ninety degrees Fahrenheit. The soldiers who fought in this battle were mostly from the Levant. They were completely acclimatized. There was a contingent of Italian soldiers who had recently landed at Acre and were supporting the effort, but these were the only ones for whom the weather could have been anything less or more than normal.

Units Involved

Frankish Forces

Sources disagree on the size and composition of the Frankish force as they rode out from Saforie. Despite this disagreement, the numbers can be compromised into a reasonable approximation of what was available for the fighting. First, it is important to provide a general description of types of forces and their uses in the warfare of the age.

The Franks had adapted their war-fighting organization and abilities to their new region over the eighty years of occupation. The primary arm of any army functioning in the Levant was cavalry. The composition and use of cavalry were what distinguished the Franks and other western Europeans from their eastern and typically Muslim opponents.

The heavily armored and mounted knight was the center of the Frankish cavalry. This was a man who tended to be armored from head to foot, mounted on a large horse, and carrying a shield and long spear or lance. The horse was specially bred for carrying the heavy weight of the knight and his equipment and specially trained to charge as directed. The spear was developing into a heavy shock weapon and was very much like the lance of the late Middle Ages. This weapon was designed to be carried in a couched grip and used to translate the force of the charging horse into an armor- and human-shattering attack on an opponent. The Frankish knights were the most feared element on the battlefield. They also represented a small percentage of the total force of a Frankish army, in this case about 10 percent, and were extremely expensive to raise, outfit, and train.

The challenge of having such a feared yet small cavalry forced the Franks in the east to come up with an intermediate force—not infantry, but not a knight. The solution was twofold. First were the mounted sergeants. These were not unique to the Levant, but they were an important part of the army of the Kingdom of Jerusalem. Since these men were not nobles, they did not possess the financial wherewithal to afford a complete armor package. They provided less of the awesome shock effect but still added mobility to the army. The second solution was the inclusion of Eastern peoples into the army—the Turkopoles. As the name suggests, they were Turkoman, or people of Turkish ethnicity. In most cases they were Christians. The Turkopoles fought much as the Muslim Turkoman—they were lightly armored and fought from horseback using a composite bow and emphasizing the horse as a mobile firing platform rather than as a vehicle of shock action like the mounted sergeants and the knights.

The importance of mobility in Levantine warfare meant that horses were a premium. The challenge faced by knights was that they could rarely use any available mount—they needed powerful horses that could carry them and their equipment into battle and deliver the shock necessary to split the opponent and cause them to break and flee. The Muslim warriors soon understood this, and the horses of the knights became a primary target of their arrows. This represented a change for both sides. Horses were not viewed as so critical a resource in warfare among the Turkoman tribes because nearly everyone had the same types of horses that were plentiful on the steppes and plains where they lived and fought. For the Frankish knights, the idea of taking an opponent's horses was usually considered wonderful compensation for battle, therefore, there was little effort made to kill the horse. Most of the nobility that were captured in this battle were horseless. This is a direct result of this Levantine clash-of-civilizations style of medieval conflict.

To address the protection of horses, the Frankish forces used infantry and dismounted bowmen to form protective squares around their knights during movement and walls in front of their knights in static positions. The infantry also wore armor, though this varied greatly based on the lord to whom the infantryman owed his feudal obligation or on other organizations to which he belonged. Most wore mail shirts and metal helmets and carried round shields rather than the kite shields of the knights and mounted sergeants. Crossbows were the missile weapon of Frankish choice, as was the spear for static defense.

The reliance on infantry protection of the mounted knight meant that a Frankish army on the move was forced to maintain the pace of their necessary but slower dismounted elements. If this formation were moving in an area where the enemy was known to be, this further slowed the column because they had to maintain a moving box formation with infantry surrounding the knights. Such emphasis on the formation required greater levels of control and discipline and would further slow the advance.

The Frankish forces in the Levant also had organizations unique from the rest of the European medieval world—the military orders. These were the groups commonly known as the Templars and the Hospitallers. Unlike regular infantry or cavalry, they were not obligated through feudal arrangements, but rather they were warrior monks who swore allegiance to the order in the form of their grand master and the Catholic Pope. In most aspects they were similar to their counterparts in armor and fighting style. The nature of their organization meant that they were raised through volunteer admittance to the order and something like a medieval equivalent of a meritocracy in terms of advancement. It was never a true meritocracy, since a peasant would not become a grand master, but an insignificant noble could rise to one of the key leadership positions if not become grand master himself, as would be the case of the Templar grand master at Hattin.

The Frankish force is believed to have consisted of about 1,200 knights, 2,000–4,000 Turkopoles and mounted sergeants, and somewhere in the neighborhood of 10,000 dismounted infantry. These numbers are designed to give reasonable approximations of the variety of reports in the original sources and the still-varied interpretations represented in the secondary analysis. It is clear that the Frankish force was large and probably the largest such force assembled in the Galilee. Regardless of the size of the force, they were probably outnumbered.

The numbers must be considered in terms of capability and the style of battle. There cannot be a one for one correlation of forces. The point of this is that the Frankish forces were slowed by their preponderance of infantry and not truly geared for a battle of movement.

Muslim Forces

Like King Guy, Saladin raised what was probably the largest army of its kind to fight in the Galilee in the crusading era to this point. Saladin ruled an empire of many kingdoms and competing tribes. Though most of his forces were either ethnically Turks or Arabs, they were from a wide variety of tribes and regions within his empire and in no way represented a homogenous army.

The Muslim armies of the medieval period were a light cavalry–based force. Their tactics were derived from generations of conflict on the steppes of Central Asia, where there is room for movement and fighting in a fixed position is weakness while mobility is strength. The central force in any Turkic army was the mounted bowman who rode a sturdy and agile horse. The concept was to approach and then attack the opponent through a hail of arrow fire and then to withdraw before the opponent could reciprocate. Strength was in mobility and not in holding to a position. This meant that if an opponent charged with determination, the Turkoman force would withdraw to allow the enemy to expend their energy, and once the energy was expended, they would attack and destroy them.

In addition to the mounted and very mobile tactics described above, the army of Saladin also included infantry and engineers. The siege engines of the Muslim forces were extremely advanced. This was a direct result of the need to capture so many fortified positions both in the wars with the Franks and with other Muslim rulers. The strength of Saladin's engineer corps was demonstrated when he breached the walls of Tiberias within a single day of siege and assaults.

Both the infantry and the cavalry were armored. The cavalry had some elements nearly as heavily armored as the Franks, and from there it rapidly declined across the spectrum. The infantry tended to be less armored than their Frankish opponents, but they also played a smaller role in a mobile battle than did the Frankish infantry. The infantry forces of Saladin also included thousands of volunteers from Damascus and other major cities who were motivated by religious sacrifice rather than through professional military service; these were the least-armored and the poorest-armed soldiers in either army.

The size of Saladin's army is widely quoted anywhere from less than twenty-five thousand up to eighty thousand. Muslim sources tend to emphasize that it was a force equal to or smaller than the Frankish army, and European sources tend to identify it as a force many times that of the Frankish king's. There is little accurate census data on the size of the force, especially when the numbers of recent religiously motivated and poorly trained volunteers are included. All of the competing sources and subsequent commentary make it nearly impossible to state the size of the army with accuracy.

This said, it is clear that Saladin commanded a vast host and that his army had many thousands of recent additions who saw this as a religious obligation and opportunity to gain an eternal reward. Saladin's total force must have been larger than Guy's and possibly twice the size. Despite this estimate, most of the battle was fought by Saladin's veterans, and the numbers of the forces were irrelevant when the very different styles were compared. As stated above, a direct correlation of forces makes for a poor analysis in this historic case.

Key Leaders in Battle

Frankish Forces

Much of what will be said in this section may seem petty and small-minded. An objective witness of the events with a modern outlook on governmental service will find it easy to criticize the people for their lack of willingness to compromise and work for the betterment of the kingdom as a whole rather than fight and argue based on personal affronts and insults. The medieval European world was one where personal honor was critical to a person's sense of self and to the perception of the individual. Slights, insults, and affronts were serious, and it was common to harbor grudges for a lifetime. The narrative that follows this section is full of such stories, and it is this tangled web of personal relationships that set the stage for the failure of the Frankish kingdom in the Levant.

The Kingdom of Jerusalem from the death of King Amalric I in 1174 AD through the Battle of the Horns of Hattin in 1187 AD was a kingdom politically divided between two competing factions. The factions revolved around two powerful personalities—Raymond III, Count of Tripoli and Lord of the Galilee, and Agnes of Courtenay, mother of King Baldwin IV. These two people drew others around them through reputation, favors, intrigues, or general ideological agreement. Both of the Frankish primary sources and most of the contemporary Muslim sources portray Raymond III as the good guy in these conflicts and cast the competing faction as schemers and incompetent courtesans or as ruthless barbarians. Hopefully this version will take a more moderate and objective course.

The faction generally associated with Raymond III attracted those of the native barony and nobles who tended to prefer a policy of long-term stability with the Muslims. Agnes of Courtenay brought those who favored more aggressive action against the Muslim opponents and many of those who were recent arrivals to the Levant. The following descriptions are brief summaries of individuals who have direct relation to the remainder of this chapter and are not intended to be a comprehensive list of all the notable personalities of the kingdom at the time of the battle. The summaries are divided into the two factions described.

Native Nobility (Polains—Frankish Term for the Levantine-born Franks)
Raymond III—Count of Tripoli and Lord of the Galilee. He was a count in his own right, and he became Lord of the Galilee through marriage to the Lady Eschiva of Bures (widow of Walter of Saint-Omer of Tiberias). He had been captured by Muslim forces and held prisoner from 1164 until about 1173 or 1174. During his imprisonment he learned the Arabic language and was reported to have read the Koran. He emerged from captivity a man who seemed to believe that the Muslims were a people with whom he could work, and he effectively built alliances and established truces with Muslim rulers on behalf of his two domains, which brought him and his areas of responsibility security and stability. He was also rumored to have developed a relationship with the Shiite band called the Assassins.

Some of his specific dealings with Saladin will be addressed in the narrative portion, but he was severely criticized for his relationship with the "infidel." His apparently positive view of Muslims is probably one reason for his positive reflection in the Muslim primary sources. He ruled the Kingdom of Jerusalem as regent from 1174 until Baldwin IV attained his majority at the age of sixteen in the year 1177. He also ruled as regent from the end of 1183 during the final illnesses of Baldwin IV and the first year of the reign of the child-king Baldwin V until his death.

The Frankish and Muslim chroniclers all give a positive assessment of his personality and leadership. This said, he was successfully outmaneuvered for the crown of the kingdom by Guy of Lusignan, and he was unable to develop a consensus among the ruling council of the kingdom. He was a source of the discontent and polarization within the kingdom.

Balian of Ibelin—He was a well-respected noble and loyal to Raymond III. He served as a peacemaker between the two camps, especially in bringing Raymond III to unite with the rest of the kingdoms' nobles against Saladin in 1187. He would later lead the defense of Jerusalem against Saladin. Muslim sources viewed him as a true noble and an honorable man.

Courtenay and Lusignan Faction

Agnes of Courtenay—first wife of Amalric I and Countess of Jaffa and Ascalon through that marriage, since she was never awarded the title "Queen of Jerusalem." She bore Amalric two children, Sibyl and Baldwin IV (the Leper King). She is infamous in the chronicles of the period as a court intriguer. She wielded influence over her son and was able to get several of her circle appointed to positions of power and influence as a result. Her moral behavior was also a matter of significant criticism.

Aimery of Lusignan—Constable of the Kingdom of Jerusalem. Aimery was a newcomer from the French region of Poitou. He was of a minor noble family. He was rumored to have been a lover of

Agnes of Courtenay, and through this relationship he attained one of the highest positions in the court. His brother was Guy of Lusignan.

Guy of Lusignan—King of Jerusalem. Most of the contemporary chroniclers and many of the later historians generally treat him as a fop and a buffoon who had the good fortune to marry well and secure himself a throne.

Several relatively recent historians have looked more at Guy through the lens of what he did following his defeat at Hattin, in attacking the city of Acre, and as King of Cyprus, as well as his ability to successfully govern there and to fashion a very successful medieval administration and relatively united nobility. This gives a lot of support to Guy as a capable person who simply suffered the misfortune of having unsupportive subordinates at the time of Hattin. Much of this will be discussed later in the narrative.

Guy arrived from France, and through his brother he was introduced to Sibyl, the sister of Baldwin IV. She was recently widowed and available. Guy married her in the spring of 1180. He was given regent-like powers in 1183 during a serious illness of Baldwin IV, but this was removed after the king received reports of his failures as a leader of the army. Guy removed himself and his wife and stepson to his domain in Ascalon, where he denied the king and the king's representatives entrance.

There were significant issues over his role as the potential future king from the beginning. His marriage was immediately opposed by Raymond III and those allied with him. Following the removal of the regent-like powers in 1183 there were attempts to have his marriage to Sibyl annulled. Despite the fact that his stepson was crowned king, he had no role as regent; instead Raymond III was declared regent. Upon the death of Baldwin V, Guy and his faction were able to outmaneuver Raymond III. The marriage was annulled, and Sibyl was crowned queen of Jerusalem with the right to choose her new husband who would become king. She chose Guy. Most of the nobles accepted this, with the exception of a few, including Raymond III.

It is unclear how to judge Guy as king of Jerusalem. He was unable to unite his nobility, though he did seem to make a serious attempt to do so. He gave the impression he was simply seeking a throne for himself and that he was not concerned about the greater good of the kingdom. He may have had the potential for greatness that was overshadowed by the pettiness of his subordinates, but he tended to act in a way that always sought personal gain and glory at the risk of the kingdom.

Joscelin III—titular Count of Edessa and Seneschal of the Kingdom of Jerusalem. The county of Edessa had ceased to exist more than forty years before the battle at Hattin, but there was still a count in name. Joscelin was also the brother of Agnes of Courtenay. He held the personal fief of Acre. Following the battle, he surrendered Acre without even attempting a defense. He negotiated the surrender, thus allowing himself and the other occupants to flee in safety with all of their possessions.

Heraclius—Patriarch of Jerusalem. He was supposedly appointed through his personal association with Agnes of Courtenay. The other candidate was the very well-respected William of Tyre. William was one of the great historians and chroniclers of his age and one of the best in the entire High Middle Ages. This slight by the Courtenays was certainly one reason why William was so critical of them. Heraclius was a man of questionable morals and education. He was responsible for bringing the "true cross" from Jerusalem to accompany the army into the field.

Gerard of Ridefort—Master of the Templars. He was a Flemish knight who had traveled to the Levant on pilgrimage. It was common for nobles to conduct armed pilgrimages to the Levant, do battle with the infidel, visit the holy sites, and then return to Europe or stay if there was a suitable enticement. Gerard sought such an enticement from Raymond III in Tripoli. According to contemporary accounts, Raymond III promised Gerard the first suitable heiress in the county and the fief that accompanied her. When just such a match became available, Raymond III reneged on his promise and wed the woman to a Pisan noble who supposedly offered to pay Raymond III her weight in gold. Gerard was angered by this treachery, though he remained in the Levant and joined the Templars. He rose through the order, and in 1186 he was named grand master of the order of the Temple of Sion (Templars). Gerard clearly despised Raymond III; he never forgave him for his failure to honor their agreement. He was also hotheaded in battle, and he sought engagements with Muslims at nearly all possible opportunities.

Reynald of Châtillon—Lord of Oultrejourdain. Without question, Reynald is one of the most colorful characters in the crusading period. As such, he has gained significant criticism. Since recent scholarship tends to be more anti-European and rely more on the Muslim sources, the reputation of Reynald suffers significantly. Saladin, who was known for his evenhanded and just approach, personally vowed to kill Reynald at least twice. From this it can be safely assumed that the Muslim chroniclers do not deal with him in an objective way. He was considered something close to an incarnation of Satan.

Some space will be dedicated here to his actions as well as in the narrative, since they are instrumental to the pretexts and causes for the battle at Hattin. Like Raymond III, Reynald was taken prisoner by the Muslim lord of Aleppo. Reynald was taken captive in 1160 or 1161 and was not released until 1175. Unlike Raymond III, Reynald did not emerge from captivity with a positive disposition toward Muslims or the Turkoman elite who had held him captive. It is relatively safe to say that Reynald emerged from captivity with quite the opposite view. Why Raymond III and Reynald came out of captivity with such opposing views of the Muslims is unclear, since there is no direct source to tell us. It is possible that they entered captivity with different approaches to the Muslims and that captivity only tipped them even more toward that end to which they were predisposed.

Prior to being taken captive, Reynald was the prince of Antioch through marriage, and it was in his role as prince of Antioch that he started his aggressive actions against Muslims in Aleppo and Christians in the Byzantine Empire. His earliest actions are not critical here, but they are useful in understanding his personality. During his captivity, his wife died. She was his tie to the rulership of Antioch. Upon his release, he was no longer welcomed at Antioch, and he journeyed south to the Kingdom of Jerusalem and found an available widow in Stephanie of Kerak and Montreal. She was the widow of Humphrey of Toron and Miles of Plancy. Miles was killed in Acre under dubious circumstances, possibly the work of the Assassins and linked by rumor to Raymond III. Stephanie attributed the murder to the Count of Tripoli, and Reynald as her husband was firmly set against Raymond III.

Reynald used his new domain—all of the area east of the Jordan River—to conduct direct attacks on Muslim caravans. The domains of Saladin were separated between Egypt and Syria. They had no Mediterranean ports in Syria, meaning that all commerce and reinforcement between the two regions had to travel inland close to the domain of Reynald. By geography alone, the domain of Oultrejordain was critical to Saladin, and the caravan routes of the Sultan of Cairo and Damascus would have been lucrative targets for any lord.

The biggest charge against Reynald is that he was a truce breaker and that he violated taboos of the coexistence of the two religions—primarily he threatened a direct attack on the cities of Mecca and Medina. These events play a direct role in the events leading to the battle and will be further addressed in the narrative.

Muslim Forces

The central figure in the Muslim forces is Saladin. There were other subordinate leaders of quality and note, but space in this chapter will not allow them to be addressed here. Saladin did not lead a unified army. As noted previously, his regular forces were in concert with the forces of other Turkoman rulers, some who had only recently placed themselves under the suzerainty of Saladin. In addition to the regular and levied Turkoman forces, there were other forces that had been raised based on the premise of waging holy war against the infidel. These forces were typically loyal to Saladin so long as they had food and victory. Once again, it is important to place Saladin in June of 1187 and not in June of 1188.

Even with the internal divisions and petty squabbling that certainly occurred within the large and disunited army, the infighting among the Franks made Saladin's army look blissfully united and

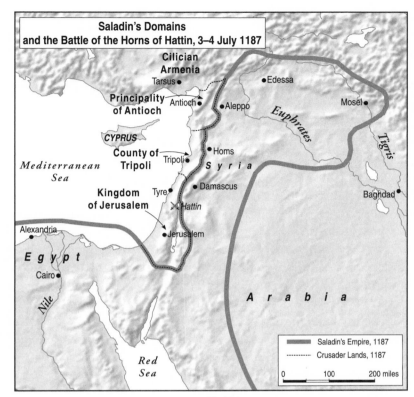

Fig. 7.1

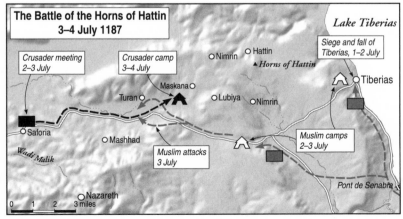

Fig. 7.2

without differences. The smaller Turkoman nobles who might have thought of making difficulties for the Sultan were silenced by the victory at Hattin and the repeated easy victories thereafter.

Yousef Salah Al Din Ibn Ayyub (Saladin)—Sultan of Egypt and Syria. Saladin was a Kurd from Tikrit. His father, Ayyub, had played a critical role in saving Zengi, the Atabeg of Mosul, from certain death during one of many Turkoman civil conflicts. Zengi would go on to have great success in welding together a large portion of Syria and Mosul under the Abbasid Caliph and conquering the crusader county of Edessa. Just as he succeeded in his triumph, he was killed. Out of the chaos rose his son, Nur Al Din, who became even more renowned by linking Mosul and all of Syria together in a powerful sultanate. Nur Al Din sent an army to Egypt under a Kurdish commander named Shirkuh, who was the uncle of Saladin. Saladin accompanied his uncle as directed by Nur Al Din, though the chroniclers say he was reluctant.

Saladin is given great credit in Muslim and Frankish Christian sources for being pious, a man of his word, and generous. He kept truces and forgave ransoms and treachery when the treachery was in the name of a higher purpose. He was a devoutly religious man who sincerely lived his religion and wanted to return Jerusalem to the control of the Muslims.

Saladin became the leader of Nur Al Din's army in Egypt when Shirkuh died and the army selected him to lead them. He captured Egypt and then ruled it under the suzerainty of Nur Al Din. At least this is what he claimed. Nur Al Din felt that Saladin had betrayed him and was a renegade, though there was no proof of disloyalty. Saladin did flee the battlefield every time Nur Al Din approached with an army to conduct a joint attack on the Franks. Saladin was constantly in fear of attacks from the Kingdom of Jerusalem under the rulership of Amalric I and from Damascus and Nur Al Din. Saladin was given the double blessing of the death of both his rivals for Egypt in the same year—1174.

Saladin then went about trying to consolidate control of the former holdings of Nur Al Din. He waged several battles against the Franks, but most of his campaigns were against fellow Muslims and Turkoman rulers. A Kurd was considered lower than a Turk in the ethnic ladder of the period, and the idea of Saladin, a Kurd who deceived Nur Al Din and had Egypt fall into his lap, as ruler was always something of an issue among the Abbasid Caliphate. This was one of the motivators for many of Saladin's actions against the Franks, and the repeated failures to deal with the Franks as effectively as he was dealing with the Turks and other Muslims left a cloud over all of his achievements.

Historical and Grand Strategy Context

Saladin's conquest of Egypt and the death of the Fatimid Caliph brought Saladin into the position of sole ruler of the most economically successful Muslim-controlled region in the Near East and North Africa. As previously noted, Saladin did recognize that he ruled under the suzerainty of Nur Al Din—the call to prayer was done in the names of the Abbasid Caliph and Nur Al Din as one example of his subordinate relationship; however, he also operated as an independent actor in all but name only. This made Nur Al Din Saladin's most feared opponent. In this initial period the other nemesis of significance was Amalric I, who seemed enamored with the idea of capturing Egypt for the Frankish kingdom. He launched multiple attacks on the area in coordination with various outside groups—armed pilgrims, Byzantine navy, and Italian city-state navies—over the years. In 1174 both of these men died, and Saladin was left as the most dominant personality in the Levant.

Saladin spent a lot of time and effort to regain control of the entire area formerly ruled by Nur Al Din. This was a campaign that took nearly nine years from the summer of 1174, when Amalric I died, until 11 June 1183, when Saladin captured Aleppo and completely surrounded the Frankish-ruled areas under a single Muslim leader. Saladin's battles against other Muslims continued for nearly three years until he gained suzerainty of the Al Jazeera[4], which was ruled from Mosul through treaty.

This meant that Saladin controlled three very important regions within the modern Near East—Egypt, Syria, and the Al Jazeera. These regions were separated by significant physical barriers—the Syrian Desert, the Sinai, and the northern part of the Nejd Desert. The lack of ports on the Mediterranean in Syria meant that all of the contact between the three regions was by land. All of these physical elements combined to create a span of control dilemma. Saladin ruled a vast region in an era of limited communications, and he was forced to govern through trusted associates, most of whom were close relatives of the Sultan, and to regularly travel from region to region.

The travel routes became strategically important in a way that they had not previously been. Of primary importance was the route from Syria to Egypt, which passed within view of the large Frankish castles of Kerak and Montreal, both of which had been ruled by Reynald of Châtillon since at least 1177. Whether through his innate sense of barbarism, brutality, and greed that some attribute to him or through an understanding of the critical weakness of Saladin—the ground caravan route—Reynald regularly affected the movement along this route through raids and attacks. It is possible that Reynald acted with a little of both motivations: that he was both a brutal and barbaric ruler who grasped the larger geopolitical weakness of his opponent and that he had the instrument to attack such a weakness.

As Saladin gained control over larger and larger areas and apparently began unifying the Muslim world in preparation for waging war against the Frankish invaders, the Frankish kingdom became less and less united. The death of Amalric I and the succession to the throne of his leprous son, Baldwin IV, meant that succession was the primary concern of the kingdom. The daughters of Amalric I, Sibyl (his daughter through Agnes of Courtenay) and Isabel (his daughter through his second wife), were both married to either native nobles or nobles recently arrived from Europe. Sibyl had a son who was to be crowned Baldwin V, but he died while still in his minority. Guy of Lusignan, the second husband of Sibyl, did not inspire the loyalty of Raymond III and those who supported him. The contentious nature of the succession was at the heart of the divisions within the kingdom. As Baldwin IV became sicker and sicker, his ability to demand the loyalty of his vassals decreased. He was still capable of leading the kingdom's army in battle, and he inflicted a heavy defeat on Saladin at Mount Gisard in 1177. Just two years later the king was nearly captured by Muslim forces during a skirmish at Jacob's Ford north of the Sea of Galilee. Another battle was lost to the Muslims at Marj Ayun, also in 1179. Guy married Sibyl in 1180, and this solidified Raymond III's opposition to the faction supporting Guy as the future heir.

Throughout the interactions with Saladin, truces were a regular occurrence. Each side proposed truces when they faced particularly challenging internal issues or opponents from other areas. In 1180, Baldwin IV requested a two-year truce, and Saladin agreed. Reynald of Châtillon broke the truce by attacking a caravan to Mecca in 1181.

Raymond III returned to the Galilee from Tripoli in 1182, and he was initially refused admittance into the Kingdom of Jerusalem by Baldwin IV, who was convinced that Raymond III was after the throne. This situation was smoothed over through the efforts of several of the other native barons, and Raymond III was allowed to return to Tiberias on the Galilee.

In 1182 Reynald of Châtillon launched a daring adventure by capturing the port at modern-day Aqaba and sending ships into the Red Sea to raid the lucrative trade routes and to pillage the annual Hajj pilgrimage. This was initially successful, but the ships were eventually hunted down by a more superior Muslim fleet and destroyed. The men from the ships landed near Mecca and threatened to attack the city, which was and still is considered the most holy city by the Muslims. There is some disagreement in reference to whether attacking Mecca or Medina was the intent, but the published reports that Mecca was the target played well in inciting Muslim anger against the Franks. It was this naval adventure, the attack on pilgrims, and the threat to a holy city that caused Saladin to threaten to kill Reynald personally.

The success of Saladin in capturing Aleppo in 1183 allowed him to turn his attention to the Franks in a significant fashion. He led an army in 1183 into the Galilee with the intent of defeating the army of the kingdom. Baldwin IV was ill, and Guy, who had the authority of the king, was leading the army. In this case both armies were large, not as large as at Hattin, but they were the largest up to 1183. The Franks did not seek battle and refused to give battle when it was offered. They occupied a defensive position near the Springs of Goliath or Ain Jalut (near the same location where Baibars would later defeat the Mongols in 1260). Saladin could not maintain his large army, and they eventually had to withdraw. He moved on to lay siege to Kerak, but that was ended when the army of Jerusalem approached.

The campaign in 1183 was viewed by the nobles of the Kingdom of Jerusalem as both a success and a failure. Those who were opposed to Guy pointed to this as a demonstration of his lack of ability to lead—he had an enormous army, but he could not engage and defeat the Muslims in battle. Others viewed this as a demonstration of the Muslim army's inability to maintain cohesion for long. In hindsight, this was probably the right course for Hattin. The cries in opposition to Guy were much louder in 1183, and it became clear that Guy could not get the loyalty of his potential vassals. The group would not conduct unified operations and, therefore, could not attack successfully. It was the failure of 1183 that was remembered by most of the nobles, and this was certainly a part of the thinking that shaped decisions four years later.

In 1184, Saladin attacked Kerak again, and when forced to withdraw, he led a lightning raid into the Samarian hills on the city of Nablus and surrounding villages. Saladin's failure to defeat his tactical opponent Reynald of Châtillon after his purportedly outrageous attacks on Muslim pilgrims, combined with his failure to defeat the army of the Kingdom of Jerusalem in battle, had shaped the regional view of Saladin. He was winning little battles but losing the major ones with the Christians.

In 1185, Saladin and Baldwin IV entered into a four-year truce. This was mutually beneficial. Baldwin IV was losing more and more control of his nobles, and the divisions were growing deeper. He was seeking alliances overseas, either through a marriage with a significant European noble or through giving homage to the Byzantine emperor in return for military assistance. The Kingdom of Jerusalem needed time to develop these relationships without fighting with Saladin. Baldwin IV sent an embassy of senior nobles to Europe and Constantinople to achieve such an end. It was on this trip that the master of the Templars died. It was also during this trip that the group secured a financial endowment from King Henry II of England for the military orders.

Saladin also needed time. He was seeking control of the Al Jazeera and needed to be able to focus his military and economic resources to the east and not the west.

Baldwin IV died within months of beginning the truce, and Raymond III became regent of the child-king Baldwin V. Saladin gained control of Mosul on 3 March 1186 when the ruler there acknowledged Saladin as suzerain. Baldwin V died later in the same year, and then came the controversial coronation of Guy, which violated the will left by Baldwin IV. The will called for an elaborate European commission to form and decide on the king if Baldwin V should die before reaching his majority. Raymond III refused to acknowledge Guy as his overlord, and he conducted a private peace with Saladin on behalf of the Galilee. In addition, he was already conducting negotiations with Saladin on behalf of the county of Tripoli, which did not fall under the direct vassalage of the King of Jerusalem.

Raymond III now had Turkoman warriors in Tiberias to assist him in defending the lordship against any attacks from Guy. The kingdom was very close to civil war.

The truce was broken by Reynald of Châtillon in early 1187 when he attacked a caravan passing close to his castle at Kerak. Saladin sent a complaint to Guy, and Guy in turn demanded that Reynald return the prisoners and merchandise. Reynald declared himself sovereign in his domains and refused to submit to the will of the king. This was the last straw, and Saladin called for a holy war against the Franks of the coast and a return of the city of Jerusalem to Muslim rule. He gathered thousands from all over his now vast domains.

Thoughts Before Battle

Guy needed to maintain the Kingdom of Jerusalem and his newly won position. He faced the challenge that all usurpers face of gaining respect. Though there are arguments that he was not a usurper, it seems clear that many contemporaries viewed him as such, and even some of his supporters questioned his legitimacy to rule, as noted by Reynald's refusal to obey a royal command. Guy needed to gain true command of his kingdom, and the best way to do so was through military success.

Saladin also needed victory, but it needed to be victory against the Christians. He received significant criticism for spending more time and effort fighting Muslims than Franks. He had to force a major battle and win it.

It is certain that Saladin knew what he wanted to do and why he wanted to do it. This was a battle he needed to force, and he was clear as to the reasoning and the urgency. It is less clear whether Guy understood why he wanted a battle. The sources are anti-Guy, and, therefore, they attribute to him a weak will and do not take into account the failure in 1183 or his need as a usurper for legitimacy. Thus, it is probable that Guy did not see himself clearly, and the decisions he was to make were flawed because he failed to know his own mind.

Operational Context

The campaign began with a direct siege of Kerak in April 1187. Saladin brought nine mangorels (catapults) to finally break through the walls of the fortress. This siege was broken as the army of the Kingdom of Jerusalem was seen moving toward Kerak.

Saladin then moved the direction of attack to the north as he sent his army to the Galilee. He coordinated with Raymond III for the rights to cross into the territory and launch a raid against the communities of the kingdom but outside the domains of Raymond III. Raymond III agreed to the request with conditions on time of crossing and limits as to their activities within his domain. The raid coincided with the movement of Balian of Ibelin and Gerard of Ridefort to try and heal the breach between Guy and Raymond III. Gerard had gone ahead of Balian by several hours, and when he heard of the Muslim raid, he gathered a group of Templars and rode into an attack. Almost the entire force was slaughtered at a place called the Springs of Cresson, being completely outnumbered. This cost the kingdom at least sixty knights at a time when every knight was critical.

Raymond III was convinced by Balian of Ibelin of his nearly traitorous association with Saladin and encouraged him to breach his alliance with the Muslim sultan. Raymond III sent the Muslim guards away, and he went to Jerusalem to offer his homage to Guy. The kingdom was finally united, at least on the surface.

The battle at the Springs of Cresson took place on 1 May 1187, only a few days after the end of the siege of Kerak. Saladin reunited his forces at the southern end of the Sea of Galilee and began crossing into the Galilee region on 26 June 1187. By this time Guy had called for a gathering of nobles. There is some discrepancy in the location because at least one source states the force gathered at Acre while others point to Saforie. The most important debate happened at Saforie, so it is the meeting placed discussed here.

The gathering of knights, nobles, and vassals included calling for the use of the money from Henry II to be spent on hiring warriors for the army. The military orders did so, further expanding the size of the army beyond what the King of Jerusalem alone could call on for vassal service.

Technical Context

Large open-field battles were rare in the medieval world. In general, such a battle required agreement by both sides to meet and fight. This was only possible if both sides thought themselves capable of such a victory. Such battles also occurred if there was an air of significant desperation on one side or the other.

The medieval period was an era in military history where defense was significantly more powerful than offense. The power of position was at its apex. The Europeans had developed fortresses and fortifications to a significant degree. They would invest an area and fortify a strategic place and then force their opponent to conduct attacks on the position. The positioning of forces in 1183 in which the Franks took control of the water source of Ain Jalut and then maintained that position, daring Saladin to attack them, meant that both armies were away from fortifications, but neither was willing to attack.

If the army could not control a fortress in the Levant, they had to control a water source. Water was the preeminent resource for all arid or semi-arid conflict. This is also the source of the advice that will be given in terms of positioning.

The Muslim military had sufficient and significant siege weapons. These were not of the most powerful kind, like trebuchets, but they were able to destroy weak or moderately constructed fortifications. Well-constructed fortresses like Kerak withstood numerous sieges and bombardments without the collapse of the walls.

Tactical Chronolgy

The order of events is somewhat muddled in terms of where it all began—Acre or Saforie—however, for the sake of this chapter and for clarity, the key events began on 2 July 1187. Saladin crossed the Jordan River south of the Sea of Galilee on 26 June 1187, and he began the siege of Tiberias on 2 July. There are accounts of Saladin leading a foray prior to 2 July toward Saforie to get the Franks to give him battle, but this was probably a reconnaissance in force, since it is highly unlikely that Saladin wanted to give battle to the Franks while they had a plentiful water supply within their camp. It would have placed him at a severe disadvantage, as it had in the campaign in 1183. The main camp of the Muslim force was at Kafr Sabt, which was east–southeast of Saforie, and positioned in such a way as to allow Saladin to intercept any movement across the plateau.

The knights and lords who discussed the events on 2 July were split. According to several accounts—Christian and Muslim—Raymond III spoke first and emphatically that the army needed to remain at Saforie and force Saladin to come to them to give battle. He predicted that the Muslim army could not hold together long and that they would eventually break up and be forced to return home on the weight of the logistical burden of such a large force. He further asserted that even though Tiberias was his city and his wife was currently besieged in the citadel of that city, this did not change his opinion or his belief in the military necessity of his advice.

At that meeting there was debate between the lords; both Reynald of Châtillon and Gerard of Ridefort disagreed with the advice and called for battle. However, most of the lords tended to agree with Raymond III's advice and recognized the problems of leaving Saforie

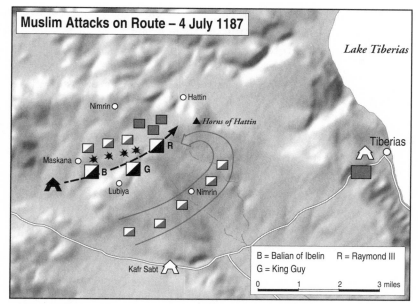

Fig. 7.3

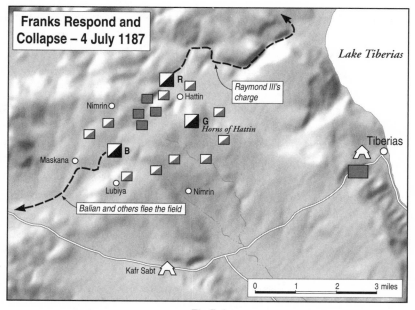

Fig. 7.4

and traveling to Tiberias with no significant water supply between the two locations. The meeting adjourned late at night with King Guy having acceded to the advice of staying at Saforie.

Following the meeting, Gerard of Ridefort had a private conversation with the king. In this conversation he said something like the following:

> Sir, do you believe that traitor who has given you this advice? It is to shame you that he has given it. For it will be greatly to your shame and your disgrace if you, who have so recently been made king, and have as great an army as ever any king had in this land ... if you allow a city only six leagues away to be lost. This is the first task which has fallen to you since you were crowned.[5]

To appreciate this advice, the vehemence with which it was given, and the manner in which it was received, the reader must reflect on the personal nature of all of the relationships, the issues of personal honor involved, and the long-held grudges common among the nobility of the era. It is possible that Gerard of Ridefort gave this advice because he hated Raymond III for denying him a marriage and a fief, for being the cause of the defeat suffered by the Templars only two months earlier at Cresson Springs, and for his associations with the Muslims. It is also possible that he truly viewed Raymond III as a traitor in the pocket of Saladin, and his advice to concede anything to Saladin must therefore have been suspect. It is uncertain which view is most true or whether it was a combination of both. It is clear now and was clear then that tactically the advice to attack was foolish and risked a great deal.

Guy accepted the advice and ordered the army to march early in the morning. The reasons for Guy's acceptance of such poor advice despite the objections of most of his nobility must also be viewed in light of his personal history. He was roundly criticized for his failure to attack Saladin in 1183 despite having a large army. Now he had an even larger army and would never have another chance to demonstrate his martial prowess and ability to command. He had the greatest military instrument of any Frankish king in the Levant. He also had to overcome the stigma of being a usurper who was only in the position because of his wife. Finally, he had spent the money from Henry II. If he did not use those knights and soldiers paid for from this money, it was highly unlikely he could ever field a force so large again. Those who claim that Guy only followed the advice because he was weak-willed and would follow whatever was said last, miss the complexity of personal history and the reasonable nature of the advice when filtered through the ears and mind of a usurper.

The army moved in the morning in three groups—the first was led by Raymond III; the second included the king and the patriarch of Jerusalem with the "true cross"; and the third included Balian of Ibelin and the military orders. Raymond III led because this was customary for the lord of a region to lead the army into that region and to be the last one out of that region if the army departed. There is a legend of the horses refusing to drink before setting out, thus giving a bad omen for the campaign. The army followed the most direct route between Saforie and Tiberias, yet away from Kafr Sabt and the Muslim camp. The route took them toward Turan.

There is an account of several knights turning traitor, going to Saladin, converting to Islam, and giving information to the sultan. These knights were supposedly from among Raymond III's vassals. Most of the accounts have this happening during the battle as the army was beginning to break down, with the vassals giving information about how close the army was to collapse. Another theory is that they abandoned the march and gave Saladin information about the route. This would have been more useful for the sultan.[6]

The army was engaged by mounted archers from relatively early on in the march. The archers seemed to focus their attacks on the rear of the column. The army did not stop at Turan to get any additional water. The reason for this is unclear, but it is probable that the most significant attacks did not come until after the second column had passed Turan. There is a lot of confusion over what, if anything, happened at Turan, but the main point is the army passed it without water and continued to the east. It appears that the army was turning more northeast to reach the water source at Hattin.

Timeline

Date	Event
1174	Almaric I and Nur Al Din die.
1177	Battle of Mount Gisard—Baldwin IV defeats Saladin.
1179	Baldwin IV is defeated at Jacob's Ford and Marj Ayun.
1180	Guy and Sibyl are married.
	Two-year truce between Saladin and Kingdom of Jerusalem.
1181	Reynald of Châtillon breaks the truce by attacking a caravan to Mecca.
1182	Reynald of Châtillon attacks Red Sea shipping and pilgrims.
11 June 1183	Saladin captures Aleppo.
1183	Campaign of Saladin—Guy leads army at Ain Jalut.
1184	Saladin attacks Kerak—campaign through Samaria.
1185	Four-year truce between Saladin and Kingdom of Jerusalem.
	Baldwin IV dies.
3 March 1186	Saladin gains control of Al Jazeera.
1186	Baldwin V dies—Guy crowned King of Jerusalem.
1187	Reynald of Châtillon breaks the truce by attacking a caravan.
April 1187	Saladin lays siege to Kerak.
1 May 1187	Battle of Springs of Cresson.
26 June 1187	Saladin begins to cross his army into the Galilee.
2 July 1187	Saladin takes Tiberias—Lady Eschiva is besieged in the citadel.
	Meeting of nobles.
	Meeting with King Guy and Gerard of Ridefort.
3 July 1187	Army of Jerusalem departs Saforie.
	Movement past Turan and toward Hattin.
	Army of Jerusalem makes camp for the night.
4 July 1187	Army of Jerusalem continues march toward Tiberias by way of Hattin.
	Guy orders defensive position at Hattin.
	Raymond III charges attackers and leaves battlefield.
	King Guy is captured.

Fig. 7.5

The attacks became more intense as the army moved, and at one point Guy asked Raymond III what to do. Supposedly, Raymond III recommended a camp. This was after being told that the Templars could not continue because they had received the brunt of the attacks and were struggling significantly. Regardless of the source of the suggestion, the army camped for the night, having only covered about half of the distance to Tiberias. The Muslim force surrounded the Franks with their camp; the two camps were close enough for the Frankish soldiers to be kept awake by shouts of "God is Great" and other Muslim religious sayings.

The army of Jerusalem moved in the morning to continue their march to Tiberias. The rank-and-file infantry were extremely thirsty. The Muslim forces brought numerous camels carrying water in order to preposition water in prepared storage areas for the army, and they also used the water to taunt the thirsty Franks by pouring some out on the ground so that they could see it. The infantry was suffering from the attacks and struggled to maintain their protective formation as they moved. Fires were set by the Muslims to blow smoke onto the Franks as they moved; the smoke and heat added to their misery.

The king moved toward the Horns of Hattin to place his tent and standard and seek a suitable defensive position. This was either his own decision or based on a recommendation from Raymond III. The discipline of the infantry deteriorated throughout the morning's march, and as it did so, the horses of the mounted fighters suffered greater and greater attrition, forcing many mounted sergeants to fight dismounted or leaving heavily armored knights at the mercy of their opponents. As the infantry approached the Horns of Hattin they broke ranks and scrambled to the top of the hill, where many simply sat, refusing to fight. After the battle, they were gathered up by the Muslims, and the survivors were sold into slavery.

Raymond III was either ordered to charge or took it upon himself to charge with the knights left to him. As they made a determined charge, the Muslim foe gave way, and they were allowed to charge down a route leading them from the plateau to the Sea of Galilee. The steep path did not allow for a return charge, and the Turkoman units closed off the lane they created. Raymond III rode off the battlefield and returned to Tripoli.

The remainder of the army that rallied to the Horns of Hattin was able to successfully repel several waves of attacks, but the process of dehydration and the attrition of horses meant that it was only a matter of time. Finally, the tent of the king was knocked to the ground, sending a symbol to all that the army of Jerusalem had fallen.

Battlefield Leadership

In hindsight it is easy to say that the army of Jerusalem was doomed from the moment it set out from Saforie. This is not entirely true, though it was mostly the case. The army could have assumed a defensive position at Turan and achieved a similar success to that seen in 1183, though as previously noted, this was a success in the eyes of only a few.

Guy did not have the loyalty or respect of any of his key vassals, so there was no trust between these key decision makers. After the battle the various accounts were clouded based on with whose side the recorder agreed. Whether it was Raymond III who recommended the stopping place for the camp and the stopping place for defense or not is moot, since the king was responsible for ordering the final decision.

Each of the decisions after leaving Saforie were of lesser importance than the decision to leave—whether or not to drink at Turan, whether or not to camp for the night, where to defend, whether or not Raymond III should charge. None of the last three decisions would have materially changed the outcome of the battle.

King Guy made two decisions before the battle that doomed his force to its eventual defeat. First was his decision to force a decisive battle rather than simply relieve the castle and follow standard patterns of military action. Second, Guy then decided to march cross-country and without sending advance units to secure water sources. These two decisions created the environment in which his force was encamped on high ground without water and surrounded by a superior force.

The reasons for the poor choices are given in the "lessons learned" section of this chapter. Guy either could not effectively lead because of all of the inter-faction rivalries and hatreds that existed, or he would not lead because he was weak-willed. The latter seems less likely, since events after Hattin show him as being aggressive and decisive. At Hattin he was also aggressive and decisive, though with disastrous results.

Saladin's decision to use the heat as his primary weapon allowed him to create panic without risking his soldiers. He exacerbated the suffering through the lighting of fires to intensify the heat and add smoke. This made worse a deteriorating situation by adding the confusion of natural disaster. Saladin also allowed determined charges of knights to break through and depart the battlefield, reducing his opponents' effective combat strength.

Significance

The Horns of Hattin stands as one of the truly decisive battles throughout history. The following are some of the results of this battle's loss:

• The loss at the Horns of Hattin directly resulted in the loss of most of the armed knights in the Kingdom of Jerusalem and left the kingdom open to easy capitulation once Saladin began his offensive. The city of Jerusalem, the spiritual and emotional prize, was taken after a siege of less than two weeks, with Saladin marching into the city on Friday, 2 October 1187, to make his prayers at the Al Aqsa mosque on the temple mount of ancient Jerusalem.

• The reports on the battle and fall of Jerusalem shocked European rulers and led the Pope to call for another crusade to regain the holy city. This became known as the Third Crusade and was led by the three great kings of Europe—England, France, and the Holy Roman Empire—and other lesser nobles. The minor successes of the crusade ensured both the continued existence of crusader states in the Levant and the incompetent and fractured ruling of those states for the rest of their existence.

• The victory for Saladin effectively ensured his safety and survival as ruler of the Muslims in the Levant and allowed his heirs to continue with an Ayyubid Dynasty.

- With the failure of the greatest of the crusader states, the local populace moved closer and closer to Islam through conversion and intermarriage. Crusader atrocities and behavior toward locals discouraged locals from moving toward Europe in culture.

Saladin earned his reputation as a generous and gracious victor by ransoming most of the nobles. Only Reynald of Châtillon and members of the military orders were executed. In the case of Reynald, it was a matter of honor for Saladin to fulfill his publicly stated vow to kill him with his own hands. The military orders were viewed as religious fanatics who would never be suitable slaves, and few had ransom value of any significance. Saladin allowed civilians to flee unharmed and typically allowed them to take their possessions as well. This was especially true of Jerusalem and Acre. But, in general, the Frankish people living in the Levant could not have asked for a better conqueror.

Lessons Learned: Principals of Conflics

The lessons from the battle at the Horns of Hattin are focused on the identification portion of the principles of conflict.

- **Identification:** Guy did not identify the cultural challenges within his opponent's political world. He did not see that Saladin needed a victory more than he did at the larger political level. Guy allowed his personal position and the challenges of loyal nobility to cloud his understanding of Saladin and his position of weakness. There was also a lack of understanding of the tactical considerations and the strengths and weaknesses of each army The conduct of an open-field battle favored the Muslim tactics over the tactics of the Franks.
- **Isolation:** The decision to move cross-country completely isolated the Frankish force from any outside assistance. It especially isolated them from the necessary water sources and forced the army to fight the summer heat as well as the Muslims.
- **Suppression:** The lack of water sources and the weakening of the infantry over time allowed Saladin to surround and

wait out the Franks. Without infantry protection the horses were prey to the Muslim arrows, and losses were enormous. The high loss of horses meant a correspondingly low opportunity to conduct maneuver. The few mounted charges of note were allowed to break out and away, and the critical combat power was lost.

- **Maneuver:** Saladin used natural means to gain the position of advantage. It is ironic that the high ground, typically viewed as key terrain in ancient and modern engagements, was occupied by those who were held impotent before the basic human need for water.
- **Destruction:** The loss of discipline of knights and soldiers was clear evidence of the emotional destruction inflicted by Saladin. Enormous numbers of prisoners meant massed surrender rather than determined fighting.

Conclusion

Leadership is essential to battlefield victory. Cannae showed what an incredible leader can do when vastly outnumbered. Here, the poor leadership and the lack of judgment of one side prevented a competent and well-matched force from making any real attempt at success. Saladin did not have to win this battle. The deck was not stacked in his favor. Rather, the battle was given to him through his opponent's failed leadership. The following quote summarizes this thought well:

A formidable Christian army, skilled in Levantine tactics and hardened by campaigns, had permitted itself to be maneuvered into a trap largely because of personal and political animosities. The irreparable blunder of the march across the arid plateau toward Tiberias was the direct consequence of Gerard's hatred and suspicion of Raymond and his baneful influence over King Guy. It is perhaps idle to speculate on what might have been; yet it seems clear that if there had been no party dissension in Jerusalem there might well have been no Hattin. But now the disasters which followed were the unavoidable consequences of a major defeat.[7]

Saladin used this success to forge a capable and relatively unified state. His actions following the battle made him legendary to his opponents and his supporters. He became the ideal of justice and chivalric behavior.

How Does It Fit Inside the Box?

- In many ways, this battle was the most normal, in that it fit the current template to a greater degree. This was a standard relief of a besieged castle, nothing more. Saladin besieged the castle at Tiberias, and subsequently an army from the Kingdom of Jerusalem was gathered and sent to relieve the besieged fortress.
- No unusual weapons, techniques, or capabilities were used. Nearly everything seen on this battlefield had been seen by the various combatants in previous engagements and battles.
- Both sides were motivated by religious and cultural idealism— true religion versus unbelievers and cultural snobbery that viewed the outsiders as uncouth savages.

Why Is It an Aberration?

- **Means:** Even though there were no new tactics or techniques, there were numerous uses of the older techniques made more relevant by the command decisions. In this case, the wells near the actual battle site either were controlled by Saladin's forces or were dry. This meant that all sources of water were controlled by a single side of the battle in July. This lack of a critical resource led to rash decisions during the actual fighting, further exacerbating previously incompetent battlefield leadership.
- **Understanding:** King Guy failed to identify the cultural and political situation of his opponent. He did not see the dynamics within the Muslim world that made Saladin's position precarious. Therefore, he did not perceive his own position of strength, nor did he recognize that it was better to be conservative in protecting an advantage. Instead, Guy perceived himself as weak and in need of executing a decisive blow that would send a message to his domestic and external opponents that he was a worthy king. This created the conditions that led to the

failed decisions on basic operational strategy.

- **Leader:** The incompetence brought to the field by Guy was vastly overwhelmed by the competent generalship of Saladin. Rarely in history do mismatches of this extreme in command ability occur. Typically something, a coup or significant competent advice, comes to even the field prior to the battle. This did not occur here. Guy refused to listen to the advice of battle-proven subordinates and followed brash and foolhardy advice to force a decisive battle in unsecured territory and with no guarantee of control of water. The advice he followed played on personal insecurities and vanity. Saladin made maximum use of the opportunity presented, and though events after the battle show his almost embarrassed response to the success, he did not lessen the efforts he put into the battle itself.
- **Target:** Once Saladin was able to encircle his opponent, he focused on the use of water as a weapon to weaken the will of his opponent, which forced them to make poor decisions out of necessity. The large number of prisoners speaks to the fact that much of the force ended up surrendering rather than fighting to the death.

Strategies (numbered based on the nine strategies for victory)

1. **Introspection:** No battle presented in this book presents a starker example of the importance of introspection as a strategy for avoiding or succeeding in aberrational environments. Guy did not see himself or his supporters in a real light. He did not perceive the conflicts within Gerard of Ridefort and, therefore, could not effectively filter his advice. Guy did not understand himself sufficiently to know why he was seeking battle; instead, he seemed to give in to the advice that pampered his vanity.
2. **Empathetic Appreciation:** Guy did not see Saladin in his weakness. This was a Muslim leader who had only had significant success against other Muslims—Egypt, Aleppo, Mosul—and had not managed considerable defeats against Christians. He was a usurper and a Kurd. Saladin was not in a position of strength in 1187. He had come off several successive failures in besieging Kerak, the fortress of his avowed enemy.

3. **Empathetic Expectation:** The failure to see Saladin properly resulted in the decision to attack him. Saladin was going to force a battle, yet he could not wait forever. It was almost certain that he would have eventually attacked Saforie as options slowly ran out. This would have meant that Guy could have used his infantry to their maximum benefit.

5. **Study of History:** There were many nobles, Raymond III most of all, who understood the Muslims and their history. They knew that large Muslim armies did not stay together for long periods, especially not after defeats or setbacks like they had experienced at Kerak.

6. **Study of Culture:** As stated above, Raymond III knew Muslims and Islamic culture. Reynald probably understood some of it, as well. Despite this, the army of the kingdom missed capitalizing on this knowledge. Guy did not understand the culture of his opponent, nor did Gerard of Ridefort. They simply saw an infidel who required destruction. Saladin clearly saw the fractures within his opponent. It is unclear how much his knowledge of the Franks led to his decision to attack into the Galilee, but the result was that he split the kingdom along its fault line of Raymond III versus Guy. By making the attack in Raymond III's domain, his advice was certain to be sought, thus eliminating the possibility of him being relegated to a mere supporting role—this forced conflict between Raymond III and those nobles in opposition to him as an attack in no other region would have.

7. **Multiple Reserves:** The nature of Frankish tactics in the Levant allowed for reserves, yet it was not suited for an undisciplined battle of movement. The reliance on infantry protection for the cavalry meant that any designated reserve could not move faster than a walking man. Saladin had a much greater level of mobility, since his cavalry was based on agility and not shock tactics. When Guy did order a charge, he could not commit a reserve to exploit the momentary opening of the lines. Each charge was a separate and uncoordinated event.

8. **Initiative:** Saladin maintained the initiative throughout the campaign. Only at Kerak did he lose the initiative, and then he quickly readjusted to attack in the north. His attack at Tiberias forced the hand of the King of Jerusalem, making him react to Saladin.

Chapter 8

CASE STUDY:
THE BATTLE OF TRENTON
(26 DECEMBER 1776)

These are the times that try men's souls. The summer soldier and the sunshine patriot will, in this crisis, shrink from the service of his country; but he that stands it now deserves the love and thanks of man and woman. Tyranny, like hell, is not easily conquered; yet we have this consolation with us—that the harder the conflict, the more glorious the triumph. What we obtain too cheap, we esteem too lightly: It is dearness only that gives everything its value. Heaven knows how to put a proper price upon its goods; and it would be strange indeed if so celestial an article as freedom should not be highly rated.

—Thomas Paine, soldier and political activist (1776)[1]

Strategies Emphasized:

1. Introspection
2. Empathetic Appreciation
3. Empathetic Expectation
5. Study of History

6. Study of Culture
7. Multiple Reserves
8. Initiative

The importance of the Battle of Trenton in the history of the United States is difficult to overemphasize. The victories won in this small New Jersey village and in the village of Princeton just a little more than a week later allowed for the survival of the Continental Army and, as such, the survival of the idea of independence from Britain. The events leading up to this fight included a series of disasters that left George Washington and his army at 10 percent of their strength only five months earlier. Bested, beaten, humiliated, and morally exhausted, the Continental Army was on the verge of collapse when George Washington explained the dangerous and seemingly crazy plan before them. The weather, their opponents, and their own condition were against them, yet with this one victory they were able to secure the opportunity to fight for another three years.

This characterization is both accurate and inaccurate at the same time. Much had been done between the staggering defeats and the spectacular victory to begin the process of turning the war around. As noted in other chapters, this more optimistic view is possible only through the lens of history. Washington and his soldiers were living in the "times that try men's souls" and not the improving fortunes of the historian. When Washington presented his plan, no one knew for sure the possibilities. Washington knew he needed a victory and felt that the conditions were appropriate for creating the circumstances that this book calls an aberration.

Geographical Setting

Location
Trenton, now the capital of New Jersey and a bustling city of significant size, was then a sleepy country village of no great consequence. The

primary reason for the selection of this location for a battle was that a garrison of Hessian soldiers was quartered there. The Hessians were garrisoned there because of the village's close proximity to crossing sites for the Delaware River, the then-existing boundary between the Continental Army and the forces of the British Empire. The village sat with the Delaware River to the west and the Assunpink River to the south. This was the western edge of New Jersey, with Pennsylvania on the western side of the river.

Terrain and Vegetation

The most significant terrain feature was the Delaware River. The river served as a formidable obstacle to both sides. The Continental Army's ability to procure, protect, or prevent the opposition from using all of the boats on the river allowed it to remain an obstacle until the severe cold caused the river to freeze. As will be discussed later, the river did freeze, creating both opportunity for mobility and hazards for defense. The route followed by Washington's army crossed one treacherous stream valley prior to entering gentler farmland adjacent to the village. Though the steep valley walls proved difficult for the marching force with their artillery, they had no direct impact on the progress of the battle. The biggest impact was that of slowing the column even more.

The terrain around Trenton consisted of rolling hills leading into farmland around the village proper. Most of the land was forested with deciduous trees that had lost their leaves, but the land immediately adjacent to the town was open. It was from this direction that generals Washington and Greene approached. The battle was fought on the outskirts of and within the village of Trenton. During the fighting, an apple orchard to the east of the village center provided some covered mobility for the Hessians, but generally vegetation was not a critical part of the battle.

Weather

Unlike the vegetation, the weather was both a hindrance and an assist in the battle. The day and night prior to the battle (25 December 1776) were bitterly cold, with high winds and snow.

The region experienced a winter storm throughout this battle. Of the three columns that were supposed to cross the river in support of the campaign only one—the column commanded by General Washington—succeeded in forcing a crossing in the demanding weather conditions. The river froze below the village, and at the main crossing point ice was in the river. The snow, water, wind, and biting cold created significant challenges to the crossing, delaying the process several hours. The weather also served the interests of the Continental Army because it forced the Hessians indoors and prevented any aggressive patrolling or outposts from providing the warning that could have allowed an attack on the crossing site itself.

Weather was an essential part of this battle. Any discussion of surprise would be disingenuous without considering how weather conditions played into the conduct of both attack and defense.

Units Involved

Continental Army Forces

George Washington commanded an army on the verge of disbanding, since many of the enlistments were scheduled to expire on 31 December 1776. He also commanded a force that had been through a series of withdrawals and retreats that began in the early fall with the battles in and around New York City. His force had been reduced by almost 90 percent through battlefield loss, desertion, illness, disease, and expiring enlistments. Washington commanded something like four thousand men as he began his operations in crossing over to New Jersey. The soldiers in his army were a combination of Continental Army regulars—the beginnings of a federal army—and militias raised and commanded by each separate colony. Washington sought to meld this force into a cohesive army. He fought a general sense of personal frustration throughout much of his command, with issues of discipline among the troops.

The forces under Washington's command consisted of about nine brigades. Each of these brigades was closer in size to a modern-day infantry battalion—typically between 500 and 900 men—as opposed to the roughly 3,000 to 5,000 men in a modern brigade. This was both a result of the historically different organization sizes—units were smaller in the eighteenth century than their comparable units today—and a result of battlefield and other losses. One example was Haslet's Delaware Continentals, an infantry unit in Stirling's Brigade that numbered 750 on 24 August 1776 and 108 on 22 December 1776.[2]

The planned offense was intended to be conducted with three separate subordinate attacks. To the south was Gen. John Cadwalader, who was supposed to cross the river with about 2,000 men and attack the Hessians under Col. Carl von Donop in an attempt to deceive them concerning the intent of the action at Trenton. In the center was Gen. James Ewing, who was to cross just south of Trenton and protect the bridge over the Assunpink River and prevent any Hessians from escaping to the south. Only the northernmost group actually crossed the river. In this group were General Washington and a force of about 2,400 men. He divided his forces into two columns under the commands of generals Nathanael Greene and John Sullivan. With Greene went four brigades, and Sullivan commanded three brigades. This northern attack was accompanied by eighteen artillery pieces.

The men who formed these units were colonials who typically made their living outdoors—fishermen, farmers, or frontiersmen. They were hardened through a lifetime of work and living in difficult situations. Though this was true of most people living in this period, the frontier had its own unique challenges. In addition, the soldiers who crossed had suffered greatly from the losses in battle, through the retreat, and from the privations of serving a nation without a preexisting logistics system. Illness and lack of material comforts— blankets, proper winter clothing, and shoes—were common in the force. This was also true of the British forces but to a lesser degree; the differences being more of degree than kind.

Forces of the British Empire

The above heading is important because in the contest at Trenton, the soldiers fought by the Continentals were not British soldiers but rather soldiers rented from the German principate of Hesse-Cassel. These soldiers were considered by many to be the most-disciplined fighting force in the world.

The British forces and their Hessian allies were considered the finest land army in the world at the time of the Battle of Trenton. The army that occupied New Jersey had bested the colonial forces on multiple occasions and consistently from August until December. They were good, and they knew it. They also tended to look down on their opponents. On the Delaware River line, there were three positions—Bordertown (center), Burlington (south), and Trenton (north). All three were manned by Hessian forces.

Colonel Johann Rall commanded the brigade that manned the defenses at Trenton. His brigade included three regiments referred to as Rall, Knyphausen, and Lossberg. The total force consisted of about 1,500 soldiers, which included 50 Hessian jagers and 20 light dragoons.

Jagers and dragoons were light and mounted infantry, respectively. These types of units were relatively new creations designed to fight in the wilds of North America and serve as both agile infiltration forces and shock troops.

The three regiments of Colonel Rall's brigade had fought at the campaign on Long Island and New York. They neither respected their opponents nor the motives for the rebellion. The unit conducted defensive patrols, and the regimental and brigade commanders were all considered good soldiers, as well as competent and aggressive fighters. The weapons for the Hessians were little different than those of the colonials. The Hessians also had an artillery of six field guns.

Key Leaders in the Battle

Most of the senior leaders in this battle were of historical significance in the birth of the modern United States of America, however, some of these names do not play prominently in this chapter. For example, both Alexander Hamilton and James Madison were participants, but neither played an important role in the events related in this chapter. The key players are listed below.

Continental Army Forces

George Washington—Born and raised a Virginia gentlemen farmer, Washington had previously served in two prominent British-sponsored or -led expeditions in the French and Indian War: Fort

Necessity and General Braddock's campaign. His experience in these ventures helped him to understand the British way of war. He admired the British Empire and had a great many friends who became Loyalists following the division. Washington's fame and experience during the French and Indian War combined with his Virginia roots made him an ideal choice for leading a Continental Army. He struggled early with the differences in culture between Virginian gentlemen and New England Puritans and rebels. He believed in the necessity of discipline, which ran counter to some of his volunteers' conception of liberty. Washington grew beyond his initial frustrations to mold the army slowly into a viable fighting force. He was a man of consensus and made decisions after council. Both of the important decisions in this battle—attack and withdrawal—came after a council of commanders.

Nathanael Greene—commander of the left (Pennington Road) column.

John Sullivan—commander of the right (River Road) column.

John Cadwalader—commander of the southern attack to fix Colonel von Donop. His attack was withdrawn because of ice and bad weather.

James Ewing—commander of the center attack to secure the bridge south of Trenton across the Assunpink River. His attack was withdrawn because of ice and bad weather.

Henry Knox—chief of artillery. A former bookstore owner who became the Continental Army's best artillerist through practice and reading books. The emphasis on artillery within the Continental Army elevated Knox's position, as did his competence.

Forces of the British Empire

This section mostly focuses on the Hessian forces under the command of Colonel Rall. The British commander in the general area is also addressed.

General Sir William Howe —He was knighted following his success in taking New York. He was the overall ground commander for the British Empire in the colonies, and he favored a measured approach both to end the rebellion and to allow a way for the rebels to repent and return to the Empire. He was generally respected as a competent commander, but he was also criticized by some subordinates for not being aggressive enough. His brother, Admiral Lord Richard Howe, was responsible for the naval activities. He shared his brother's competence and his view of bringing the wayward back into the British imperial fold.

Major General James Grant—Scottish officer who commanded New Jersey for defense and occupation.

Colonel Carl von Donop—Hessian brigade commander. He was responsible for both the Burlington and the Bordertown defensive positions. He and Rall did not get along.

Colonel Johann Rall—commander of a Hessian brigade with three subordinate regiments, one of which was named for him. He spoke neither English nor French. He spoke German, but typically used the Hessian dialect when speaking with his men.[3] He was proud and thought very little of the rebels. He led a regimental attack at White Plains and Fort Washington in the New York area during the August campaign. Despite his disdain for the Americans, he did conduct the defense along the Delaware River in a very professional manner, with patrols and outposts even during the Christmas holiday. The idea that the Hessians under Rall were caught napping as a result of a party the night before is not true. Rall ignored intelligence based on his low opinion of the Americans, and the storm prevented the outposts from being out at their normal strength. A particularly good quote comes from one of Rall's junior officers, Lieutenant Jakob Piel of the Lossberg Regiment:

It never struck [Rall] that the rebels might attack us, and therefore he had made no preparations against an attack. I must concede that on the whole we had a poor opinion of the rebels, who previously had never successfully opposed us.[4]

Historical and Grand Strategy Context

The American Revolution is an event in U.S. history that can sometimes be shrouded in the mists of foundation mythology. Since this chapter only looks at the events from a military viewpoint, the larger political reasons for the war and the subsequent battles are beyond its scope. The events of 1776 began in the fall of 1775 with the decision by the English Parliament to enforce its right to tax the colonies to pay for the costs of the previous war—known in U.S. history as the French and Indian War. The decision met with stubborn resistance among many American colonialists, and the firebrands of the revolution used the printing press to spread their views in what may have been the first mass-publicity revolution in history. The pamphlet *Common Sense*, written by Thomas Paine, was particularly stirring, and his words written later in the year as things became dire would inspire a sense of unity among what were thirteen very different colonies, causing them to recommit to the revolution upon which they had embarked with the signing of the Declaration of Independence.

The year 1776 began with great fanfare and splendid success. These are the battles of the American Revolution that are taught in U.S. history classes from elementary school to college—Lexington and Concord and Bunker Hill. The ability of the colonials to drive the greatest army in the Western world out of Boston and much of New England was staggering in its accomplishment. The success, unexpected in its achievement by nearly everyone, caused even greater visions of future success, and the new American or Continental Army could see itself defeating the British. Flushed with this excitement, the colonial forces moved to New York, where the next major engagement was expected to occur.

General Washington was right in understanding that the next target of the British would be New York, but in this minor achievement he was to enjoy his only glory for nearly six months. As brilliant as his inspiration, organization, and decisiveness were in leading to the eviction of the British from Boston, Washington was unsure, often mistaken, and completely outgeneraled in New York. He seemed unable to fathom what the British could do and how well they could do it. He changed subordinate commanders on Long Island several times before the fighting, giving no one the full opportunity to know the ground, the plan, or their subordinate units and commanders. Rather than inspire his men, he was frustrated by their lack of discipline, and he often bemoaned the fact that he had little of what could be called an army.

In his opponent, Washington was faced with both a blessing and a curse by the Howe brothers—Admiral Lord Richard Howe and General Sir William Howe. The blessing for Washington was that neither man wanted to crush the rebellion in a brutal fashion, since their primary purpose was to create an environment where reconciliation was not only possible but would be seen as the preferable option. Their willingness to continually hold out an olive branch meant that Washington and his Continental Army were never pursued with the vigor that could have caused their complete destruction. The curse was that both of these brothers were as competent in their assignments as any professional soldier or sailor in the world at the time. Their only mistake was in believing that the American revolutionary leaders were inclined to seek terms when they were not.

Washington lost Long Island. The combination of British dominance of the waters around Manhattan Island and the capability of the British and Hessian soldiers meant that Washington had to deal with landings at multiple sites with little warning or opportunity to prepare defenses that could prevent the landings. Washington's greatest achievements in the various battles and debacles that occurred were his ability to withdraw and to avoid being destroyed. The weather, either through providence or luck, assisted Washington in withdrawing forces from Long Island when potential loss in detail loomed large and again from Manhattan under similar circumstances. Finally, Washington was forced to concede all of New York. He came upon the plan to conduct a strategic withdrawal, attacking only when the situation was favorable with the opportunity for great gain and the chance of only limited loss.

As is true of other great generals, Washington understood what was most critical, and he was willing to do what was necessary to accomplish the critical. In this case what was critical was preserving the Continental Army. Other than the Continental Congress, this was the only institution that truly bound the colonists together in a common cause. The army was a place where average people could become a part of the collective cause in a way that the congress would never be. The institution had to be preserved.

The institution was preserved by Washington's retreat through New Jersey and across the Delaware River into Pennsylvania. The

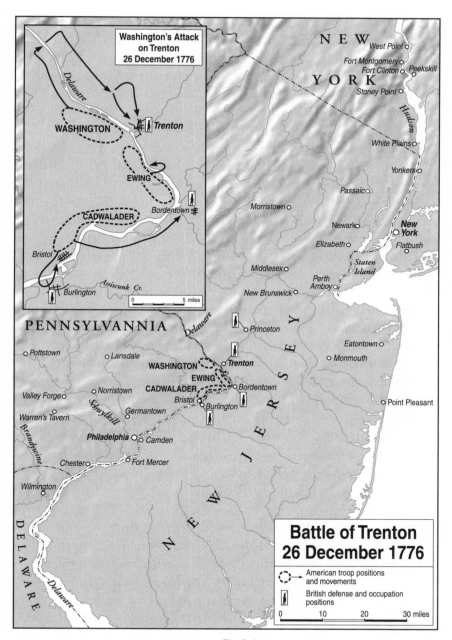

Washington's Attack
on Trenton
26 December 1776

Delaware

WASHINGTON

Trenton

EWING

CADWALADER

Bordentown

Bristol

Assicunk Cr.

Burlington

0   5 miles

N E W   West Point
         Fort Montgomery
         Fort Clinton   Peekskill
Y O R K
         Stoney Point

                    White Plains

                    Yonkers

              Passaic

Morristown

         Newark   New
                               York
    Elizabeth   Flatbush
                   *Staten
                    Island*
         Perth
         Amboy
New Brunswick

PENNSYLVANNIA   *Delaware*

Pottstown   Lansdale   Princeton
                                          Eatontown
                 WASHINGTON   Trenton   Monmouth
                 EWING
Valley Forge Norristown CADWALADER Bordentown
                        Bristol
Warren's Tavern *Schuylkill* Germantown Burlington   Point Pleasant

              Philadelphia   Camden
Brandywine
         Chester   Fort Mercer

Wilmington

D E L A W A R E

Delaware

N E W   J E R S E Y

Battle of Trenton
26 December 1776

American troop positions
and movements

British defense and occupation
positions

0   10   20   30 miles

Fig. 8.1

retreat included fighting and some spectacular evidence of quality soldiering by the Continentals, but it was a nearly continuous withdrawal throughout the entire campaign. Washington and the American effort enjoyed yet another providential aspect of the retreat across New Jersey in the form of the opposing commander—Charles Cornwallis. Like the Howes, he felt that reconciliation was crucial and that it was better to allow the colonial effort to maintain some dignity, thereby making it easier for them to return to the British fold. He pursued but only to keep Washington moving, never with the intent of destroying the force.

Thoughts Before the Battle

Washington had suffered a brutal string of defeats. His men were tactically demoralized, though many still possessed the spirit of the rebellion. Washington desperately needed a symbolic victory, something that could be used to bolster the cause to allow men to rally in both a spiritual and physical sense. He needed to keep the army in existence with himself in command, and to allow for the potential of greater internal and external support. All of this meant victory.

The British did not see the events as we do, looking back. It was the most logical thing for them to imagine the colonials' return to the British Empire. Destruction of the Continental Army was not an imperative, but pacification was. By December 1776, the British had regained, in some measure, three of the thirteen colonies, and the Howes wanted to bring these colonies back into the fold through recognition of the inevitable and logical conclusion more than through occupation.

Operational Context

The operational level of this campaign was. On an operational level, Trenton was the first battle of the December and early January campaign by the Continental Army into New Jersey. Because this campaign included the crossing of a major obstacle, the Delaware River, under extremely hazardous conditions, the preparation for and crossing of the river were as crucial as the battles themselves. Since the focus of this chapter is Trenton (26 December 1776), the recrossing of the Delaware River and the later battles in Trenton (2 January 1777) and in Princeton (3 January 1777) are not addressed.

In the time between the Continental Army's flight into Pennsylvania and the occupation of New Jersey by the British and the Hessians and Washington's subsequent attack, a great many events transpired within New Jersey and the movement of the colonial rebellion. The publication of Thomas Paine's inspiring words, which opened this chapter, had a dramatic effect both on those serving and on those supporting the soldiers. The impending expiration of enlistments spurred several creative ways of encouraging soldiers to lengthen their service through the end of the proposed campaign.

Additionally, a great many spontaneous resistance groups formed within New Jersey, and they began to harass and assail the occupying forces without coordination with the Continental Army. These attacks served to make the occupying forces leery of moving in small groups as foraging parties, and couriers were regular targets. The attacks, in general, served a purpose useful to Washington's overall plan, but some of the attacks threatened to alert the very targets of Washington's attack plan. Specifically, on the night of Washington's crossing, a group attacked the pickets of Colonel Rall's Hessians. The regiments were called out, and the attackers moved off after wounding six Hessians.

Technical Context

The fighting in the American Revolution featured the direct clash of the disciplined version of European open-field battle with the less disciplined and less classroom-educated behavior of the American soldiers. In many ways there are similarities to earlier discussions of clashing cultures in conflict—particularly the clash at Yarmouk where warriors and soldiers met, as discussed in chapter 6. The American experience, a few senior leaders excluded, was not one of open-field battle. It was typically drawn from fighting with Indians or hunting, and, as such, the skill sets and views of battle were completely different from those of their opponents. Armed conflict was a thing pursued as a result of need, not as a result of policy. The technical details of how soldiers fought were also different.

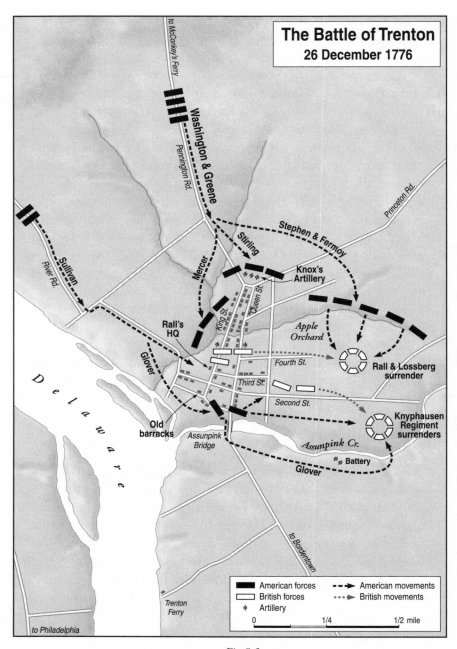

Fig. 8.3

At Trenton and throughout the war, Washington sought to make the Continental Army like European armies, and therefore much of what was seen at Trenton was a European-style battle. Even though this is true, what was inside each soldier and how each perceived war was not the same, and this did matter.

The Hessian soldiers were trained and prepared to fight in a very specific way, on line and in formation. The weapons and tactics of the eighteenth-century battlefield were truly suited for formation warfare, much as the weapons and tactics of the Greek Phalanx were. Soldiers required something like a half a minute to load and fire their weapons. Though there were accurate rifled weapons that allowed the engagement of targets at hundreds of yards, most of the smooth-bore muskets needed very close ranges and the massing of weapons to be able to mass effects—killing many people. The closeness of the formation allowed for the men to move forward in the face of opponents shooting at them at close ranges. The formation was important to support the weapon, the psychology, and the soldier.

Artillery in this period was much more like the tank is today—it was a direct fire support. The artilleryman aimed his weapon at an opponent or location he could see. The role of artillery in the battle was important because it provided shock effect, as well as direct casualties. The American use of artillery was critical in this battle and throughout the war. In general, Americans used artillery in greater concentrations than their opponents. Soldiers and leaders perceived that having artillery nearby emboldened the generally new American soldiers as they faced well-trained and disciplined British and Hessian veterans. Additionally, the firepower presented by the artillery made up for the lack of experienced musketry of the infantry. In this battle, the Continental Army enjoyed three times the artillery pieces of the Hessians and nearly twice the ratio of artillery to infantry. The Hessians had about one artillery piece for every 250 soldiers, whereas the Americans had one for every 133.[5]

Tactical Chronology

The biggest challenges presented in this battle were weather and river related. The battle itself was relatively simple. The weather

Date	Time	Event
Timeline		
27–29 August 1776		Battle of Long Island
15 September 1776		Battle of Harlem Heights
28 October 1776		Battle of White Plains, New York
9–10 November 1776		Cross Hudson River
28 November 1776		Evacuate Newark, New Jersey
1 December 1776		Evacuate New Brunswick, New Jersey
7 December 1776		Cross Delaware River to Pennsylvania
25 December 1776	Dusk	Delaware River crossing begins
26 December 1776	~0300	Crossing is completed
	~0400	March south begins
	~0800	Engagements with pickets
27 December 1776		Continental Army returns to Pennsylvania camps
2 January 1777		Second Battle of Trenton
3 January 1777		Battle of Princeton

Fig. 8.4

was cold, and ice was forming in the upper river, but below the falls near Trenton, ice had already formed, causing Ewing to deem the passing of troops impossible. The ice was not thick enough to walk across, but it was too thick to move boats through it. To the south, Cadwalader did get some men across, but they could not get the guns across because ice had formed on the far bank, making a landing impossible. Cadwalader withdrew those who had crossed and waited on the Pennsylvania side of the river.

In the north, the plan had been to begin crossing at dark and be finished by about midnight, giving roughly five hours for the nine-mile movement from the crossing point to Trenton. This would have placed Washington's men arriving at first light. The crossing did not work out that way. The ice slowed the movement of the boats, and then the sleet and hail came, further adding to the misery of boat crews and waiting soldiers. The crossing was complete by about three o'clock, and the movement south began about an hour later. The roads were slippery with the precipitation and the freezing temperatures. Movement of the guns was slow and a further delay.

Washington had his force divide to attack the town from two sides nearly simultaneously. Greene led his brigades down the Pennington Road, and Sullivan led his down the river road. The Hessians had pickets placed of between twenty and fifty men on either road about a half a mile to a mile from the town. In both cases, the Americans were able to carry the positions with a spirited charge that sent the pickets back to the town in good order.[6] The rout of the pickets happened in close time proximity; therefore, the American plan to hit the town from multiple directions simultaneously was working. The Hessians began their preparations for battle. The two main streets that ran north–south were called King and Queen streets. Knox was able to get his guns set up in the north so that he could fire directly down the streets.

The firepower of the artillery, combined with the simultaneous attack, caused serious problems for Rall. Sullivan's forces captured two Hessian artillery pieces and turned them on their previous owners. The battle was a relatively short and sharp engagement, since Rall was overwhelmed. While Greene's forces dominated the ground north of town, Sullivan's men moved through the town fighting a building-to-building battle. This forced the Hessians back slowly but inexorably.

Washington occupied a position north of town and close to the artillery. He was able to see the movements of the Hessian regiments that charged up King and Queen streets and the later flanking attempt. As he observed these actions, he ordered appropriate reactions from his own forces. This allowed him to prevent being flanked and, at the same time, to flank those attempting to flank him. The city fighting was difficult, but the large maneuver decisions made by Washington allowed him to move his units as effectively as a chess master positioning pieces.

Many of the senior Hessian officers were killed. Part of the chaos in decision making resulted from a false report that the Assunpink

River bridge had been taken by the Americans much earlier than Sullivan's force had actually done so. It is possible that Rall chose to fight in the town rather than withdrawing to the better terrain south of the Assunpink because he believed that option was already closed to him. Either way, the battle was over, and it was a clear and dominant victory for the Continental Army.

Battlefield Leadership

George Washington made the decision of his career in forcing the crossing of the Delaware River in such horrible weather conditions. He clearly had a vision of what he had to do, and he unhesitatingly did so. The decision to attack at all was the most fundamental in shaping the battle. A regular commander and any competent commander of the day probably would not have done so, but Washington did, and that really did make all the difference. This decision was not made by Washington alone, but it came as a result of consensus created through council. It is clear that Washington was looking for this type of opportunity. The fact that Washington used a collegial rather than a dictatorial approach shows strength of character and an understanding of his subordinates.

The fact that he originally planned to attack in the early morning in either pre-dawn darkness or just after dawn made the plan more palatable to his more skeptical subordinates, but when it became abundantly clear that it would not happen, Washington made the next related decision—to continue with the operation. Two capable subordinate commanders abandoned the attack based on their assessments of the weather and their perceptions of the ability to accomplish the mission.

The commands at the battle itself and the various technical and tactical decisions were necessary, since the battle did not have an inevitable destined outcome. The initial decisions were the ones that took the courage of character and creativity that made Washington a greater household name and gave him much of his deserved mystique in American history. Creativity and the ability to see possibilities when others do not are crucial in the creation of aberrational events.

Significance

Trenton was a tactical success for the American forces because they killed or captured more than 900 of the estimated 1,500 Hessians and attached British soldiers present. That is more than a 60 percent casualty rate for the Hessians—a great accomplishment by any army against an opponent. This is in direct comparison to American casualties, which vary by account but tend to be two or so killed in action and maybe as many as five dead from exposure with less than five wounded. Trenton was even more important both domestically and internationally at the strategic level.

Trenton was crucial to the continued American effort. The revival of spirit that occurred in December 1776 may have progressed and sustained the cause without the stunning victories in the winter of 1776–77, but it is clear that these victories made so many of the subsequent events possible. One of the most important results of the battle is that the Continental Army continued to exist after December 1776. There was considerable doubt that this would be the case in early December.

The victories gave some of Britain's European enemies thoughts of potential American success. American colonials had defeated Hessian and British regular troops, and it became conceivable that the Americans might be able to win if they were to receive some help. This was a significant turning point in the battle to get international acceptance.

The events in the winter of 1776 began the creation of what is an "American." The Continental Army shaped Virginians and Pennsylvanians and New Yorkers into Americans in a way that only combined effort, sacrifice, and commitment could.

Lessons Learned: Principles of Conflict

Surprise can sometimes be achieved through serendipitous events, though this is highly unlikely and rarely occurs in conflict. As in this case, more often it happens as the result of a deliberate choice or decision.

- **Identification:** Washington knew his opponent's expectation of his army, and because of this, he believed he knew the conceptual box in which his opponent operated. By identifying his opponent in all aspects and by having the empathy to recognize how his opponent perceived him, Washington had a distinct advantage in being able to choose an option that he knew would be completely unexpected. The use of the word "knew" does not denote metaphysical certitude, but rather a reasonable understanding.

- **Isolation:** The timing of the attack in the day and in the year was instrumental in keeping the opponent separated from outside assistance. Additionally, the operations conducted by nonassociated militia from New Jersey kept each post isolated physically and emotionally. Weather, celebration, and expectation kept Washington's opponents from seeking or being able to rapidly reinforce each other.

- **Suppression:** Similar to isolation, the timing of the attack in relation to Christmas and in relation to a powerful winter storm meant that the Hessians were caught unprepared. The use of two columns to attack from multiple directions simultaneously also denied Rall the ability to mass his regiments against a single target. Further, the disruptive nature of American artillery allowed Americans to mass effects, while at the same time the guns silenced the Hessian artillery. The fact that most of the Hessians fought within the village also limited their movement.

- **Maneuver:** The position of advantage here was threefold— time, weather, and geography. By attacking in the middle of a storm following Christmas celebrations and from two directions, Washington was able to gain an immediate advantage. The Hessians were unprepared emotionally. The aggressiveness and unexpected competence of the attack further affected the Hessian will.

- **Destruction:** Aberrational surprise was complete, and the Hessians never fully massed their units or their firepower. A less-disciplined force of the time might have surrendered outright, but the Hessians continued to attempt to organize and fight until complete capitulation.

Conclusion

Understanding the mental conceptual box of the opponent, combined with a willingness to accept risk, led to a critical victory. The enemy defeated at Trenton was relatively insignificant in comparison to the overall British force; however, it was crucial to the morale and existence of the Continental Army. Washington saw what was necessary, understood how it could be done, and was willing to do it. This is rare in a commander and is one of the key dividing lines between good and great ones. The fact that Washington sought to create an aberration and was successful in doing so also demonstrates his impressive vision and leadership.

The timing of the battle in the day, in the year, and in the war created the position of advantage. This is an important lesson of this battle and is instructive of the breadth of the definition of maneuver. Hopefully, a reader outside the military can glean some insight from this about how to apply lessons from this book beyond a military or geopolitical scope. Vision, empathy, risk, and timing are components that apply to all competitive human interaction and are also necessary for success in all these venues.

How Does It Fit Inside the Box?

- The American Revolution had been in progress for more than a year, and the men fighting on both sides had fought each other and similar forces many times. By the end of 1776, most soldiers expected a battle to progress much as it usually had, and the mental box of the war was pretty fixed.
- The consistent battles between the two forces created an understanding and appreciation of opponent fighting prowess or lack thereof. The Hessian forces, quartered at Trenton, New Jersey, in the winter of 1776, were viewed by the Americans as among the best of the British forces—they had an aura about themselves unlike other forces. The Americans had likewise developed a reputation for being a beaten and poorly led force. They would not last the winter and could not mount a competent military campaign.
- Many considered the Christmas holiday season to be off limits in

terms of major combat operations. The religious significance of the period combined with inclement weather to create in this period an expectation of peace and rest for the British and their allies.

- As noted, the weather was cold and stormy. Climate and disease were some of the biggest killers in the modern period because soldiers were poorly equipped and logistics were insufficient to provide for the needs of cold, hungry, and wet soldiers.
- American forces were on the eastern side of a major river with the opponent on the other side. The river had ice floating in it, and boats were scarce. It was expected that the river would be used by the colonists as a defensive measure throughout the winter.
- Battles were typically fought in a generally symmetrical manner, with opponents facing off in an open field and fighting a major engagement, or through the use of defensive positions and fortifications to protect critical terrain or towns. Conduct of a battle within a town was less common.

Why Is It an Aberration?

- **Means:** General Washington chose to cross the river at night and to conduct a night attack in the middle of a winter storm and in association with a holiday.
- **Understanding:** Washington had every expectation that his decision would be unexpected—he was seeking to create not just surprise, but an aberration through his use of timing, weather, and time of day. He expected the surprise would render the superior disciplined tactics of his opponent ineffective.
- **Understanding:** The Hessian leadership, as well as that of the higher British command, failed to identify the conceptual and cultural issues facing the American leadership. They did not perceive the commitment to the revolution and the issue with expiring enlistments to be sufficiently motivational for aggressive or even desperate decisions. The failure to recognize desperation as a motivator for Washington led them to discount intelligence reports of Washington's impending attack.
- **Leader:** Though previously stated as desperation, it is

uncertain that Washington acted out of such an emotion. The political and military situations were clearly desperate, but Washington was able to see both the short- and long-term implications of success. His vision of the potential for success and the ramifications of failure or inaction, which he saw as similar, led to his decision to take the risks necessary for victory.

The risks were large, but Trenton and battles associated with this offensive campaign in New Jersey

showed that the decision was reasoned and visionary.

- **Target:** Washington's target was not the Hessian force in Trenton as much as the will of his own soldiers and citizens. He also sought to influence an international audience to prove the viability of the revolution. The target of his actions also changed the definitions of reasonable actions and possibilities and reshaped the box.

Strategies (numbered based on the nine strategies for victory)

1. **Introspection:** In this book, George Washington demonstrates the ideal for this strategy. Though it is often difficult to read the minds of leaders from history books, in the thinking and actions of George Washington in this campaign we have his letters and the thoughts of those close to him, which have survived. From these we learn that Washington knew of the plight of the army and the potential catastrophe to independence if the army ceased to exist. He also knew what his opponents thought of the army and of him as a leader. The information flow both ways was generally good, and it was clear then that the British command and the Hessians thought little of their American opponents. Washington was able to assess all of these things, and within his own mental box he created an aberration for his opponent because his honest introspection allowed him to broaden his own box while clearly perceiving that of his opponent. I am certain that George Washington would not use these words to explain his actions and intent, but I believe they are an accurate representation.

2. **Empathetic Appreciation:** As stated above, Washington knew

what his opponent expected or did not expect. Colonel Rall, on the other hand, did not know the mind of his opponent. At best, he had reports from spies, but his cultural egotism did not allow him to put himself in Washington's shoes.

3. **Empathetic Expectation:** Though Washington did not predict how Rall would react, he did have enough understanding to appreciate what Rall would *probably* try to do. As a result, he created a plan that would give him the advantage of overwhelming Rall. If Ewing had been able to cross, Rall would have started the battle surrounded.

5. **Study of History:** Washington understood the British. He had fought with them, for them, and against them. Washington knew British history and knew of the military history and culture of the opponents. His understanding, compared with the ignorance of American colonial history by the Hessians and most of the British officers, put Washington in a position of asymmetrical dominance.

6. **Study of Culture:** The arrogance of the British and Hessian leadership responsible for defending New Jersey allowed this attack to take place. They did not understand the Americans as a people with a culture, nor did they understand the draw of the words "liberty" and "freedom." The spontaneous New Jersey insurgency was a direct result of affiliation with these two words rather than with some hierarchical structure.

8. **Initiative:** The timing of the attack, the placement of the artillery at the ends of King and Queen streets, and the attack from different directions meant that Rall was always reacting to Washington. Washington was in a position where he could see the Hessian movements, so he was able to react to Hessian decisions faster than they could make those decisions.

Chapter 9

CASE STUDY:
THE BATTLE OF GROZNY
(31 DECEMBER 1994–
3 JANUARY 1995)

Welcome to Hell!
—Chechen fighter (1994)[1]

Strategies Emphasized:

1. Introspection
2. Empathetic Appreciation
3. Empathetic Expectation
4. Study of Language
5. Study of History
6. Study of Culture
7. Multiple Reserves
8. Initiative
9. Think Science Fiction

The events that happened in the city of Grozny at the end of 1994 and early into 1995 represent yet another key change in the transformation of warfare and present an aberration for the Russian soldiers and commanders who fought. This was both a civil war and a revolution, depending on the perspective of the person applying the labels. It also functioned in both genres, as did Trenton (discussed in the previous chapter), by providing an asymmetry of knowledge. The rebels understood the Russian soldiers because they had formerly been Russian soldiers, but the Russian soldiers could not really understand the Chechen rebels. The issues creating this problem are at the heart of the discussion in this chapter.

An understanding of the opponent and an understanding of the importance of international media served in tandem to create a change in perspective of how to fight the Russian soldiers. This battle and the war surrounding it existed at the edge of the explosion of international media access and internet connectivity. It also existed in the control of the Russian government establishment, who still functioned in a Cold War media-access environment. Because of this, media was not a transformative effect in the response of the Russian military, as it would have been ten years later or will be in the discussion of the following chapter.

This battle features the engagement between irregular forces and unprepared forces. The plans used by the Russians are distinct in the differences between the initial entry and the subsequent reentry. This chapter will focus on the tactics and events of the initial attack and will discuss the changes applied in the re-entry.

Geographical Setting

Location
Chechnya lies in the northern Caucasus Mountains. It is a relatively small, land-locked country about a third of the way inland from the Caspian Sea toward the Black Sea. It is south of Russia and north of Georgia. Georgia lies to the southwest with a variety of other Russian republics surrounding Chechnya on every other side. The republic with the greatest common border with Chechnya is Dagestan, which shares the southern, eastern, and northeastern borders of the country. Grozny is the capital of Chechnya and is centrally located at a bend in the Sunzha River and to the west of the Argun River. The city itself was originally built as a Russian fortress in 1818. Strategically, the most important aspect of geography deals directly with the fact that pipelines and railroads transit Chechnya,

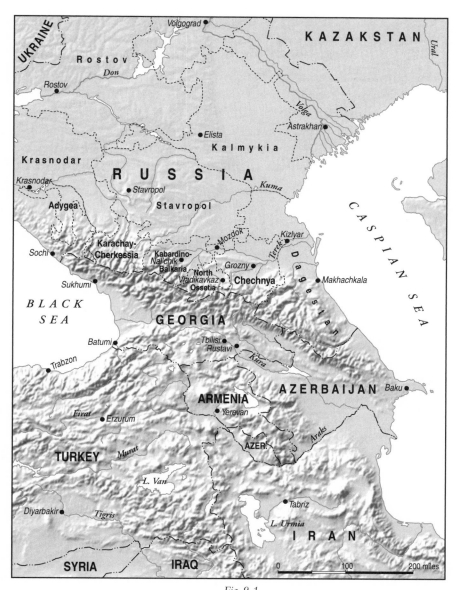

Fig. 9.1

carrying Caspian Sea oil en route to Russia itself. The city is the center of the national and regional road network.

Terrain and Vegetation

Chechnya is a generally mountainous country with most of the ranges running from west to east. The northern third of the country is a plain. As forces travel south they encounter a series of mountain belts. Grozny, at the eastern edge of the second mountain belt, is a natural junction of multiple trafficable routes, and a key to trans-Caucasus movement.

The events discussed in this chapter happen within the city itself, and the terrain is the complex terrain of an urban center. The buildings were typically of Soviet-era concrete and usually multiple stories.

Weather

Weather played no significant role, though it was winter in the northern Caucasus Mountains. This meant cold and snow.

Units Involved

Chechen Forces

Not all Chechens wanted independence from Russia; in fact, depending on the source, it seems likely that most Chechens did not want conflict with Russia over any issue. As is true with most revolutions, this one was started and fueled by a minority. Understanding the forces fighting for Chechen independence requires a great deal of patience and a willingness to accept ambiguity. It is probable that there will never be a definitive account of how many rebels actually fought because there is a wide disparity concerning numbers even among those supportive of independence. The Russian commanders' beliefs about the intentions of the Chechens varied from the initial assumption that the Chechens would not fight prior to the movement into Grozny to a view of their opponents as ubiquitous and omnipresent. They understood the composition of the opposition to be about 10,000 soldiers, 25 tanks, 35 armored personnel carriers, and 80 artillery pieces. Most of the equipment and personnel came from former

Soviet Union inventory and former Soviet Union soldiers. A pro-independence Chechen political leader explained that the Chechen fighters had between 4,500 and 6,000 soldiers. A Chechen fighter said that there were only about 450 permanent fighters. This information is indicative of the confusion of the Chechen forces involved.

In an attempt to provide a consensus view of what existed in the city, the following information is provided. It is certain that this information is open for dispute, but this gives a rough opening figure. The organization fighting the Russian army was composed of separate groups who combined against a common enemy. Their weapons included armored personnel carriers, artillery pieces, and several tanks. The equipment and numbers of personnel vary wildly based on accounts, but for the purposes of this narrative the force was about one thousand to two thousand strong with about ten or so tanks and an equal number of artillery pieces. Other unorganized and some organized groups adhered to this general organization for the conduct of the defense.

Russian Forces

The Russians brought a significant force into Chechnya, and they conducted the operation from multiple directions. Three different battle groups entered the country. Each battle group divided into two groups to approach the city from six different directions. For the most part, this chapter focuses on one unit—the 131st Independent Motorized Rifle Brigade, which was part of the Northern (sometimes referred to here as the Northwestern) Battle Group.

The Northwestern Battle Group began their attack from the city of Mozdok in North Ossetia and consisted of the 131st Independent Motorized Rifle Brigade (IMRBr), the 106th Paratroop Division, and the 56th Independent Paratroop Brigade.[2]

The Western Battle Group attacked from Vladikavkaz in North Ossetia. The Eastern Battle Group attacked from Kizlyar in Dagestan. The total force was something along the lines of thirty-eight thousand soldiers. The south was left open to allow escaping refugees to clear the city.[3] This was a conscious decision primarily designed for humanitarian reasons, though it also served to allow those fighting against the Russians an open corridor for supply and reinforcement.

As noted above, the focus here is on forces from the Northwest Group, specifically the 131st IMRBr. The lead battalion of this brigade was the battalion that attacked all the way to the railroad station. Other units that entered Grozny on 31 December 1994 are the 106th Paratroop Division with subordinate units of the 81st and the 276th Motorized Rifle Regiments (MRR). The 56th Independent Paratroop Brigade also played a role in this initial penetration. The total composition of these forces in this first major encounter was 80 tanks, 208 BMP (armored fighting vehicles), 182 artillery pieces, and 90 supporting helicopters.

Key Leaders in the Battle

The leaders at the tactical levels are unclear in most cases and are therefore not mentioned here. There is some reference to people who did not fight in this battle, but they were important after the battle and gained importance as a result of the events in Grozny.

Chechen Forces

Most of the Chechen fighters had experience in the former Soviet Union military. Many also had combat experience in Afghanistan or in stability operations within the former Soviet Union.

Dzhokar Dudayev—a former Soviet Air Force general major. He became the elected president of Chechnya and publicly sought to create a single trans-Caucasian republic stretching to include parts of Russia and Ukraine ,as well as the entire Caucasian and trans-Caucasian region.

Shamil Basayev—He served as the senior field commander in Grozny. He later became infamous for attacks on a hospital, a Moscow theater, and a school in Beslan.[4]

Russian Forces

Boris Yeltsin—the Russian president.

General Lieutenant V. M. Chilidin—Commander of the Mozdok Group. He was relieved during the course of the approach.

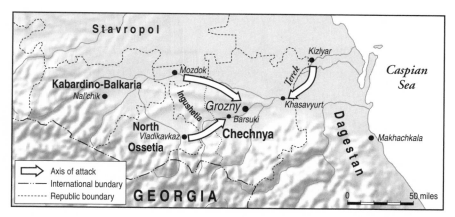

Fig. 9.2

Battle of Grozny, 31 December 1994 – 3 January 1995

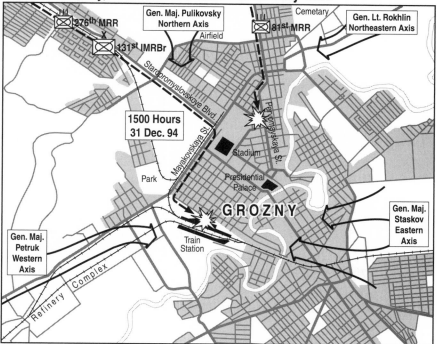

Fig. 9.3

General Major K. Pulikovsky—He commanded the actual assault into the city from the north.

Colonel Ivan Savin—Commander of the 131st Independent Motorized Rifle Brigade.

Historical and Grand Strategy Context

The fighting in the city of Grozny took place within a larger dynamic series of events for Russia and the various federated states, independent states, and neighboring states of the former Soviet Union. The Iron Curtain had fallen, Germany had become united, and the Cold War had been lost by the USSR. The USSR broke up, and many states became independent. Many states within the Russian Federation also sought independence in this era of dissolution and Chechnya was one of these states. The decision to force Chechnya to remain a territory of the Russian Federation was based on the theory that granting sovereignty would guarantee a wave of secession by other territories containing minority Russian populations. As the concentration of Russian majority populations extends only a few hundred kilometers around Moscow, such an inclination toward independence would reduce the remaining Russian state to a shadow of its former self. A secret military campaign was launched against Chechnya and Dudayev by Boris Yeltsin. These efforts failed. Over a period of years—from 1991 to 1994—the Russian and Chechen politicians worked at diplomatic solutions to the problem. Finally, following a failed coup attempt in Russia, Boris Yeltsin sought a military solution to the problem. He ordered the attack to begin and gave the ultimatum to the Chechens to return to Russian control on 29 November 1994.

Chechnya's economic significance is also worthy of note. Chechnya contains significant amounts of oil, accounting for 18 percent of total Russian oil output. Such an important source of a strategic material would not simply be allowed to walk away from Russian control. A final note on this struggle relates to religion. The ethnic Chechens were and are Muslims. Ethnic Russians tend to be either non-religious or Russian Orthodox Christian. This difference in religion played a part in creating a different view of accommodation.

Thoughts Before the Battle

Russia tended to view the conflict in a strategic sense, believing that if this small republic were allowed to depart then an avalanche of secessions could follow. Russia could not risk accommodation. Chechnya had taken advantage of inner turmoil to declare independence, and now a message of Russian resolve and strength needed to be sent. Most soldiers and leaders did not foresee a major battle. It was generally believed that the campaign was more along the lines of an occupation than an attack.

The Chechens needed to seriously bloody the Russian army and force the government in Moscow to reconsider negotiated independence. The memory of the withdrawal from Afghanistan was still fresh, and the hope of forcing a similar event was a driving factor in decision making.

Operational Context

The Russian army sought to encircle Grozny by sending forces from three different cities in neighboring republics to attack on six different axes. The intent was to create a series of concentric circles of control, with the innermost circle being that around the capital, Grozny. The air campaign began on 30 November 1994, with ground troops entering on 11 December. Access for foreign as well as Russian media was severely restricted. This played against the Chechens, since they wanted to use the media to demonstrate Russian brutality. Media restrictions became harsher after initial reports of Russian aircraft bombing columns of fleeing refugees. Because the cry for independence among ethnic Chechens was not universal, the early media coverage and the harsh actions by the Russians helped bolster the resistance. Despite these restrictions, there were Western journalists present in Grozny, and the Chechen rebels used this fact to their greatest advantage in telling their side of the story. The fact that nearly all reporting to the West was coming from Chechen-protected journalists and all the reporting inside Russia was coming from state-sponsored media indicates why the accounts of this battle require significant reading between the lines.

As the Russians advanced, they were greeted with resistance. Entire villages in some regions mobilized against them. The signals of Chechen anger and resistance were missed. Russian officers did not see the minor attacks and snipers as indicative of something more but simply as a nuisance. By 31 December the armies were on the outskirts of Grozny. The original plan called for Grozny to be reached by not later than 9 December. The delays were a result of the terrain and weather, but most of all they were a result of the constant attacks by the Chechens along the route of march.

The battle for Grozny was intended to be a simple show of force by the Russian military. The occupation of the capital would signal, it was believed, the end of the drive for independence. The massive concentration of tanks and armored personnel carriers was intended to intimidate the populace into foregoing any ideas of independence, similar to the Czechs' response to the uprising in Czechoslovakia in 1968.

Technical Context

The battle in Grozny was a battle between soldiers of the former Soviet Union. Fighters on both sides had learned military discipline and tactics through the same training and on the same Afghanistan battlefields. This common understanding of equipment and tactics gave a distinct advantage to the Chechen rebels. They understood the Russian soldier. They knew the weaknesses in the armor of their vehicles and what techniques could defeat the Russia tactics and equipment. Most of them also understood the Russian language. The Russian soldiers and officers did not have a similar understanding. They did not speak Chechen. They did not understand Islam, and they did not fully understand the guerilla tactics to be employed against them. This was true asymmetry of knowledge and understanding.

The Chechens followed some equipment-based tactics. They had access to Soviet weapons, and they used them to target those weaknesses they knew existed in the equipment of their opponent. They used thermobaric weapons—flame throwers or fire-based projectiles—to mark targets. They also used massed rocket propelled grenade (RPG) fire against tanks or to clear buildings. The command and control were based on standard phone and radio technology. Digital cameras came into play as well as the internet as numerous images of Russian atrocities were uploaded to pro-independence websites. Communications security came through the use of the Chechen language, which was a dialect that few, if any, Russian soldiers understood.

The Chechens used a tactical concept called a defenseless defense. This means that they did not defend a specific objective. There was not a single site that they felt they could not surrender. Thus they chose to defend from numerous locations simultaneously, and they moved frequently, surrendering buildings and other positions to large-scale Russian efforts only to flow to another position or return to the same position later once the Russian soldiers moved on. They organized in small mobile groups or cells of three to four personnel or tank-killing teams of eight personnel. Typically the group included one or more RPG gunners, snipers, machine gunners, and other fighters. To imply a rigid organization would give a schematic vision to something that was neither schematic nor truly ordered along a template.

Rebels fought from upper floors of buildings—usually the third floor or higher—or from basements. In both cases this assisted them in avoiding the overwhelming firepower of the Russian conventional forces. Tanks could not elevate their gun tubes sufficient for close-range engagement above the second floor, nor could they depress the gun for close-range engagement of basement positions. The Russians would later counter these techniques by placing antiaircraft vehicles as the lead vehicles of columns. These weapon systems had greater elevation and depression capabilities.

The result of these techniques was the loss of 225 armored vehicles—61 of which were tanks—by the Russian forces in the first month. This represented more than 10 percent of all armored vehicles initially committed to the campaign.[5]

Chechnya followed the trend of Bosnia—it was another sniper war. Single riflemen with high-quality training and good weapons created a disproportionate number of casualties on the battlefield. Chechen snipers used and improved on the techniques learned in Bosnia—firing from the back of rooms to mask the location of the shot was one of the most effective of these techniques.

Tactical Chronology

Russian commanders chose to attack into Grozny with only about six thousand of a possible thirty-eight thousand soldiers. By the Russian intelligence estimates of about ten thousand Chechen rebels, they knowingly went in outnumbered more than 1.5:1. This resulted in more than two thousand Russian soldiers killed and seventy-five armored vehicles destroyed on the first day alone. The Russians reentered the city in early January 1995, and the second time they made extensive use of artillery, attack helicopters, and smoke.

The attack on New Year's Eve 1994 was done as a primarily armored force. No dismounted infantry were used. The infantry that were present were in the back of armored vehicles. Many were asleep as they moved in the city. Not all had weapons. The soldiers were told to expect a police action. In some cases, the machine guns on the tanks did not have ammunition.

Despite the goal of concentric rings of defense and blockade, the Russians never completely blockaded the city as noted previously—they wanted to leave a corridor for fleeing refugees to the south. Of the three different groups approaching the city, elements of only one (the Northern Group from Mozdok) entered the city on the first afternoon. The other commanders complained of fading daylight and exhausted soldiers. The two regimental-sized units that entered the city that afternoon were the 131st IMRBr and the 81st MRR. They attacked south toward the center of the city on parallel axes, the 131st in the west and the 81st in the east. They did not attack simultaneously but sequentially, with the 81st moving first into the city. Instead of massing two powerful, regimental-sized units against an unconventional opponent, the Russians sent essentially one unit at a time and allowed the Chechens the opportunity to mass on each separately.

This they did, engaging and defeating the 81st relatively early as they moved through the city. The regiment stopped and began to withdraw after heavy contact. The buildings created line-of-sight difficulties for communication, so no word was received by the 131st, and they continued toward the city center alone. The 131st was allowed to progress all the way to their objective. It is unclear why the 131st reached the train station without contact. Some secondary sources attribute this to the fact there were limited Chechen fighters who were all fixated on fighting the 81st, and therefore they could not engage the 131st until later in the day.[6]

They arrived at the train station, and some of the officers dismounted their vehicles and went into the café and bought sandwiches. Things seemed to be going exactly as planned. Then the Chechen forces opened fire. The opening quote of this chapter was a line supposedly heard over the radio by the 131st IMBr communications officer just prior to the beginning of the Chechen attack. The Chechens had created a trap around the station, and they were able to mass RPGs on the vehicles lined up as if in a parade. The armored vehicles could not bring their main armaments to bear, and since many of the machine guns were without ammunition, the soldiers were simply targets. The unit suffered heavy casualties. The brigade lost 102 of 120 armored personnel carriers, 20 of 26 tanks, all of their surface-to-air missile systems, 1500 soldiers killed or wounded, and 74 captured.[7] This was a brutal fight.

Unlike the 81st, the 131st was stuck in the center of the city. They struggled through several attempts to break out, but no external unit would come to their assistance. The battalion that reached the train station was completely isolated. The other two battalions from

Timeline		
Date	Time	Event
1818		Grozny is founded as a Russian bastion in occupied territory.
1944–1957		Chechens are removed from Chechnya.
21 August 1991		Localized revolution begins.
6 September 1991		Chechnya declares independence from Russian Federation.
November 1994		Chechen opposition fighter attacked Grozny with Russian support.
29 November 1994		"Disarm and Surrender" statement made by Boris Yeltsin.
11 December 1994		Ground campaign begins.
31 December 1994	~1500	Russian troops enter Grozny.
3 January 1995		Russian troops withdraw from Grozny.
7 January 1995		Russian troops re-enter Grozny.
19 January 1995		Russian troops capture Presidential Palace.

Fig. 9.4

the brigade struggled to get to them, but they were cut apart as they used side streets to bypass blockades. Eventually the surviving soldiers used the remaining operational armored vehicles to escape. The brigade commander—Savin—was killed in this escape.

The first stage had gone to the Chechens. The failure to note the commitment of Chechen resistance cost the Russians dearly. The Russians would return and eventually capture the city, but they wreaked terrible damage to do so and inflicted thousands of casualties on civilians in the process.

Battlefield Leadership

Battlefield decisions by the Russian leadership were poor. Too much was left to assumption. It was assumed that such a significant show of force would cow the opposition and that they would not fight. This assumption continued despite evidence to the contrary. Leaders at all levels did not ensure that soldiers and equipment were properly prepared for battle. All of this led to a decision to move directly into the city center under the assumption that the routes in and out were secure, or at least posed no significant threat. The sequential nature of the attack allowed the Chechens to focus on only one Russian unit at a time. The decision by General Pulikovsky to allow the 131st IMRBr to continue the attack toward the train station even though the 81st had been forced to withdraw from the city was fateful.

Conversely, Chechen leaders either decided to allow or simply decided to focus on one unit at a time, which meant that they allowed the lead unit to arrive safely at the railroad station without engagement. The decision to use loosely defined tactics and to allow freedom to low-level leaders also allowed Chechen rebels to make maximum use of the urban terrain. They created terrain advantage by drawing the unit into the city, where the buildings negated the superior firepower of the Russian tanks and armored vehicles.

Significance

At the strategic level, the world was exposed to the inadequacies of the contemporary Russian military in general.

From a global perspective, Chechnya served as a validation of insurgency, even against a modern opponent in one's own country. This was not Afghanistan, yet insurgency worked almost as well. In the end, the Russians were able to force compliance, yet the price for this compliance was very high.

The shock from the destruction of the initial elements into the city reverberated throughout the Russian command structure. The renewed assault in early January used significant firepower and destroyed huge portions of the city. Even after this, the Chechens retook the city in August of 1995. The atrocities inflicted as a result of the Russian frustration played a direct role in justifying the subsequent terrorist tactics used by groups like that led by Shamil Basayev.

One of the outcomes of the war was the loss of many civil liberties in Russia, with general public acceptance. Russia slowly backed away from democratic reforms in the light of ethnic rebellions and the use of terrorism to influence public opinion.

It is too soon to fully understand the effect of this battle from a cultural perspective. A challenge with this battle is that the long-term implications are still developing. Relationships with the West have been damaged, reforms stopped or slowed, and the concept of an open and free Western-style democracy seems no longer to be a likely outcome of Russian political developments.

Leasons Learned: Principles of Conflict

The debacle faced by the 131st IMRBr was a direct result of the asymmetry of knowledge mentioned earlier.

- **Identification:** The fact that most of the Chechen leadership and many of the fighters had experience with the Russian military resulted in a complete asymmetry in identification. The Chechens understood the Russian army, but the soldiers and leaders in the Russian army did not understand Chechen language, culture, religion, or motivation. They failed to identify their opponents at any level and did not empathize with them. The surprise of the initial attack was unnecessary, since there had been warning signs throughout the approach to Grozny, but the complete ignorance allowed the untenable plan to be executed. Items as simple as maps at the correct scale for the city, all soldiers having weapons, and other simple requirements of military operations were ignored, since the Russians expected merely to give a show of force. Basic rules and principles must be followed, and reassessments must be repeatedly made to allow for the use of the latest information.

- **Isolation:** In an urban environment it is essential to maintain line-of-sight communications, which may mean seizing and controlling tall buildings to allow for radio antennae placement. It is also crucial to understand the relationship of adjacent forces upon entering the urban landscape.

- **Suppression:** The very shape of infrastructure in the urban environment exists to canalize movement. The nature of the ground means a force must follow linear movement patterns with little width for dispersion.

- **Maneuver:** An emotional position of advantage was achieved through the dominance of identification. The Chechens completely controlled the initial engagement and were able to surprise their opponent effectively, thereby creating an aberration through this dominance. The use of upper floors and subterranean basements that were above and beneath the shooting ability of Russian tanks also served as a physical position of advantage from which the Chechens dominated the battle. In later engagements, the Russians had to change tactics radically to reach these locations.

- **Destruction:** The initial Russian brigade moving to the railroad station was physically and emotionally destroyed. The complete destruction of this force is a demonstration of the risks inherent in urban combat for a force inadequately trained and poorly informed. As in all of the previous battles discussed in this book, preparation before the battle is critical to the decisions and actions made during the battle. Failures in identification may be overcome if the force is sufficiently well trained and prepared. Grozny was not such a case for the Russian army.

Conclusion

The Russian leaders and soldiers were completely overwhelmed by events. They had a very small box of possibilities in mind. Once the world changed, they could not change the box quickly enough to make the necessary adjustments. The leaders and soldiers expected the Chechens to act in a way similar to previous East European peoples or to many other former Soviet Union residents. They did not realize that their perceptions and prescribed boxes of behavioral responses were taken from the wrong shelf. They did not perceive that the changes in war outside the borders of Russia were being brought within Russia.

How Does It Fit Inside the Box?

- For the majority of soldiers and officers moving into Grozny, the capital of Chechnya, the attitude was that the operation was going to be similar to the action in Czechoslovakia in 1968—a show of massive force that would almost immediately end the unrest. This was a rebellion, but most saw it as a rebellion without the will to stand against the might of Russian military strength.
- The Chechen rebels were irregulars without discipline or training. This line of thinking by Russian commanders allowed the planning conducted to discount the idea of an intelligent, integrated, and well-coordinated response by the Chechens.
- This was not a war, but intimidation. The rebels had tried and failed to intimidate the Russian government, and now it was the Russian government's turn to intimidate the rebels and end the uprising.

Why Is It an Aberration?

- **Means:** The Chechen rebels used the urban terrain to accomplish principles of conflict that they could not do on their own. For example, they allowed the Russian forces to enter the city uncontested, and then the buildings and other urban infrastructure did the isolation and suppression. The limited ability of the Russian tanks to elevate or depress their main guns meant that the basements and upper floors of buildings were ideal positions of advantage at the tactical level. Once again, the very urban infrastructure facilitated a principle of conflict—maneuver. The Chechen rebels simply had to identify and destroy.

- **Leader:** Russian leaders moved in without any proper identification of their opponent at any level. Because of this, they assumed they were occupying a hostile city and not fighting to gain and maintain control of it. This left leaders and their soldiers unprepared for the violence of the engagement. As the emotional will of soldiers and then leaders was broken, there was a complete loss of control.
- **Understanding:** As previously noted, the Russian leaders at nearly all levels perceived the event as similar to Hungary or Czechoslovakia. They did not grasp how the events of Vietnam, the Palestinian Intifadah, and Somalia had changed the equation of state versus non-state actors on a modern battlefield.
- **Target:** The Chechen rebel leadership understood that it was not sufficient simply to kill Russian soldiers but that they needed to attack the will of the Russian populace. The actions in the theater in Moscow, the hospital in Budennovsk, and the school in Beslan are all severe examples of this targeting of civilian will. All of these came after the initial success and then the subsequent loss in Grozny. The ferocity of attacks by the Chechen revolutionaries on civilian targets grew over time. Initially, the focus was to attack the Russian military and demoralize the soldiers, much as had occurred in Afghanistan. However, even within Grozny, there were significant efforts to play to the media to portray the Russian army as indiscriminate killers. The Russians changed tactics as well, virtually annihilating the city center over time to allow for a successful retaking of the city. There was a general acceptance that to win this kind of war, civilians were legitimate targets for either physical destruction or destruction of will.

Strategies (numbered based on the nine strategies for victory)
1. **Introspection:** The Russian leadership from the top down did not understand the state of their own military with regard to the force necessary to successfully conduct the operations required to win in

Grozny. Those who did understand the poor condition of the military did not conduct the necessary steps to prepare their forces.

2. **Empathetic Appreciation:** It is difficult to say whether anyone understood the force size, composition, or capabilities of the Chechen rebels, including the rebels themselves. This said, it is clear that the Russian commanders could not appreciate who or what they were dealing with. This seems to be a flaw in state leadership, both military and political, in assessing the capability of the nonstate actor. The boasts of Russian leaders about what it would take to successfully bring an end to the rebellion showed the same naiveté that was demonstrated by U.S. Army officers in dealing with the Indians in the nineteenth century or British officers in dealing with the American Revolution in the eighteenth century. The revolutionary is almost universally underestimated, especially in his ability to garner and maintain popular support.

3. **Empathetic Expectation:** No Russian leader knew what the Chechens would do. Even after the initial engagement, there was no commander who came forward to say that he had warned the establishment. Part of this may be that Russian military culture would not allow for such a statement, but I believe that, in fact, none of the commanders expected the Chechens to mount a competent defense. This lack of empathy was true even after several weeks of delaying attacks from Chechen rebels along nearly the entirety of the approach march to Grozny.

4. **Study of Language:** The Chechens had complete asymmetry of language understanding—most, if not all, of the rebel fighters knew Russian, but few, if any, of the Russian soldiers knew Chechen. This allowed for secure communication in the native language, making it nearly as good as a code. No entity should enter a conflict environment without having some level of understanding of the opponent's language.

5. **Study of History:** The history of conflict in the Caucasus is filled with events like Chechnya. The ability of small, irregular forces to delay and stop larger forces riddles the military history of the region. Grozny and the campaign that preceded it in 1994 are

only two examples in a series of similar campaigns. Though history is never a complete or perfect predictor of events, one should not discount the weight of history out of a sense of ethnic superiority or simply because of convenience.

6. **Study of Culture:** Islam was an important part of Chechen culture, as was a strong sense of independent will. These two aspects were never fully addressed in preparing for the conflict. Russian soldiers did not understand their opponents in any way—why they were fighting, how they might fight—and as a result they lost any ability to link what they saw and experienced with what might be happening in a larger sense.

7. **Multiple Reserves:** The commitment of two regimental- or brigade-sized organizations without any unit prepared to relieve or assist them meant that the higher commander could not react in any way to unforeseen contingencies. Those units were on their own, even though the plans called for additional units to be moving or at least ready to respond. Some of this was a result of bureaucratic organizational issues.

8. **Initiative:** The movement into the city seemed to provide the Russian force with the initial advantage. The fact that soldiers then lost their sense of discipline and alertness by buying food at the train station café surrendered any initiative to the attacking Chechens. From this point forward in the initial three to four days, the Russians could only react. It took a complete withdrawal, regrouping, and subsequent attack before the Russians could regain the initiative.

9. **Think Science Fiction:** This battle demonstrates a compelling need to think beyond the standard patterns. Even if the Russians had gone into Grozny completely ready to fight in an urban environment, they would still have faced a challenging opponent, since the Chechens were not fighting using conventional techniques. The loose organizational structure and the free-flowing method of fighting would have stressed conventional thinkers. How is the future different from the present? What is out there that is changing? These things must be considered.

Chapter 10

Levantine Nonstate Conflict (1967–Present)

Strategies Emphasized:

1. Introspection
2. Empathetic Appreciation
3. Empathetic Expectation
4. Study of Language

5. Study of History
6. Study of Culture
9. Think Science Fiction

There is neither time nor space left in this book to attempt anything approaching a comprehensive review of the events that have occurred since 1967 in the world, not even those specific to the Levant. There are a great many books that discuss the nature of conflict in this region in detail. In this chapter are brief pieces of information of key events that may have direct relevance on the discussion of moving toward a greater propensity of aberrations in the future.

In many ways this progression from state versus state conflict to state versus non-state conflict has an ancient tradition in the region.

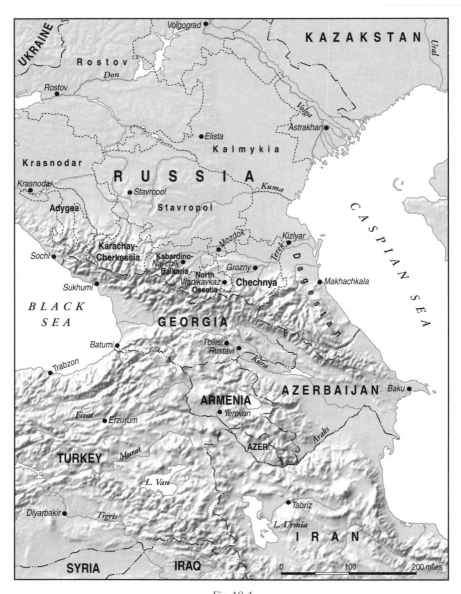

Fig. 10.1

Some of that was addressed in the previous chapters with the rise of an Islamic empire and the nonstate actors common in the crusader era (Assassins, Templars, Hospitallers, etc.). Here the discussion could go back even further to the Maccabean revolt against Seleucid rule in the region in the second century BC. Since the cultures and religions in the region trace their histories in terms of millennia, the associations and inspirations drawn from earlier eras are powerful and should not be discounted. The ancient nature of the nonstate actor in the region is crucial to appreciating the modern incarnation of the same types of power centers.

The birth of the modern state of Israel saw a significant role for nonstate actors. Some of this was a result of the Jewish people feeling that there was no state that represented their interests with which they could associate. Thus groups formed whose avowed purpose was to fight the British mandate and the local Arab organizations. The focus of these groups was to inflict an unsustainable pain level on the British people and government and to discredit the British occupation of Palestine. This culminated in the UN vote in 1947, favoring partition of the British mandate into an Arab state and a Jewish state, and the 1948 declaration of independence by the state of Israel. At this point, the nonstate organizations began to coalesce into the state organizations of the nation of Israel.

With the wars that followed, and especially the 1967 Arab-Israeli war, the Palestinian Arabs, both within the Israeli-defined state boundaries of Israel and outside those boundaries, either as a result of expulsion and intimidation or as a result of chosen flight and departure, then saw themselves as being in a similar position to the Jewish groups of earlier decades—they no longer had a government that they could rely upon to represent their interests. Palestinian-Arab organizations formed to begin a fight for their own state and independence. These groups covered a large portion of the political and military spectrum. They ranged from groups primarily motivated by religion to those who were closely aligned politically with communism and nearly everything in between. These nonstate actors grew in size and complexity and eventually expanded to a position where they felt they could intimidate and threaten the overthrow of the Hashemite monarchy in Jordan in 1970. The failure of the Palestinian Liberation Organization (PLO) to achieve the overthrow of the Jordanian monarchy led to their expulsion from Jordan.

The PLO moved to Lebanon, and there they continued attacks against Israel until Israel felt compelled to attack in 1982. The Israeli invasion and eighteen-year occupation acted as the genesis of the non-state Hezbollah organization. It was this actor that would claim responsibility for driving Israel out of southern Lebanon in 2000 and would execute the events that precipitated the Israeli invasion of southern Lebanon in 2006. Though not directly linked to Hezbollah in religious ideology, support, or training, it can be argued that Hamas developed its power and influence from the successes achieved by Hezbollah. Hamas seemed to follow a pattern of social assistance and military resistance, effectively linking itself to the people as a beneficial social and political organ for Palestinians while also being a dynamic and aggressive military opponent of Israel. The line of logical progression moves through the Israeli withdrawal from southern Lebanon to the withdrawal from Gaza in 2005 and the political victories of Hamas in Palestinian elections in 2006. Hamas, like Hezbollah in southern Lebanon, claimed and was given credit by the Palestinian people for the Israeli withdrawal from Gaza.

The dual successes of both these nonstate actors against opponents who had soundly defeated state actors on battlefield after battlefield and in engagement after engagement came within a generation of the success of similar organizations in a much more rural environment in Afghanistan. The remainder of this chapter discusses some of the snapshots of means, methods, and events that have facilitated the transformation from the modern construct of state versus state conflict to the current rise of nonstate actors on the modern battlefield and their foreseeable importance in the future.

Russia had a brutal introduction to fighting nonstate actors in Afghanistan. The Red Army of the 1980s and 1990s understood the challenges of fighting such a force. However, the Russian leadership could not imagine that the Chechens could transfer the lessons of fighting the Mujahideen to their conflict within Russia.

It was not just the Mujahideen who caused this transition. A line of knowledge and tactics can be drawn from China to Vietnam to revolutions in South America to Palestine to Bosnia and to Somalia. The actions in Palestine and later in Bosnia are contemporary links in this transformation. In the spectrum of state participation and support versus independent action, the Palestinian struggle for an Arab-Palestinian state and the Bosnian-Serb struggle for a greater Serbia are at the crossroads of this struggle. There has been and continues to be outside support from states and state-level entities, but the actual conflict is waged by nonstate individuals and organizations.

The most recent example of a nonstate organization waging a war with external support is the 2006 fighting between Hezbollah and Israel mentioned earlier. In this example, a state fought a nonstate organization within the borders of a neighboring state that stood helpless to control the activities of either party in the conflict yet suffered standard industrial-age destruction as in previous state versus state conflicts.

Because of the nature of this type of conflict and the tactics used, Western governments typically label these nonstate groups and their individual fighters as terrorists. Whether this label is accurate or appropriate is irrelevant. As this book now transitions to draw critical relevance to today and the future, it is essential that we see that these fighters, regardless of label, represent the future of conflict to a much greater level than in previous times. These types of fighters have always existed, but the changes in degree and the changes in information technology have created differences from our recent post–World War II history.

In this book so far, six battles or engagements have been presented. Of these, only two could be labeled as battles between accepted peer states—Cannae between the Roman Republic and the Carthaginian Empire and the Horns of Hattin between the Ayyubid Sultanate and the Kingdom of Jerusalem. The other four all included the dynamic of state versus nonstate. Arguments could be made against Yarmouk being so considered, but it is certain that the Roman Empire of that period did not consider the expanding

Arab tribes as anything like equals and did not recognize them as anything more than a tribal conglomeration. As we have seen, they ruled through arrogant ignorance. At the Little Bighorn, the U.S. government was seeking to force peoples rebelling from governmental overlordship to return to their subordinate positions. At Trenton, we have colonial rebels fighting a world superpower, not unlike Chechnya. Many might take offense at the comparison, so it is important to note that the comparison is one of roles in opposition rather than tactics and individual leaders. History is replete with numerous examples of nonstate actors defying or opposing the will of states. It would, therefore, seem that revolutionaries tend to seek aberrations. In fact, it may be said that they require them in order to succeed.

In the contemporary world, there are dynamics in existence that make this interaction more common and more likely than ever before. When such clashes occur, it is also more likely that the engagement or battle will be outside the conceptual box of those members of a state military who are fighting.

The following are observations on nonstate conflict in general and on what has changed or may change to make it different from our historic examples in both the contemporary and future worlds:

Means

Destroying an Idol

On 17 February 2002, Hamas, a nonstate Palestinian organization, detonated a 100-kilogram (approximately 220-pound) roadside bomb, severely damaging a Merkava III Israeli main battle tank and killing three of the four crewmembers inside. The use of a roadside bomb was not in itself remarkable. They had been used in Afghanistan against Soviet armored vehicles and columns and also in southern Lebanon during the later stages of the Israeli occupation. The remarkable nature of this date and event lies in the vehicle targeted. The Merkava III was considered nearly indestructible and the crew completely safe from such attacks. The scale of the explosive communicated the intense desire to destroy such a vehicle for the public relations coup and the ability to communicate power to the Palestinian community and the Arab world. Coming only eighteen or so months before the increase in insurgent attacks in Iraq on coalition convoys, this event was a harbinger of the changes coming in this new nonstate opponent.

The importance of this event lies in the fact that this was the destruction of a modern idol; the main battle tank and the attack helicopter represent idols in the religion of technological warfare, just as a stone-carved figure might have represented an animistic god in the ancient world. The Jewish, Christian, and Muslim historical-religious traditions have powerful images of leaders throwing down the idols of the opposing religions to remind the populace where their spiritual loyalties should lie. In this modern and secular example, Hamas placed a great deal of effort to do the same thing—cast down the technological idol of the main battle tank to remind the Palestinian people of where they should place their loyalties and who they should support: Hamas. This served as both a domestic and an international message.

Transmitting Images of Terror

Late in 2003 and throughout much of 2004, television news stations were consistently showing some of the most horrific images possible of the suffering and emotional torture of captured civilian workers in Iraq and Saudi Arabia. The images of beheadings and pleading kidnap victims were intense. The horror on the faces and in the voices of these victims broadcast a message as chilling as the brutal acts depicted in the video images.

The use of terror and horror are by no means new. Ancient armies used to flay the skin off victims before the walls of besieged cities. Victorious armies would rape and pillage and toss living infants from city walls following the capture of a city. These actions were meant to discourage cities and opponents from resisting the will of the attacker. These actions were not limited to seemingly barbaric and non-Western Mesopotamian armies like the Assyrians or Babylonians or to supposedly uncivilized and non-European Aztecs or Native Americans; the Greeks, Romans, crusaders, and Spanish conquistadors all applied similar tactics. The terms "barbaric" and "uncivilized" are used to connote the misapplied labels for behavior in conflict. One side's barbarism is another side's necessity—the use of an atomic weapon against Hiroshima in 1945 being a very good example of the difference of opinion.

What made the images of 2003 and 2004 so brutal was that the U.S. audience, and maybe Western audiences in general, had become used to the sterile video-game presentation of war—Shock and Awe was a lot more like a fireworks display when watched on television than it was like the brutal realities of war. Television and the internet provide propaganda media unlike any enjoyed by the historical forces who used terror. One image, successfully downloaded or distributed, can now send waves of horrific emotions through millions rather than only those who walked past the crucified bodies lining the ancient road.

A Transforming Enemy

Consider the transformation in suicide bombers. Initially, nearly all suicide bombers could be effectively characterized by a common template—young (18–30 years old) Arab men with basic education though not with advanced degrees. Since the events of 11 September 2001, the template no longer applies. Women have been involved— single women, married women, and possibly mentally handicapped women. In England in 2007, medical doctors from Muslim countries were implicated in a terrorist-related event. The opponent realized the strength of the existing template and made alterations to ensure that the means can no longer be easily identified.

Understanding

The fact that tactics and techniques used by the Mujahideen in Afghanistan were then seen in Bosnia and later in Chechnya and then still later in Lebanon, Palestine, Iraq, and again in Afghanistan should be no surprise. Military tactics never remain secret for long, and rarely do they remain the sole province or possession of a single side in the conflict. The accessibility to text and image media is unparalleled in the historic record. Unlike the centuries it took for gunpowder to travel from China to Europe, today a new technique can be transmitted within hours of a successful operation, and the new idea implemented within days or weeks. Personal experience of such operators can now be multiplied by the vicarious experiences of similar-minded individuals operating nearly simultaneously around the globe. In addition to technical and tactical application of such activities, the ability to develop far-reaching strategy through comparative and collective discussion and action exists. A single revolutionary mind does not have to think up how to defeat his much larger opponent all by himself. Nor is he relegated to reading the words of bygone revolutionaries. Now he can access the minds and thinking of successful contemporaries. The power of globalized information increases his ability to resist or destroy like never before.

Leader

The power of leadership is based, in great measure, upon culture. That said, regardless of culture, a charismatic leader can still motivate dedicated groups. Nonstate organizations tend toward a cell-based or family-like network. This is certainly not always true, as demonstrated with the Battle of Trenton and numerous other large-scale revolutions and uprisings; however, in the small-scale events and among tribal-based societies this does apply. This old-style heroic and charismatic leader serves both as the motivation and the inspiration for the organization— meaning he pushes them forward with his will, and he pulls them forward with his vision. This is different from the Western bureaucratic leader. This means people become more important than organization. The difference in this leadership comes about when the idea itself—freedom from occupation, for example— becomes so compelling that real organization or leadership at a high level is irrelevant. In this environment, leaders are of smaller and smaller groups with a loose combination of alliance based on the overriding idea. It is for this reason that this type of resistance may be extremely difficult to defeat, but if they win they are ineffectual at governance.

Target

The focus of revolution is rarely the military defeat of the state or the state's military. The focus is typically on the people—the idea being to dissuade the people from involvement with the government or to gain outright support. This remains true, but the means to do so have become more sophisticated through the modern media. Satellite television can communicate the shooting of a supposedly surrendering prisoner concurrent with the event. No comment or clarification means that people are free to interpret the event as they want, and then the images take on a life of their own as they remain caught in the media atmosphere, being recycled as desired to make a point. The support of the state is eroded through these images, and support of, or at least sympathy for, the nonstate organization is increased without a real armed engagement occurring. The waters can be muddied, and by doing so everyone gets covered with filth so that there are no good guys and no bad guys anymore. The impact on the state is similar to defeat because the perception results in a loss of credibility or competence.

The Results of this Transformation

Information Transfer: Why Does Moore's Law Have Relevance?

The amount of time it takes to transfer technology, technique, and engagement method from one group or region to another is growing shorter and shorter. As already stated, in previous eras up to and including the recent past, the transfer of ideas and techniques required time and access. How could a Viet Cong insurgent (circa 1960s) learn about revolutionary techniques in South America or even in Malaysia? It took time to smuggle this sensitive information from one place to another because governments had greater control of information and the ability for humans to communicate with each other. Now, this information can be text messaged from one country to another in minutes, or multiple groups can simultaneously review the same information on a website using their cell phones, Blackberries, computers, or other electronic devices. As quickly as one government shuts a site down, another one or more opens up. The explosion of technological advancement only means that this will become more and more difficult to combat.

Technological Mismatch

Many roadside bombs and other explosive devices are triggered by simple consumer electronic devices like cell phones. Cell phone triggers prey on the very infrastructure development that the state opponent creates to facilitate a better life in the country. As the state improves the infrastructure they, in turn, create more ways to empower the actions of the nonstate actor. Even though the nonstate actors have more avenues, they cannot match the military muscle of the state and, therefore, recognize their inability to engage the national or organized opponent in any set battle. Thus the nonstate group must have a focal point, or center of gravity, of information control and manipulation—horror in developed societies and rumor or preconceived theories in developing countries. Secrets of insecurity whispered on the street are better than headlines proclaiming a better life in the official newspaper.

The nonstate actor seeks to use religious zealotry and perceptions of ethnic superiority to create conditions of mental or physical salient that can then be enveloped. This salient can be created through an emphasis on expectation and perception and can create conditions for overreaching and overextension. What this means is that a nonstate group creates the perception of weakness in the minds of their opponents—rock-throwing children, weapons made from regular household materials, simple shepherds shaking a frustrated fist in anger. Then when the state responds, competent and dedicated individuals use modern or near-modern weapons and equipment to kill an unexpectedly large number of their state military opponents. This exact scenario was seen in Somalia in 1993 and again in Lebanon in 2006. The nonstate forces did not create the poverty and ignorance that they used to create this salient, nor may they even use this salient as a conscious part of their overall plan; however, it exists, and such failures have significant consequences in policy decisions. Withdrawal without achieving objectives was the result in both previously stated examples.

Information Dominance:
Tribal Mindset, Security and Resources

In tribal societies, there is usually an egalitarian ethic that says all members of the tribe are relatively equal and have a say. The leadership of such a society is chosen because that person has shown that he or she can provide the two critical aspects of leadership—security and additional resources. Loyalty is given to such an individual. Any leader who is shown to be consistently ineffective in these two areas will be replaced. The information campaign and, when possible, the military campaign of the nonstate actor must be directed against these two things, or the perception of them. The leader must be shown to be ineffective. The military use of force is primarily in support of this broader information goal.

As part of this, the military actions seek to demonstrate that no place is safe—mosques, churches, synagogues, restaurants, etc.—the more common or sacred the target the better. If people cannot be safe shopping, riding public transportation, in their homes, or talking with god, then where and when can they be safe? Suicide attacks in Israel, as part of the Second Intifadah begun in 2000, existed to demonstrate this. The attacks focused on restaurants, buses, shopping centers, etc.

Cultural Perspective: Too Soon to Tell

This tactic is not new in the history of mankind, but the ability to get the information out is new. The culture of the world is changing as people are seen sending text messages and talking on cell phones in places where the printed word was rare, other than in religious texts, only a handful of decades earlier. What this means for conflict and the perception of it is uncertain. Will the population become desensitized and accepting of a level of nonstate violence and destruction? The development of state military power may also adjust and become more agile in infiltrating organizations and preventing attacks.

The world has seen revolutionary fervor expand over the globe—in east Asia, southwest Asia, and South America, and on every continent. The ability of governments to understand the revolutionaries and to develop policies that encourage inclusion and internal discussion, debate, and referenda as the means of reformation and change, rather than resorting to military action, are the challenges of modern man. The actions visible on television on a daily basis reflect the frustrations of many, both the opponents who conduct the operations and the populace who supports them.

The State Adjustment: Create Nonstate Actors

The explosion of security companies, both from Western nations and from China and others, is a clear demonstration of one response from the state—create your own nonstate actor. Such actors allow the plausible deniability that Hezbollah provides to Iran or Syria. They also can operate at a level beneath congressional or parliamentary oversight and usually underneath the standard media interest. In addition, they are not direct representatives of a specific government. Thus, they can do the will of a state entity yet free that state from the responsibility of criticism for atrocities or even questionable behavior. One specific example is as follows:

> If China had announced that it planned to send multiple field armies to Angola to assist with security and construction there, the UN would at least have opened up a dialogue. Yet a Chinese company has signed a contract to do just that, except that it will substitute 850,000 armed and unarmed contractors for the field armies. This event has simply not shown up in international discussion. It is particularly interesting because China has just signed a 10-year contract with Angola to purchase oil at $60 a barrel. While the contractors are not an official branch of the Chinese Government, their presence clearly puts China in position to "resolve" any disputes with the Angolan Government over that contract.[1]

The rapidly increasing existence of private contracting firms with global reach, especially those within the security arena, demonstrates a real transformation of war to the dominance of the nonstate actor. It is uncertain what role these contractors will have in the future.

The 2007 hearings and media explosion over the role of Blackwater International in the killing of Iraqi civilians elevated the existence of such companies from the obscurity of the military-security arena of the developing world to front-page status on a global theater. Within a year of the event, this company and others are once again nondiscussion points in the international security debate. The ability for such companies to seek and maintain anonymity is vastly superior to that of the security forces of any state.

Another point often lost in the criticism of the private security companies operating in Iraq was their success in executing their designated missions. Regardless of all of the discussion about Iraq being a poor place for security and the dangers of movement through Baghdad in 2004–2007, Blackwater International and companies of equal experience maintained a perfect record of protection of those they were assigned to guard. These companies have demonstrated a level of professional competence that has exceeded that of most of the elite military units of the world—they get the job done.

In a world where securing multinational corporate interests becomes more and more critical, the role of the corporate nonstate actor will probably continue to grow in proportion with the growth of the influence of nonstate opponents of those corporate interests.

Strategies (numbered based on the nine strategies for victory)
1.   **Introspection:** What is the position of the state? The U.S. in 2004 and Israel in 2006 demonstrated a failure to appreciate the difference between constabulary tasks and combat tasks and how an army needs to prepare for one after being proficient at the other. The two cited examples are polar opposites, yet they reflect similar problems. In neither case did the senior hierarchy foresee the changes needed by their own forces prior to committing them to the task.
2.   **Empathetic Appreciation:** Who is the opponent? How do they see themselves? The challenge is especially great when the opponent is closely known and associated with. The fact that they seem to be a neighbor with whom one can work and then become an opponent indicates that one side did not know the

other from the beginning. The challenge for Israel was in truly understanding the Palestinian people and their motivations.

3. **Empathetic Expectation:** Hamas and Hezbollah have created the definition of how nonstate actors fight. They have learned and developed. The challenge for Israel was to see this development in order to stay ahead of it mentally. How will nonstate actors behave in the future? Will they continue to evolve into semi-legitimate agencies as well as conflict opponents?

4. **Study of Language:** In this chapter the importance of nuance is critical. It is insufficient to understand the translation of words. It is the ideas they convey that matter. This is similar to when generations speak the same language, yet they don't speak the "same language." The same words have sometimes vastly different meanings between generations and even within cultures. This is also true when the opponent comes from within a society or from a closely associated society.

5. **Study of History:** How people see themselves and their own history is as important as the history itself.

6. **Study of Culture:** From where does each opponent draw his or her source of conflict? The villages and urban squalor among Palestinians resulting from occupation and exile created a completely unique culture.

9. **Think Science Fiction:** How is the opponent adapting as they perceive the world around them? The use of an enormous roadside bomb to destroy a single armored vehicle was both within a set of values and outside them at the same time. The use of civilian locations for weapons caches and firing positions is directly related to the changing perceptions of an opponent and the future possibilities.

Chapter 11

ANSWERS AND CONCLUSIONS

By design, this book has asked many questions, and it is one of its purposes to leave readers with more questions that will hopefully result in a greater level of interest and a desire for learning more about the complexities of conflict. At the beginning, the intent of making this book accessible and worthwhile for a wide spectrum of readers was established. Throughout the middle portion, the book used entirely military examples of aberration and the challenges associated with them. In answering questions, this chapter will attempt to make the lessons relevant to all readers. The answers to the following questions are encapsulated within the discussion of the strategies set forth in the introduction.

- How do you recognize aberration?
- How do you prepare for aberration?
- How do you predict aberration?
- How do you react to aberration?
- How do you preempt negative aberrations?

Strategies to Achieve Victory in a World of Uncertainty and Change

The first three strategies outlined here are the essential goals of this process. The critical recognition of aberration needs to begin with understanding how the individual perceives the world around him or her. What does or would he or she expect? How does the current situation fit the contemporary and personally accepted model? Once a person understands his or her own perspective and expectation—the definition of one's own box, as it were—it is then possible to reach out mentally and seek to empathize and see the box from the perspective of the opponent. Both steps are necessary in this process, but empathy requires the greatest knowledge and understanding. The first step is one of introspection, and the second is one of using this introspection to understand the opponent by putting oneself in the opponent's place. One needs to divorce oneself from the expected and traditional and see the world without shading from the other side.

The example is one of observing a pyramid—the geometric shape, not the monumental architecture. Depending on the angle from which one observes this shape, there can be a variety of answers about what one sees—a square, a triangle, a square with intersecting diagonal lines, or a pyramid. First one must be able to define what one sees—a square, triangle, etc.—from one's own perspective and then be able see what one's opponent sees. Once it is possible to define both sides of observation, then it is possible to increase the personal conceptual box and be prepared for new and more possibilities to occur.

Introspection

Aberrations are a result of the failure of individuals to see the world and opponents as they really are; these occur when the opponent is viewed in the standard, existing format. The box metaphor is crucial, since one perceives the world within one's own box of expectations, experiences, cultural preparation, mental flexibility, and training.

Self-reflection is a critical skill in any environment. It is necessary to see oneself as one is, and ideal to see oneself as an opponent sees one. This touches on the next strategy, so it will not be addressed in detail here. Honesty is at the heart of this strategy—an honest appraisal of self, skills, abilities, attributes, and capabilities. This strategy was used in all of the case studies, which is the reason it begins the list of strategies. If any entity does not see itself accurately, it will not last long in any difficult conflict environment. The primary examples presented within the case studies emphasized the ability of the individual commander to see his forces, thereby empowering himself in decision making.

Introspection was first introduced in the concept of empathy and understanding how a suicide terrorist sees himself or herself within the context of cultural terrain and the world. In chapter 3, a section was dedicated to how the individual sees himself and also how the U.S. is perceived by those attackers. In the other case studies, there are examples of successful and unsuccessful introspection.

Hannibal saw himself clearly, as demonstrated in the Battle of Cannae (chapter 5). He knew the abilities of each of the various national contingents within the army. He placed those forces in a manner appropriate for the tasks he assigned. Khalid bin Walid knew of the strength of conviction possessed by his forces, and because of this he knew what risks he could assume in the Battle of Yarmouk (chapter 6). Washington knew what his forces could do at Trenton (chapter 8), and he strengthened the force with a greater preponderance of artillery to provide encouragement and empower units to stand and fight. In all of these cases, a successful understanding of self empowered commanders to take risks and act in a way that facilitated aberrational success.

Custer saw his forces as sufficient to deal with any opposing force at Little Bighorn (chapter 4). He also saw his subordinates as generally loyal and willing to follow orders as given in the conduct of the campaign. His arrogant presumptions led to the decision to send Benteen far away and to place Reno on the most important mission. All of these assumptions proved false and were directly responsible for the mission failure. Guy also struggled with his perceptions as he both saw himself and did not see himself accurately preceding the Horns of Hattin (chapter 7). He knew action was needed to cement his position, yet he allowed himself to be bullied into an unwise course of action because he failed to grasp the power of division within his own forces. The commander of the 131st IMRBr did not recognize the unprepared nature of his soldiers at nearly every level as he conducted his attacked into Grozny (chapter 9). Finally, the failure of state actors to perceive their weakness with regard to the nonstate actor has conceded great moral authority and power to the opponent in the Levantine conflicts post-1967 (chapter 10).

It is essential to see oneself clearly in conflict. Only from a sound understanding of self can a person see what is possible. This is where the personal or collective box is defined. How big, what shape, how much room exists for expansion or innovation are all necessary questions to consider before making critical decisions.

Empathetic Appreciation

Empathetic appreciation is the critical strategy of seeing the opponent as he or she sees him or herself. This is a logical step beyond the first strategy, since it is impossible to see anyone else clearly if one cannot see oneself clearly. Again, this strategy is a part of every case study.

As is the case with each of the strategies discussed in this book, much can be learned from our case studies about the importance of exercising empathetic appreciation. When this strategy was understood and put to use in these battles, the result was success on the battlefield.

Hannibal (chapter 5) had watched and learned through prior encounters that one of his opposing commanders was considerably more aggressive than the other. He had also seen and heard the friction between the commanders. Washington (chapter 8) knew that he could surprise the Hessian garrison because he understood their disdain for him and his army. This allowed him to effectively predict actions and reactions.

Custer (chapter 4) did not understand that the Indians were ready and willing to fight, irrespective of the number of Indian warriors present. There had been a fundamental change in how the Indians perceived themselves and their opponent, and Custer completely missed this. The failure of Vahan or Heraclius (chapter 6) to understand the role of Islam in driving the Arab tribes forward at Yarmouk meant that the Roman commanders always fought in a vacuum of knowledge. Guy (chapter 7) did not perceive Saladin in his weakness. He did not realize that he could outwait the sultan and have a strategic victory, he only perceived the need to achieve an immediate victory. The Russian commanders (chapter 9) failed to identify the fighting commitment of the Chechen rebels and the prior experience gained by the rebels through their service with the Russian military. States (chapter 10) have consistently missed the influence and capabilities of non-state players, and they have failed to see their intent and commitment.

This is the definition of the physical and conceptual box. Creation of a successful box, or escape from a too-narrow or rigid conception, can only be achieved when one observes the opponent with true empathy—seeing them as they see themselves. This also includes seeing them as they are and appreciating the difference between the two.

Empathetic Expectation

Empathetic expectation is the strategy that allows one to see the possibilities envisioned by one's opponent. What does the opponent see as an opportunity? Where does the opponent see weakness or strength? What is the opponent's perceived base of strength or center of gravity? These are some defining questions. See yourself from the opponent's perspective. How are you perceived? Understanding of how an opponent perceives your strengths and weaknesses will forecast the list of possible actions he or she may take against you. Much of the discussion of an opponent in the current military focuses on the idea of a capabilities-based opponent. This means that the opponent will use his or her capabilities to determine what is done and how it is done. With empathetic appreciation one seeks to see what the opponent understands to be his or her capabilities. In empathetic expectation, one tries to understand what the possible uses of those capabilities are as the opponent might understand them.

Throughout the case studies this was illuminated, but nowhere as clear as in the discussion of suicide terrorism. In chapter 3 an example discussion of this very strategy was laid out. This path included how the opponent, in this case the suicide terrorist, saw the circumstances in which he found himself, how he saw the opponent, and what techniques seemed the most logical. This example of empathetic expectation could be expanded to allow one to fully grasp any opponent based on the opponent's definition of the field of conflict and his perception of means available. Such command of this strategy would allow for the ability to predict such aberrational events as the attack on the school in Beslan or the attacks on the World Trade Center. Those who predicted such events employed this strategy.

Each of the other case studies also demonstrated this strategy either in success or failure. This strategy directly comes from empathetic appreciation, and the examples in the case studies are similar to those outlined above.

ONCE ONE DEFINES ONE'S OWN BOX, then the box of the opponent needs to be recognized. What are their rules and what game are they playing? This empowers one to know which piece to protect and which to go after. These three primary strategies—introspection, empathetic appreciation, and empathetic expectation—allow each person to clearly define the expanse of the space of conflict, the rules of conflict, and the objectives of the conflict. The respective boxes must be defined for aberration to be predicted or prevented. Without these steps occurring successfully, then, as noted in each of the prior case studies, an aberration is not just likely but probable.

The irony is that the discussion of conflict tends to define conflict in terms of conventional or unconventional. Even this book has used those two words. The very meaning of those words implies that the opponent is judged and categorized based on whether or not he or she fits inside a prescribed box of behaviors. The use of the first three strategies should be a logically employed process of assessment for each possible opponent or conflict, helping one to define the appropriate box in which to place the opponent.

As a note, the most capable managers of conflict will be able to keep all of their opponents out of boxes but be able to see them in the dynamics of the world at large. As commented previously when discussing the statement of "thinking outside the box," this is nearly impossible for most of us. This is why the recommendation here is to define a box in which to place the opponent. For most who have to understand conflict, it will be easier to create a box for the opponent and define them, their worldview, and their behavior through this box.

Through employment of the first three strategies, a person can recognize that he or she is entering an event or time period, based on observation and analysis, that may produce an aberrational event. It is through the combination of introspection and understanding personal expectation, empathetic appreciation, and empathetic expectation that one can truly be prepared to recognize an aberrational event as it occurs. Obviously this requires personal preparation in developing the skills and knowledge prior to the event.

To develop empathy, as stated, requires preparation. Study, study, study. This means language, history, culture—all the things that make people think the way they think. This is neither simple nor easy. If it is impossible for one person to do all of this, then it is incumbent on an organization to prepare people on their staff to be able to do so—experts in various cultures and regions.

The next three strategies all are part of the personal preparation just mentioned and are supportive of the first three. They empower one to gain greater insight, understanding, and eventual empathy for the opponent.

Study of Language

Language is one of the foundation points—not just the ability to translate words, but the ability to understand the context and connotation of words. Words carry meaning beyond dictionary definitions and can incite emotions and reactions beyond a reasonable understanding of the word. One of the best words in this category is "crusade." Spelled with a lowercase letter in English it means a complete commitment of resources to achieve an important objective. With an uppercase "C," it now has historical meaning denoting a period of religious wars wherein religious benefits were granted by Christian leaders for military acts, usually killing people and capturing places. That is in English. In Arabic, where there are no lowercase and uppercase letters, there still exists the two technical meanings, but to many, if not the vast majority of Arabic speakers, this word connotes Christians killing Muslims. As identified earlier, the same is true in the reverse for the Arabic word "jihad."

Another example of this challenge was identified in chapter 3 with the discussion of the two primary words in the chapter's title—"suicide" and "terrorism." Terrorism is a great example. There are dozens of definitions of this word throughout the world, maybe hundreds, since nearly every country has an official definition that allows that nation to identify those nonstate actors causing the greatest problems to the state to be classified as terrorists. The plethora of definitions means that the word has nearly lost all meaning. The ability to understand a word in its context and the emotions and reactions it elicits is more essential than the ability to translate the word itself.

One of the greatest examples of this in the case studies is in Chechnya (chapter 9). The Chechen rebels were allowed to communicate in their native tongue on an open radio because their opponent—the Russian army—did not understand that language. This was a significant concession of understanding by the Russians and an emotional strongpoint for the Chechens.

If a language is not understood, how can real understanding of a thought process occur? Language misunderstanding does not occur only with foreign language, but it can be a result of dialect or slang within a specific market target audience. If a company is targeting a certain age demographic, then their advertising needs to be in the age-appropriate speech. This is also true of understanding the language of a competing company. What are their specific acronyms and buzzwords? These provide keys to how people think and what is important within their culture, especially if a specific word is used for certain techniques or products.

Study of History

To prepare for aberrations it is necessary to study and understand precedent. As a result of this study, the crucial task is to understand not just what has happened but why. A full appreciation of the "why" in this manner means much more than a surface understanding of facts or explanations but an empathetic understanding of the reasoning behind the events. What were the perceptions that both sides had that allowed them to create a world where an aberration could occur? Why were boxes rigidly fixed and unable to be adjusted to accept the changing dynamics?

This is not the simple study of history as provided in a survey course on world history or even a specific course on regional or national history. It involves understanding the history as the opponent understands it. I often encourage students and other professionals interested in learning about the Near East simply to listen to the portrayal of history as it is given by those who live there. Even if one disagrees with the facts presented, these facts reveal a great deal about how that person perceives his or her people and the events that have transpired over time.

As indicated in chapter 10, the understanding of history created a fascinating point of discussion about who was at fault for the 2006 war between Hezbollah and Israel. The answer to any question about blame was based on how a person perceived the historical record. Another example of this comes from a teaching experience. One student was presenting a battle analysis on a battle in one of the Arab-Israeli wars. Several international students were present. Most of them were from the Arab country discussed in the analysis. As the U.S. student asked for questions, he was bombarded with challenges on his facts by the Arab students. They wanted to know where he learned about the battle—were the books written by Israelis or Jews? The U.S. student's sources gave a number for the Arab troops present in the battle that the Arab students had learned in their native country was grossly exaggerated. I spoke with the presenter after the brief and pointed out to him the value of his experience—he had just learned the historical interpretation of one of the combatant countries in the battle he had studied.

As a specific recommendation, it is important for students of and those who work in the Near East to understand the period of the Crusades in its complexity and detail. The Hollywood and standard high school or college survey versions of crusading history are insufficient and in many ways damaging to gaining the insight recommended here. The complex relationships revealed in chapter 7 present just a portion of the numerous issues confronting leaders and common people throughout the region in the two hundred years represented by the period. The political alliances between states and non-states provide a great window for viewing the current political machinations of the current states and nonstate actors in the region. The importance of this era in appreciating the contemporary issues is difficult to overstate. The challenge is to see the crusading era in a nonjudgmental way. Too many scholars present the events in the contemporary world of political correctness. This path will never provide the student the opportunity to gain the empathy necessary for the effort to have value. Those who study this period need to seek the reasons why the characters acted, just as it is crucial to do the same when seeking empathy of a contemporary person or opponent. Those who judge Reynald of Châtillon as a crazy man miss the point of his actions, just as do those who simply dismiss suicide bombers as crazy.

In addition to understanding interpretation and perspective, there is the basic understanding of objective history. What has happened in the past, where has it happened, and how did it happen? The answers to these questions and many other historical interrogatives provide the foundation upon which the interpretation can add detail and color.

Study of Culture

Culture is in many ways a combination of historical interpretation and language, along with the traditions and behavioral actions common to the people. In what ways do the people behave? The offenses generated by Reynald of Châtillon's attacks on Muslim pilgrims and the perceived threat against Mecca mentioned in chapter 7 so enraged the Muslim populace that this act alone could be given credit for uniting a historically disunited tribal culture against the crusaders. This was a case where the common culture was threatened, therefore the groups who held to some form of that culture united against the threat. The discussion in chapter 3 also elucidates much of the importance of cultural understanding in shedding light on the reasons behind events. In many ways, studying the culture of an opponent brings one's own culture into greater focus. This assists with both introspection and empathy at the same time.

The Indians at the Little Bighorn (chapter 4) attacked Custer from multiple directions, not as a result of some great tactical maneuver plan by Sitting Bull, but because it made logical sense within their cultural construct of conflict—the hunt. Crazy Horse knew that a band was already attacking up the Medicine Tail Coulee, so the logical move in a hunt-based tribal tactical culture was to move to find a flank of the "herd" and hit it there. This is what he did. I do not say this to lessen Crazy Horse's tactical abilities. I say it to identify where they came from. The same can be said for why Khalid bin Walid (chapter 6) sent his cavalry to find the Roman flanks—it was what Beduoin raiders and tribal warriors did. It was who they were and the cultural-tactical construct from which all conflict was derived. The same holds true for the war in southern Lebanon in 2006. The fighters for Hezbollah come from a semi-rural village construct where they had lived and developed their tactics under an occupied culture. The use of clandestine weapons caches and firing positions from within an urban environment and close to traditionally off-limits structures was a manifestation of who they were and their cultural template.

This may sound like a form of cultural determinism. I am unsure whether or not it is. I do believe that our ways of participating in conflict are very strongly shaped by our culture—as yet another example, Americans seek technological solutions to conflict because this is ingrained in our culture. The challenge for scholars of and participants in conflict is to understand what cultures will be shaping our opponents in the future and how these will change their views of conflict.

IN CHAPTER 7, THE TWO CHARACTERS of Raymond III, Count of Tripoli, and Reynald of Châtillon were introduced. Both men spent years in Muslim prisons. Raymond III, we know, learned Arabic and was able to speak it with sufficient fluency to allow him to have and control a personal bodyguard of Arabic-speaking Muslims provided by Saladin. It is unclear whether Reynald ever learned Arabic. Raymond III was able to use his understanding of language, history, and the culture of his Muslim opponents to allow him to conduct negotiations and successfully work for peace and agreement between his realms and his opponent. Reynald came away from similar experiences (though it is unknown whether one experienced different treatment than the other) with a nearly polar opposite view. It seems clear from the record that though one man saw the Muslims as intractable opponents with whom negotiation was fruitless and war inevitable, the other man envisioned an opponent of honor with whom he could effectively work. This is a great lesson on the fact that though one develops a detailed understanding of these strategies, there is no certain definition of the derived understanding.

An idealized example of a person who pursued excellence in the previous three strategies—study of language, study of history, study of culture—was John Bagot Glubb. There is no space to discuss the long and varied history of this British Army officer, but a brief summary is worthwhile. Glubb was tasked with the organization and leadership of the Arab Legion, which eventually evolved into the Jordanian Armed Forces. He began this work in the 1930s and continued until 1956. He had previously served in Iraq. In both Iraq and Jordan, he lived for years among the Bedouin. He spoke nothing but Arabic, and he became at home in the culture and was immersed in the history. He knew how the Jordanians thought. He had an ideal form of empathy and served as one of the great examples of the type of person these strategies are designed to create. The challenge is that very few organizations or individuals will invest the resources in time or treasure necessary to achieve this level of proficiency.

The key lesson for corporations and government agencies alike is to invest in developing expertise in language, history, and culture. These are soft skills that must be valued for organizations to truly excel in the global marketplace. The U.S. position is certain to continue to decline in relation to its historic highs, and because of this, the expectation that other cultures will work to understand us is less and less valid. One of the contentions here is that other cultures have not truly understood U.S. culture, and that is a part of the challenge in a globalized market. The U.S. system of liberal arts education allows for the concept of empathy, whereas few other educational systems around the globe present an equal opportunity for this.

THE FINAL FOUR STRATEGIES DEAL with application in the time or space adjacent to the potentially aberrational event itself.

Multiple Reserves

A reserve provides the last chance, and sometimes the only ability a leader has, to influence events once action has begun. This reserve can be one of forces in conflict, money or other resources (capital) in economic or business ventures, or personnel in any of a variety of situations. The freedom to move resources from one point of decision to another potential point of decision is critical for leaders reacting to aberrational events.

The Battle of Cannae (chapter 5) demonstrated clearly the failure in this strategy. Here the Roman commander, Varro, committed all of his forces to the attack. Once the Carthaginians appeared to give way, the entire Roman army moved forward, seeking to maintain contact with an enemy being forced back. This allowed the Romans to be enveloped as they pushed themselves into the ever-increasing bag the Carthaginians created. Had Varro kept several legions back in case of success or surprise, he could have reacted by allocating resources either to pursuit or defense of a threatened area. Nearly every losing commander in the case studies could have benefited from a supportive and redundant reserve plan. Grozny (chapter 9) provides a poignant case, since the existing forces either were unprepared to assist or refused to risk themselves for their compatriots. The higher commander either would not or could not commit forces that existed within the larger battle area. In most cases, the losing side had a greater number of forces and the ability to have reserve forces identified.

Custer (chapter 4) represented an example of reserves poorly allocated, costing the mission and assisting in the creation of the aberration. The additional dynamic of subordinate-leader personality conflicts also effectively negated Benteen as a true reserve, though his appearance later in the fighting allowed him to serve as a reserve for Reno and arguably saved that portion of the 7th U.S. Cavalry that survived the battle.

It is important not to overemphasize the use of reserves. There are plenty of times in military history where events went against a commander who was too cautious and unwilling to commit all of his resources when they could have turned the tide of battle. The idea of multiple reserves is to allow a leader to invest one force to react to opportunity or challenge and still have forces available to react yet again. Aberrational events do not present a simple challenge but one that is outside the experiential box of the opponent and, therefore, requires the ability to react more than once.

An aberration does not require an aberrant response. It is not necessary to be as innovative in response as the aberrant action. The key is to have an open mind that can recognize the aberration and then search for the possible response through personal experience. It is also critical to provide the ability to react and react again. This means multiple reserves. A single reserve will only address the obvious situation, but in an aberration the situation is not as obvious as it appears. The ability to react and protect what appears to be weakness, or exploit what appears to be success, can then be augmented by a secondary or tertiary reserve, which will help to regain the initiative lost. Reaction alone will only prevent defeat, but to achieve victory or dominance requires the ability to dictate the requirements and actions of the subsequent engagement.

Initiative

In so many cases, the failure of a leader to clearly see himself and to empathize with his opponent created surprise and placed the leader in a state of shock. This allowed the opponent to get ahead in the decision cycle and forced the leader in question to play a mental and strategic game of catch-up. The ability to see the area of conflict accurately—battlefield, game board, or market—allows one to be prepared for the possibilities and, therefore, think through reactions to potential events.

Everyone wants to have the initiative, but it is clear that many do not know how to gain it or regain it once it is lost. This strategy requires commitment to the struggle and not the emotional collapse witnessed in Grozny (chapter 9) once it was clear the initiative was lost.

Custer (chapter 4) is one of the best positive and negative examples of this, even in a losing effort. First, Custer thought he had lost the initiative when reports of Indians spotting the column were received. One of his key decisions following receipt of this information was to announce the attack on the village—he immediately sought to regain the initiative. He did so as Reno and his troops charged the village. The misidentified size of the village resulted in an encounter with more warriors than anticipated and the fact that Reno was rapidly overwhelmed—initiative lost. Custer again sought to regain the initiative by attacking the village at the opposite end, thereby throwing the Indians into confusion and possibly creating the shock he desired. His movement failed to find the north end of the village—initiative lost—and he was forced up on to high ground for the famous Last Stand. Despite the failures, Custer never stopped seeking a way to regain the initiative.

At the operational and strategic levels, Washington (chapter 8) demonstrated a similar tenacity for seeking to regain the initiative. His efforts at Trenton (26 December 1776) and then again at Trenton (2 January 1777) and Princeton (3 January 1777) were both examples of seeking to gain initiative and force the British to react to him. The decisions for both of these operations were made despite logic and statistics arguing against offensive operations in the face of an opponent superior in both size and experience.

In a proactive aspect, initiative can be called preemption. This is the ideal of maneuver and is facilitated by empathy and identification of the position of advantage, whatever or wherever that position might be—time, location, person, idea, product. The intent is to gain the position or remove the opponent from the position prior to its use. This is directly linked to understanding the position itself and focusing resources against that position to gain it.

It is much better to act than to be acted upon. This implies a significant challenge of risk acceptance, which many cultures avoid. To preempt means to act on something before it acts on you, and possibly before it has done anything offensive or wrong. In the defense of criticism following such preemptive action, the actor will be called upon to justify his or her actions and will be put in the position of defending a negative—an impossible task. Preemption cannot occur without the moral willingness to endure the fallout and the certitude that the preemptive actions are correct.

Because initiative relies upon the actions and reactions of the opponent, it is always fluid and changing. Therefore, once initiative is gained, it is necessary in planning and preparation to ensure the maintenance of the initiative through continual offensive actions. Once again, the best example of seeking initiative and trying to preempt the opponent is that provided by Custer in chapter 4. Even in loss he was tenacious in trying to gain, maintain, and regain the initiative.

Think Science Fiction

What is out there that could be used and what is coming that will change the world? Science fiction often accurately forecasts the techniques and technologies that may be used now and in the future. This may seem odd, but those who consistently think about future fictional possibilities are rarely surprised by the real innovations that occur. Leonardo de Vinci, Jules Verne, and Gene Rodenberry all forecasted through one medium or another current gadgets. What is being imagined and written now that will be common to us in future decades?

I vividly remember watching the television program *Star Trek* as a child and being amazed by the "communicator" used by the characters and wishing that I could have such a device. Now mobile phones are ubiquitous, and nearly all of them have significantly more features than did the communicator of the television show. So many of the devices used in that program have been surpassed in a few decades, though the show was supposed to depict life several hundred years in the future. This is equally true of those who read the books written by Jules Verne or see the sketches made by Leonardo de Vinci. Both of these men described through words or pictures devices currently in use.

Who is writing now about a future that we will see? Someone certainly is describing accurately the devices, techniques, behaviors, or cultures of the future. Many more are writing pure fantasy that has no relevance to any future reality. The point here is that solutions to aberrational events or preparation for aberrational events should not be expected to come from the conventional sources. One must have a broad sweep of information to collect those ideas that will be the most useful in the aberrations of today and tomorrow. Conservative thinking and conventional ideas will make one more susceptible to experiencing aberration rather than being equipped to excel in the event or to create such an event oneself.

What are the current capabilities? It is important in answering this question that capabilities are not viewed in a standard list of possibilities but that a much wider scope is taken to imagine what items may be used by the opponent that now could be classified as a capability. In answering this question, a person can create the greatest risk for aberration if he or she only reviews those capabilities that are typical.

Conclusion

War has changed. Obviously! The issue at hand with the obvious nature of that statement is that we missed it the first time—1945–1949 with the use of two nuclear devices and the success of a guerrilla campaign against a Western-backed nationalist government in China. The small war was back, and the massive engagements of the Napoleonic era of war were over. The U.S. has only recently grasped the first change, and as they now address that change of sixty years ago, we are probably missing the second change—2000–

2006 and the Levantine Intifadah and Israeli War with Hezbollah. These two events can be linked by incremental and evolutionary steps back to the tactics of the Mujahideen in Afghanistan and probably to the use of similar tactics by Jewish groups against the British in Mandatory Palestine in the 1920s–1940s. The U.S. missed the changes, mostly because those changes had been lumped in the wrong boxes and also because our box had been shrunk to include only wars against peers or near-peers.

The era of the large war and Napoleonic battles was dominated by the belief taken from Carl von Clausewitz that war was politics by other means. However, this conceptualization of conflict misses the fact that there have always been cultures that have viewed conflict as an end unto itself—warrior cultures. By definition, warriors live to fight wars. Those cultures have moved forward again, and they have done so generally empowered with ideological beliefs not based on Western views of rights of man, Declaration of Independence statements of inalienable rights, or Marxist views of conflict as class struggle. These ideas have been at the center of conflict for centuries, whether the conflicts were large or small, conventional or unconventional.

The "'net-wars" and "networks" used to explain Al Qaida–like organizations miss the point and discuss this as if it were a new way of waging war. The common narrative used by the insurgents or terrorists today is no different than the common fear and anger over white western expansion in the nineteenth century felt by the Indians or the religious piety and infusion of energy created by the Islamic conquests of the seventh century. Neither group conducted highly centralized battles, though in the case of the Muslims, there were senior commanders and a caliph, but the style of fighting was still tribal and personalized.

The newest changes deal primarily with ideological foundations (religion being the single biggest motivator for armed conflict rather than political objectives), the return to warrior culture and the move away from soldier culture, and the urbanization of fighting. This is currently a conflict scenario of Yarmouk meets Grozny. Just as the U.S. military was still fighting large, conventional battles in 1950 while others were fighting small wars against nonstate opponents, now there are nonstate opponents who are fighting in urban environments while others seek the Maoist model and rural and wilderness safe areas.

Early 2008 provides a great example of this spectrum. Northern Iraq saw battles between the Turkish military and the Kurdish Workers Party (PKK) in the mountains and wilderness. In Gaza, Hamas battled Israeli military in city streets. Iraqi suicide bombers and snipers targeted Iraqi civilians and military in the streets of Baghdad. Afghanistan saw a blending of the rural insurgent and the urban one.

Loose networks, or those associated by common ideologies, will adapt in unforeseen ways when faced with positions of perceived direct conflict. Much as Glubb described how the Bedouin fighter would react in unexpected ways that demonstrated tremendous initiative when in the heat of battle, this will be true of modern nonstate actors. They are free from the fixed conceptualization of conflict created by state-run bureaucracies.

As an example, network-like organizational dynamics in Iraq are not there as a result of a concerted plan but rather through a means of behavior. The insurgents who fight the U.S. military do not use loose organizations and networks because of a complex bureaucratic model but as a result of an applied and tested model of insurgency overlaid on top of tribal Arab culture. This is reminiscent of the reasons why Crazy Horse flanked Custer. He did it because that was the natural thing for a buffalo-hunting Indian to do in a conflict environment. Why do Arabs fall back on loose family-sized organizations? It is their cultural construct and something that seems natural. It is true that this model is facilitated by the explosion of communication media, but that is not necessarily the cause of the behavior, it is merely a facilitator for it.

CONFLICT HAS ALWAYS CHANGED and will continue to do so. Human beings think so they can survive—this means human conflict must evolve or the species would quickly cease to exist with the modern ability to kill. The march of technology and the reality of progression predicted by Moore's Law mean that change can occur at an increasing rate. Because revolutionaries tend to seek for surprise and possible aberration, and because the nature of armed conflict for the foreseeable future is to have nonstate actors fighting states and other nonstate actors, aberrational conflict will increase. Aberrations, or the drive for them, will become more common. As each of us moves from the known into the unknown it is incumbent on those desiring to be prepared for aberrations to seek awareness.

Great empires at their height rarely fell to an enemy they perceived (Carthage excepted) but usually to the unexpected and sometimes aberrational enemy. Rome did not fall to Carthage, Parthia, or Sassanid Persia. It fell to German and Muslim tribal warriors. These were not the focus of the legions in their prime— the focus was rather on a peer competitor. Though adjustments were made historically, it is interesting to think of what great powers perceived as their primary threat in their prime and what ultimately led to their downfall. Other examples of this sort of failed vision include the following:

- Assyria perceived its primary threat from Egypt, not Babylon.
- Babylon perceived its primary competitor as Egypt, not Median Persia.
- Persia did not perceive Macedonian Greece to be the perpetrator of its conquest.
- The Abbasids saw their threat as the Fatimids, not the Mongols.
- The Ottomans saw the Hapsburgs of Austria as their primary threat, not England.
- The Russians fell to internal revolt and not French imperialism.
- France did fall to the British, but first it fell to internal revolt.
- The Aztecs did not perceive the Spanish conquistadors to be the harbingers of their destruction.

How we define the opponent in conflict is crucial. Not all competition equals opposition, nor must it. The definition of all nonreservation tribes in nineteenth-century America as "hostile" led to conflicts that may have been unnecessary, not to mention costly. It is possible that part of the current changes in conflict exist because the era of destruction may be returning to an era of defeat. One is a physical and measurable conceptualization and the other an issue of will and conviction. Think of changing conflict from destruction of regimes or capabilities to simple reduction of capabilities. We do not have to destroy the army or remove the regime—we can just reduce the threat to an acceptable level. This is a Desert Storm versus Iraqi Freedom conundrum. Which one was more successful?

BY DEFINITION, AN ABERRATION CAN OCCUR anywhere and at anytime, otherwise it would not be an aberration—the unexpected. So the point here is to try and answer the question, how do you expect the unexpected?

The answer: You do not.

This is a problem.

What *may* be possible is to recognize events or time periods where a person is entering personal uncharted water. Varro, as he led his army for the first time into Cannae (chapter 5) and a major battle with an experienced opponent, was in the position of a possible aberration. His arrogance and pride prevented him from admitting the potential for aberration. He lacked the introspection necessary to forecast the potential for aberration.

It is not enough simply to seek to survive aberrations—Reno and Benteen did so at the Little Bighorn (chapter 4), but neither would have characterized their survival as success. It is best if one can transform the situation to achieve positive aberrations if there are any.

Culture is the terrain on which long-term and truly important battles are won and lost. The understanding and control of the *physical* land only grants limited and temporal gains, but the long-term conquests have come from the understanding and dominance of the cultural terrain. The empires and small nations of the past that have lasted longest and left the most indelible marks on human culture and society are those that reshaped how mankind thought, and not just where they lived. The victories of the future need to be won through engagement of culture rather than focus on military forces—transforming a people to accept the concept of rule of law will go further than brutal oppression of those same people.

Organizations must invest in the understanding of the opponent. There is no simple answer to overcoming aberration. Custer was no fool and no incompetent. He was considered by most of his peers as the best Indian-fighter of his time. He allowed arrogant presumptions to dominate his thinking, and, as a result, he made a series of mistaken decisions based on his assumptions. There are more Little Bighorns with more Indian villages, more Crazy Horses and Sitting Bulls waiting to crush some similarly arrogant commander who is unwilling to expand his box because the world fits so well in the box as it is.

Notes

Preface

1. The story of John Boyd is related in the book *Boyd: The Fighter Pilot who Changed the Art of War*. See bibliography.

Introduction

1. These battles are wonderfully described by the 1st Battalion commander, Hal Moore, in his and Joe Galloway's book *We Were Soldiers Once . . . and Young: Ia Drang, the Battle the Changed the War in Vietnam*. There is a complete battle analysis of the Battle of LZ Albany in *Armed Conflict: The Lessons of Modern War*.
2. Neither of these events appears in this book because they are discussed in another book by the author: *Armed Conflict: The Lessons of Modern War*.

Chapter 1: The Nature of Change and the Wizard of Oz

1. The "Levant" is a French word used to denote the eastern Mediterranean region generally consisting of the modern countries of Syria, Lebanon, Israel, and Jordan.
2. Moore. "Cramming more components onto integrated circuits."
3. Hiremane, "From Moore's Law to Intel Innovation—Prediction to Reality," 4.
4. Ibid., 3.
5. Ibid., 4.

Chapter 2: Building the Schoolhouse: Principles of Conflict

1. Han-chang, *Sun-Tzu's Art of War*, 99. The quote is "For to win one hundred victories in one hundred battles is not the acme of skill. To subdue the enemy without fighting is the supreme excellence."

Chapter 3: Case Study: The Suicide Terrorist

1. Robinson, *Dungeon, Fire, and Sword: The Knights Templar in the Crusades*, 201.
2. *Holy Qura'an, 4:29–30*. "*O ye who believe! . . . [do not] kill yourselves, for truly Allah has been to you Most Merciful. If any do that in rancor and injustice, soon shall We cast him into the Fire.*"

3. The same could be asked of those who walk into a crowded
    building and start shooting people and finish their act by shooting
    themselves. Because this chapter seeks to develop empathy for
    a different cultural and religious worldview than the common
    American one, this very relevant question is not pursued in this
    chapter. Despite this, the same arguments and reasoning could
    be used in trying to understand those labeled as domestic
    terrorists. It is interesting to note that many of those who attack
    with weapons within the U.S. have been diagnosed or treated for
    mental illness. This presents an argument in favor of the "they are
    crazy" line of reasoning.
4. Ghosh, "Inside the Mind of an Iraqi Suicide Bomber." Ghosh,
    "Professor of Death." These two articles provide insight into the
    minds of those who wish to conduct suicide attacks and those
    who support them with explosives and intelligence.
5. Han-chang, 118. The quote is "Know the enemy, know yourself;
    your victory will never be endangered. Know the ground, know
    the weather; your victory will then be complete."
6. Cowan, *The Hans Wehr Dictionary of Modern Written Arabic*, 168.
7. In general vocabulary there are two divisions in the Muslim
    worldview—the House of Islam and the House of War. Those
    who live in countries not controlled by Islamic governments are
    part of the House of War. This does not mean that Islam requires
    or orders war against all countries that do not believe,
    but it does mean that those countries fall into the category of
    "acceptable to go to war against."
8. This was the written statement by British Prime Minister Arthur
    James Balfour in 1917 that Great Britain looked favorably on the
    establishment of a Jewish homeland in Palestine.

Chapter 4: Case Study: The Battle of Little Bighorn (25 June 1876)
1. Godfrey, "Custer's Last Battle 1876, 19.
2. Utley, *Cavalier in Buckskin*, 42.
3. A coulee is a western U.S. term for a deep gulch or ravine usually
    dry in the summer—*Webster's New World Dictionary and Thesaurus*.
4. Ibid., 44.
5. Ibid., 177.
6. Utley, *Frontier Regulars*, 253.

7. Ibid., 254. Also Graham, *The Reno Court of Inquiry: An Abstract of the Official Record of the Proceedings*, 28–30. This is the best discussion of numbers in any of the sources referenced here. Graham suggests four thousand.
8. Utley, *Frontier Regulars,* 262.

Chapter 5: Case Study: The Battle of Cannae (2 August 216 BC)
1. Polybius, *The Histories, Book III,* 29.
2. Goldsworthy, *The Punic Wars,* 368.
3. Polybius, *The Histories, Book II,* 83, 85, 101, 136.
4. Ibid., 206, 208-209.
5. Ibid., 287.
6. Livy, *The War with Hannibal,* 50–51.

Chapter 6: Case Study: The Battle of Yarmouk (16-20 August 636)
1. Khaldun, *The Muqaddimah,* 107.
2. Glubb, *The Great Arab Conquests,* 240.
3. An absolutely outstanding explanation of the importance of this piece of terrain: ibid., 140–142.
4. Good discussion on Roman force issues: Kaegi, *Byzantium and the Early Islamic Conquests,* 40–41.
5. Glubb, 192.
6. Ibid., 199.
7. Blankinship, *The History of al-Tabari,* 74, note 421.
8. Ibid., 82.

Chapter 7: Case Study: The Battle of the Horns of Hattin (3-4 July 1187)
1. France, *Victory in the East,* 42.
2. Lane-Poole, *Saladin: The All-Powerful Sultan and the Uniter of Islam,* 216; this is an unabridged reprint of the edition first published in Great Britain in 1898.
3. There is a great description of the road network in Prawer's *Crusader Institutions,* 488–491. The descriptions are technical and sometimes complicated, but there does not seem to be a better explanation.
4. The Al Jazeera is a name given to the grasslands between the Tigris and Euphrates Rivers in what is today northern Iraq.
5. Kedar, Mayer, Smail, *Outremer,* 173. (Quoted from *Raymond III of*

Tripolis and the Fall of Jerusalem [1140–1187] by Marshall W. Baldwin, Princeton, 1936, 113)
6. Runciman, *A History of the Crusades, Volume II,* 486.
7. Setton, *A History of the Crusades, Volume I,* 614.

Chapter 8: Case Study: The Battle of Trenton (26 December 1776)
1. Paine, "The American Crisis," 456.
2. Fischer, *Washington's Crossing,* 387, 391.
3. Ibid., 183.
4. Ibid., 190.
5. Ibid., 404.
6. Ibid., 243.

Chapter 9: Case Study: The Battle of Grozny (31 December 1994–3 January 1995)
1. This is a quote associated with this battle in almost all of the narrative sources. It is unconfirmed by a source quote or reference. The story goes that the 131st IMRBr communications officer heard this come across his command radio net in Russian just prior to the rockets hitting the armored vehicles outside the railroad station. Though unconfirmed, it is one of the great and telling quotes from this battle.
2. Thomas, "The 31 December 1994-8 February 1995: Battle for Grozny," 167.
3. Ibid.
4. Jenkinson, "Tactical Lessons from the Grozny Combat Experience," 42.
5. Grau. "A Weapon for All Seasons."
6. Thomas, 170.
7. Grau and Thomas. "Russian Lessons Learned From the Battles For Grozny."

Chapter 10: Levantine Non-State Conflict (1967–Present)
1. Hammes, "Fourth Generation Warfare Evolves, Fifth Emerges," 18.

SELECTED BIBLIOGRAPHY

Bill, Alfred Hoyt. *The Campaign of Princeton 1776–1777*. Princeton, NJ: Princeton University Press, 1948.

Blair, Clay. *The Forgotten War: America in Korea 1950–1953*. New York: Times Books, 1987.

Blankinship, Khalid Yahya, translator and annotator, Temple University. *The History of al-Tabari: An Annotated Translation, Volume XI: The Challenges to the Empires AD 633–635/AH 12–13*. Albany: State University of New York Press, 1993.

Bowden, Mark. "Blackhawk Down: An American War Story." *The Philadelphia Inquirer*: 16 November to 14 December 1997.

Cary, M., and H. H. Scullard. *A History of Rome Down to the Reign of Constantine*. 3rd ed. London: MacMillan, 1974.

Chiaventone, Frederick J. *A Road We Do Not Know: A Novel of Custer at the Little Bighorn*. New York: Simon & Schuster, 1996.

Clausewitz, Carl von. *On War*. Edited and translated by Michael Howard and Peter Paret, Princeton, NJ: Princeton University Press, 1976.

Cobb, Hubbard. *American Battlefields: A Complete Guide to the Historic Conflicts in Words, Maps, and Photos*. New York: Simon & Schuster, 1995.

Coram, Robert. *Boyd: The Fighter Pilot Who Changed the Art of War*. New York: Little, Brown and Company, 2002.

Cowan, J. M., ed. *The Hans Wehr Dictionary of Modern Written Arabic*. Ithaca, NY: Spoken Language Services, 1994.

Dupuy, R. Ernest, and Trevor N. Dupuy. *The Harper Encyclopedia of Military History: From 3500 BC to the Present*. New York: HarperCollins Publishers, 1993.

Edbury, Peter W. *The Conquest of Jerusalem and the Third Crusade: Sources in Translation*. Aldershot, England: Scolar Press, 1996.

Fehrenbach, T. R. *This Kind of War: The Classic Korean War History*. Washington, D.C.: Brassey's, 1994. First published in 1963 by Macmillan.

Fischer, David Hackett. *Washington's Crossing*. New York: Oxford

University Press, 2004.

France, John. *Victory in the East: A Military History of the First Crusade.* Reprint, Cambridge, England: Cambridge University Press, 1996.

Friedman, Thomas L. *From Beirut to Jerusalem.* Paperback edition, New York: Anchor Books, 1995.

Friedmann, Yohanan, translator and annotator, the Hebrew University of Jerusalem. *The History of al-Tabari: An Annotated Translation, Volume XII: The Battle od al-Qadisiyyah and the Conquest of Syria and Palestine AD 635–637/AH 14–15.* Albany: State University of New York Press, 1992.

Gabrieli, Francesco, ed. and trans. *Arab Historians of the Crusades* selected and translated from the Arabic sources. Translated from the Italian by E. J. Costello. Berkeley and Los Angeles: University of California Press, 1984 (English paperback edition).

Ghawanmeh, Yusuf. *The Battle of Yarmouk.* Irbid, Jordan: A Publication of the Department of Public Relations, Yarmouk University, 2004.

Gibbon, Edward. *The History of the Decline and Fall of the Roman Empire, Volume V.* Notes by Dean Milman, M. Guizot, and William Smith. New York: A. L. Burt Company, Publishers, n.d.

Gil, Moshe. *A History of Palestine 634–1099.* Translated by Ethel Broido. Paperback edition, Cambridge, England: Cambridge University Press, 1997.

Glubb, John Bagot. *The Great Arab Conquests.* First American edition, Englewood Cliffs, NJ: Prentice-Hall, Inc., 1954.

Goldsworthy, Adrian. *The Punic Wars.* London: Cassell & Co, 2000.
———. *Roman Warfare.* London: Cassell & Co, 2000.

Graham, W. A. *The Story of the Little Bighorn.* Originally published 1926. New material copyright, Mechanicsburg, PA: Stackpole Books, 1994.
———. *The Reno Court of Inquiry: An Abstract of the Official Record of the Proceedings.* Originally ublished 1954. New material copyright, Mechanicsburg, PA: Stackpole Books, 1995.

Hamilton, Bernard. *The Leper King and His Heirs: Baldwin IV and the Crusader Kingdom of Jerusalem.* Paperback edition, Cambridge, England: Cambridge University Press, 2005.

Hammer, Kenneth, ed. *Custer in '76: Walter Camp's Notes on the Custer*

Fight. New edition, Norman, OK: University of Oklahoma Press, 1990.

Han-chang, T'ao. *Sun-Tzu's Art of War: The Modern Chinese Interpretation.* Translated by Yuan Shibing. New York: Sterling Publishing Co., Inc., 1987. *Holy Qur'an.* Modern English translation with meanings and commentary by A. Yusuf Ali. Kansas City, MO: Manar International, 1998.

Hastings, Max. *The Korean War.* New York: Simon & Schuster Inc., 1987.

Kaegi, Walter E. *Byzantium and the Early Islamic Conquests.* Paperback edition, Cambridge, England: Cambridge University Press, 2000.

Kedar, B. Z., H. E. Mayer, and R. C. Smail, eds. *Outremer: Studies in the History of the Crusading Kingdom of Jerusalem* presented to Joshua Prawer. Jerusalem, Israel: Izhak Ben-Zvi Institute, 1982.

Lane-Poole, Stanley. *Saladin: The All-Powerful Sultan and the Uniter of Islam.* This is an unabridged reprint of the edition first published in Great Britain in 1898. New York: Cooper Square Press, 2002.

Livy. *The War with Hannibal.* Paperback edition, Middlesex, England: Penguin Books, Ltd., 1983.

Longacre, Edward C. *Custer and His Wolverines: The Michigan Cavalry Brigade 1861–1865.* Conshohocken, PA: Combined Publishing, 1997.

Luttwak, Edward N. *Strategy: The Logic of War and Peace.* Cambridge, MA: The Belknap Press of Harvard University, 1987.

Lyons, Malcolm Cameron, and D. E. P. Jackson. *Saladin: The Politics of Holy War.* Cambridge: Cambridge University Press, reprinted 1990.

Malouf, Amin. *The Crusades Through Arab Eyes.* Translated by Jon Rothschild. New York: Schocken Books, 1984.

Marshall, S. L. A. *The River and the Gauntlet: Defeat of the Eighth Army by the Chinese Communist Forces, November, 1950, in the Battle of the Chongch'on River, Korea.* Nashville, TN: The Battery Press, 1959.

Matloff, Maurice, ed. *American Military History: Volume 1: 1775–1902.* Conshohocken, PA: Combined Books, Inc., 1996.

McCullough, David. *1776.* New York: Simon & Schuster, 2005.

Moore, Harold G., and Joseph L. Galloway. *We Were Soldiers Once . . . and Young: Ia Drang, the Battle the Changed the War in Vietnam.* Paperback edition, New York: Harper Perennial Publishers, 1993.

————. *After Action Report of Operations in the Ia Drang Valley.* November 1965.

Newby, P. H. *Saladin in His Time.* London: Phoenix Press, 1983.

Nicolle, David. *Yarmouk AD 636: The Muslim Conquest of Syria.* Westport, CT: Praeger Illustrated Military History Series, 2005.

————. *Hattin 1187: Saladin's Greatest Victory.* Westport, CT: Praeger Illustrated Military History Series, 2005.

Oliker, Olga. *Russia's Chechen Wars: 1994–2000.* Arroyo Center: RAND, 2001. Downloaded from http://www.rand.org/pubs/ monograph_reports/MR1289/MR1289.ch2.pdf.

Patai, Raphael. *The Arab Mind.* Paperback edition, New York: Hatherleigh Press, 2002.

Polybius. *The Histories, Book III.* Loeb Classical Library, 6 volumes, Greek texts and facing English translation. Tranlated by W. R. Paton. Cambridge: Harvard University Press, 1922 through 1927. Taken from http://penelope.uchicago.edu/Thayer/E/Roman/ Texts/Polybius/home.html

Prawer, Joshua. *The Crusaders' Kingdom: European Colonialism in the Middle Ages.* London: Phoenix Press, 1972.

————. *Crusader Institutions.* Oxford, England: Clarendon Press. Special Edition for Sandpiper Books Ltd., 1998.

Richards, D. S., trans. *The Rare and Excellent History of Saladin or al-Nawadir al-Sultaniyya wa'l-Mahasin al-Yusufiyya by Baha al-Din Ibn Shaddad.* Crusader Texts in Translation. Burlington, VT: Ashgate Publishing Company, 2002.

Ridgeway, Matthew B. *The Korean War: How We Met the Challenge; How All-Out Asian War Was Averted; Why MacArthur Was Dismissed; Why Today's War Objectives Must Be Limited.* Garden City, NY: Doubleday, 1967; paperback edition, New York: Da Capo Press, 1986.

Robinson, John J. *Dungeon, Fire, and Sword: The Knights Templar in the Crusades.* New York: MJF Books, 1991.

Rosenthal, Franz, trans. *The Muqaddimah: An Introduction to History, Ibn Khaldun.* Abridged and edited by N. J. Dawood. London: Routledge & Kegan Ltd., 1987.

Runciman, Steve. *A History of the Crusades, Volume II: The Kingdom of*

Jerusalem and the Frankish East 1100–1187. Cambridge: Cambridge at the University Press, 1952.

Savas, Theodore P., and J. David Dameron. *A Guide to the Battles of the American Revolution*. New York: Savas Beattie LLC, 2006.

Scales, Robert H., Jr. *Certain Victory: United States Army in the Gulf War*. Fort Leavenworth, KS: Command and General Staff College Press, 1994 (select reprint).

Schubert, Frank N., and Theresa L. Kraus, eds. *The Whirlwind War: The United States Army in Operations Desert Shield and Desert Storm*. Washington, D.C.: Center of Military History Press, 1995.

Schwarzkopf, H. Norman, and Peter Petre. *General H. Norman Schwarzkopf: The Autobiography: It Doesn't Take a Hero*. New York: Bantam Books, 1992.

Setton, Kenneth M., general ed. *A History of the Crusades*. Marshall W. Baldwin, ed. *Volume I: The First Hundred Years*. Madison, Milwaukee, and London: The University of Wisconsin Press, 1969.

Steed, Brian. *Armed Conflict: The Lessons of Modern War*. New York: Presidio Press, 2002.

Utley, Robert M. *Frontier Regulars: The United States Army and the Indian 1866–1891*. Lincoln: University of Nebraska Press, 1973.
———. *Cavalier in Buckskin: George Armstrong Custer and the Western Military Frontier*. Norman: University of Oklahoma Press, 1988.

Von Schlieffen, Alfred. *Cannae*. A Military Classic Reprint. Fort Leavenworth, KS: U.S. Army Command and General Staff College Press, 1992.

Ward, Christopher. *The War of the Revolution*. New York: The MacMillan Company, 1952.

Website, Journal, and Magazine Articles

Bateman, Robert L. "Shock and the Digital Battlefield." *Armor* (January–February 1998): 14–19.

Celestan, Gregory J. "Wounded Bear: The Ongoing Russian Military Operation in Chechnya." Downloaded from http://fmso.leavenworth.army.mil/documents/wounded/wounded.htm#19a, Foreign Military Studies Office, Fort Leavenworth, KS,

1996.

Faurby, Ib, and Märta-Lisa Magnusson. "The Battle(s) of Grozny."
    Baltic Defence Review 2 (1999): 75–87. Downloaded from http://
    www.caucasus.dk/publication1.htm.

Galloway, Joseph L. "Fatal Victory." *U.S. News and World Report*, 29
    October 1990, 32–35.

———. "Vietnam Story." *U.S. News and
    World Report*, 29 October 1990, 36–46.

———. "Where Have All the Young Men Gone?" *U.S. News and
    World Report*, 29
    October 1990, 50–52.

———. "Once More, Into the Valley of   Death:
    American and Vietnamese Soldiers Meet Again." *U.S. News
    and World Report*, 6 December 1993, 32–34.

Ghosh, Aparisim. "Inside the Mind of an Iraqi Suicide Bomber." *Time*,
    4 July 2005.

———. "Professor of Death," *Time*, 24 October 2005.

Godfrey, E. S. "Custer's Last Battle 1876." originally
    published in *Century Magazine*, January 1892, reprinted
    Silverthorne, CO: VISTABOOKS, 1995.

Grau, Lester W. "A
    Weapon for All Seasons: The Old But Effective RPG-7 Promises
    to Haunt the Battlefields of Tomorrow." Downloaded from
    http://fmso.leavenworth.army.mil/documents/weapon.
    htm#N_19_, Foreign Military Studies Office, Fort
    Leavenworth, KS. This article first appeared in *Infantry* (May–
    August 1998) under the title "The RPG-7 on the Battlefields
    of Today and Tomorrow."

Grau, Lester W., and Timothy Smith.
    "A 'Crushing' Victory: Fuel-Air Explosives and Grozny
    2000." Downloaded from http://leav-www.army.mil/fmso/
    documents/fuelair/fuelair.htm, Foreign Military Studies Office,
    Fort Leavenworth, KS. This article first appeared in *Marine
    Corps Gazette* (August 2000).

Grau, Lester W., and Timothy L.
    Thomas. "Russian Lessons Learned From the Battles For

Grozny." Downloaded from http://fmso.leavenworth.army.
mil/FMSOPUBS/ISSUES/Rusn_leslrn.htm, Foreign Military
Studies Office, Fort Leavenworth, KS. This article first appeared
in *Marine Corps Gazette* (April 2000).

Hammes, T. X. "Fourth Generation Warfare Evolves, Fifth
Emerges." *Military Review* (May–June 2007): 14–23.

Hiremane, Radhakrishna. "From Moore's Law to Intel Innovation—
Prediction to Reality." *Technology@Intel Magazine*, April 2005, 4.

Jenkinson, Brett C. "Tactical Lessons from the Grozny Combat
Experience," Master's thesis from the U.S. Army Command and
General Staff College, 2002.

Keller, Brian A. "Intelligence Support to Military Operations on
Urban Terrain: Lessons Learned from the Battle of Grozny." U.S.
Army War College Strategy Research Project. Carlisle Barracks,
PA, 2000.

Moore, Gordon E. "Cramming more components onto integrated
circuits," *Electronics* 38: 8 (19 April 1965).

Paine, Thomas. "The American Crisis." *The Annals of America:
Volume 2: 1755–1783 Resistance and Revolution*. Chicago:
Encyclopedia Britannica, Inc., 1968, pp. 456–461.

Thomas, Timothy L. "The 31 December 1994–8 February 1995:
Battle for Grozny," downloaded from http://www.globalsecurity.
org/military/library/report/2002/MOUTThomas.htm.
———. "The Battle of Grozny: Deadly Classroom for Urban
Combat." *Parameters* (Summer 1999): 87–102.

INDEX